# lonely planet

JOSH WEST, ANNA KAMINSKI, MONIQUE PERRIN,
CHARLES RAWLINGS-WAY, GLENN VAN DER KNIJFF, STEVE WATERS

# Contents

## PLAN YOUR TRIP
- Welcome to Australia ........................... 4
- Our Picks ............................................... 6
- When to Go ........................................ 14
- Get Prepared for Australia ................ 16

## EXPLORE ........................ 18

### SYDNEY & AROUND .......... 21
- Prince Henry Cliff Walk ..................... 24
- Wattamolla to Otford ......................... 26
- Bouddi Coastal Walk ......................... 28
- Jerusalem Bay Track ......................... 30
- Bondi to Coogee
  Clifftop Walk ...................................... 32
- Also Try ............................................... 36

### BYRON BAY TO THE
### SUNSHINE COAST ............. 39
- Tibrogargan &
  Trachyte Circuits ................................ 42
- Mt Mitchell ......................................... 44
- Mapleton Falls
  to Gheerulla Falls .............................. 46
- Cape Byron ........................................ 50
- Minyon Falls Loop ............................. 52
- Also Try ............................................... 54

### THE DAINTREE
### & THE FAR NORTH ............ 57
- Mossman Gorge ................................ 60
- Pine Grove & Broken River .............. 62
- Best of Great Keppel Island ............. 64
- Mt Sorrow Ridge ............................... 66
- Carnarvon Gorge .............................. 68
- Also Try ............................................... 72

### THE OUTBACK ..................... 75
- Valley of the Winds ........................... 78
- Kings Canyon Rim .............................80
- Mt Sonder .......................................... 84
- Ormiston Pound ................................ 86
- Above Standley Chasm .................... 88
- Edith Falls &
  Sweetwater Pool ............................... 90
- Motor Car Falls ................................. 94
- Florence Falls ................................... 96
- Also Try ............................................... 98

### THE KIMBERLEY
### & PILBARA ........................... 101
- Emma Gorge ................................... 104
- Punamii-Unpuu/
  Mitchell Falls ................................... 106
- Bell Gorge ........................................ 110
- Bungles Gorges ................................112
- Mt Bruce ............................................114
- Weano & Hancock Gorges .............. 116
- Dales Gorge Circuit ..........................118
- Also Try ............................................ 120

### SOUTHWEST
### FORESTS TO THE SEA ..... 123
- Bluff Knoll ........................................ 126
- Nancy Peak & Devils Slide ............. 128
- Bald Head ........................................ 130
- Nuyts Wilderness ............................ 132
- Hamelin Bay to Elephant Rock ...... 134
- Also Try ............................................ 138

### FLINDERS
### TO FLEURIEU ..................... 141
- Mt Remarkable Summit ................. 144
- The Riesling Trail ............................ 146
- Morialta Gorge Three Falls ............ 148
- Mylor to Mt Lofty ............................ 150
- Belair National Park Waterfall ...... 154
- Marion Coastal Trail ....................... 156
- Blowhole Beach
  to Cape Jervis ................................. 158
- Also Try ............................................ 160

### GRAMPIANS TO
### THE HIGH COUNTRY ........ 163
- Wonderland Loop ............................ 166
- Mt Stapylton .................................... 168
- Mt Buffalo Plateau ...........................170
- The Razorback
  & Mt Feathertop ...............................172
- Mt Cope ............................................ 176
- Also Try .............................................178

### THE PROM TO THE
### GREAT OCEAN ROAD ....... 181
- Lilly Pilly Gully & Mt Bishop .......... 184
- Oberon Bay ..................................... 186
- Squeaky Beach ............................... 188
- Lorne Forests & Waterfalls ........... 190
- Wreck Beach ....................................194
- Also Try ............................................ 196

### TASMANIA'S HIGHLANDS
### & COASTLINES .................. 199
- Dove Lake Circuit ........................... 202
- leeawuleena/Lake St Clair ............ 204
- Cataract Gorge Adventure ........... 206
- Wineglass Bay
  & Hazards Beach ............................ 208
- Organ Pipes Circuit ........................ 210
- Cape Hauy ........................................214
- Crescent Bay ................................... 216
- South Cape Bay ...............................218
- Also Try ............................................ 220

## TOOLKIT ........................ 223
- Arriving ............................................ 224
- Getting Around ............................... 225
- Accommodation ............................. 226
- Hiking ............................................... 227
- Health & Safe Travel ...................... 228
- Responsible Travel ........................ 229
- Nuts & Bolts .................................... 230

# Welcome to Australia

Long before European boots stepped onto this sunburnt earth, Aboriginal Australians had forged a deep kinship with the land, creating Songlines (walking routes) across the continent and nurturing its biodiverse habitats. This environmental and explorative legacy has become the cornerstone of Australia's bushwalking ethos.

Thousands of well-maintained trails now snake across the country. Within these pages, you'll find a collection of curated walks showcasing Australia's natural diversity. From the lush rainforests of Tropical North Queensland to the vine-striped hills of South Australia's wine country, these hikes are vast and varied. Climb the jagged peaks of Victoria's High Country, admire the tainted haze over the Blue Mountains or sift through the Red Centre's ochre sands. Horizons shift seamlessly from the coastal serenity of Western Australia's bone-white beaches to Tasmania's eucalyptus-scented valleys. Australian bushwalks are not just a physical exploration, but an insight into the wide-ranging environments that define the continent.

**Acknowledgement of Country**
Lonely Planet would like to acknowledge all Aboriginal nations throughout this country, who have nurtured and maintained the land since time immemorial. This guide was written on, and is written about, the lands of many diverse nations. We recognise the unique and ongoing connection that Aboriginal peoples have to land and waters and thank them for their efforts to preserve them. We pay our respects to Elders past and present and extend this respect to any Aboriginal or Torres Strait Islander people who may be reading this guide. We also recognise the ongoing efforts of Aboriginal peoples for reconciliation, justice, and social, cultural and economic self-determination. Sovereignty was never ceded. Australia always was, and always will be, Aboriginal land.

**Cultural Sensitivity Warning**
Aboriginal and Torres Strait Islander readers are advised that this guide may contain names and images of people who have since passed away.

**Kings Canyon (p80)**
MMARTIN/SHUTTERSTOCK ©

# Our Picks

## BEST WILDLIFE WALKS

As you drift further from the urban centres, the likelihood of meeting Australia's unique fauna grows. Rustling leaves hint at grazing marsupials or retreating reptiles, and eucalypt-topped canopies bring kookaburra laughter, flashes of kaleidoscopic feathers and the fluffy backsides of dozy koalas. Each region has its headliners and there are immersive wildlife experiences across the country.

**TOP TIP**

Unshackling your backpack for your bottle can quickly become annoying. Carry a water bladder with a long tube for easy sipping.

### ❶ Hamelin Bay to Elephant Rock

Pack your best lens for Margaret River's menagerie of snakes, lizards, birdlife and offshore humpback whales.

**P134**

### ❷ Blowhole Beach to Cape Jervis

Keep your eyes peeled for pods of dolphins and migrating southern right whales along SA's dramatic coastline.

**P158**

### ❸ Punamii-Unpuu/ Mitchell Falls

Venture to WA's northwest for lizards, goshawks and rock wallabies, but steer clear of the water; crocs lurk below.

**P106**

### ❹ Lorne Forests & Waterfalls

Turn your walk into a game of 'spot the koala' in Great Otway National Park's leafy canopy.

**P190**

### ❺ Pine Grove & Broken River

Tread quietly around Eungella National Park's lowland creeks for your chance to spy an elusive platypus.

**P62**

Koala

**TOP TIP**
Beat summer's heat by embracing short twilight strolls, returning before nightfall. Pack an emergency headtorch for navigation.

Mitchell Falls (p106)

**TOP TIP**
Struggling with achy knees? Trekking poles can relieve stress on joints, especially on steep gradients.

# Our Picks

## BEST VIEW-INSPIRED WALKS

Australia is a living postcard of panoramas, where every walk unveils unique geographical features. Outback trails deliver desert dunes and ochre-tinged gorges, while Tropical North Queensland's palm-shaded paths provide vistas over the world's oldest rainforests. Admire endless horizons atop the thigh-thumping peaks of Tasmania and Victoria's High Country, or breathe the briny air of WA's rugged south coast. Clear your camera storage and charge your batteries; Australia's scenery-packed terrain awaits.

### The Razorback & Mt Feathertop

Absorb Victoria's High Country peaks along the Razorback ridgeline towards the lofty Mt Feathertop summit.

**P172**

### Organ Pipes Circuit

Survey Hobart's sunken cityscape, capturing the skyline from the rocky slopes of kunanyi/ Mt Wellington.

**P210**

**TOP TIP**

You'll need a permit to fly drones in most parks across Australia. Organise in advance or leave it at home.

Kings Canyon (p80)

### Mt Sorrow Ridge

Set your gaze across the ancient rainforest towards Cape Tribulation in Tropical North Queensland.

**P66**

Mt Feathertop (p172)

### Bald Head

Spend the day hiking to this rocky headland promising unobstructed ocean vistas in WA's southern reaches.

**P130**

### Kings Canyon Rim

This desert canyon delivers a breath-stealing spectacle, but save some puff for climbing the rocky ridge.

**P80**

# Our Picks

## BEST SUNSET-SIP WALKS

As the trail's shadows lengthen, the promise of a tasty tipple quickens your steps. In Australia, post-hike sundowners are more than just a beverage; they're a motivating ritual, a reflective finale to the sights, sounds and scents experienced on your walk. You'll find locally brewed ales and Australia's world-class wines gracing the drinks menus of cafes, pubs and hotels in urbanised outposts, country towns and remote communities.

### Mt Remarkable Summit
Having conquered the mountainous summit, take your pick of Melrose's two charming pubs.

**P144**

### Wonderland Loop
Visit Paper Scissors Rock Brew Co in Grampians National Park's foothills for a craft beer.

**P166**

### Bouddi Coastal Walk
Bookended by NSW surf life-saving clubs, you'll have a brew waiting whichever end you start.

**P28**

### The Riesling Trail
Stroll through the historic Clare Valley wine region, sipping and tasting as you go.

**P146**

### Bondi to Coogee Clifftop Walk
Rooftop bars, cocktail lounges, sports taverns, upmarket hotels, chic restaurants…you won't go thirsty in Coogee.

**P32**

**TOP TIP**
Replace your minerals, as well as your fluids, after a sweaty stroll. Electrolyte tablets and sachets provide a quick rehydration boost.

Bouddi National Park (p28)

# Our Picks

## BEST SWIM-WORTHY WALKS

Against the backdrop of Australia's drought-prone landscapes, a surprising number of inland waterholes emerge, providing sweat-cleansing dips on arid walks. Dunk your head at plunge pools in northern Western Australia and the Northern Territory (first ensuring the waters are croc-free). Less surprisingly, the country's windswept coast is primed and ready for a mid-hike splash. Prepare to get your feet sandy on beach-bound walks across the mainland's southern coast and Tasmania.

**Bell Gorge (p110)**

**TOP TIP**
Don't let Australia's cloud cover fool you; daytime UV rays are constant. Reapply sunscreen every two hours and immediately after a dip.

### Cape Byron
Take in a lighthouse, coastal cliffs and a sweep of swim-ready beaches on the mainland's eastern edge.

**P50**

### Edith Falls & Sweetwater Pool
This relaxing route leads past scenic swim spots, plunge pools and waterfalls along the NT's Edith River.

**P90**

### Bell Gorge
Cool your heels in cliff-encircled swimming holes after crossing the Kimberley's sun-soaked savannah.

**P110**

### Oberon Bay
Take your pick of three superb beaches along this half-day trek through Wilsons Prom.

**P186**

### Wineglass Bay & Hazards Beach
Pack your swimsuit for this popular coast-hugging loop through Tasmania's Freycinet National Park.

**P208**

# Our Picks

## BEST SECLUDED WALKS

With over 5% of Australia's landmass – nearly 400,000 sq km, an area larger than Germany – protected and maintained by national parks, the Aussie bush hosts a wealth of isolated escapes. These hidden walks uncover marshland plains, untouched beaches, distant waterfalls and native woodlands, offering a tranquil refuge in nature's embrace. Lace up your boots and let the outside world fade away in Australia's secluded landscapes.

**TOP TIP**

Get to know your first-aid kit, snake kit, PLB and maps before hitting the trail. The internet can't help in a signal-free ravine.

### South Cape Bay

Navigate southern Tasmania's bracken, bottlerush and marshy boardwalks at the edge of the world.

**P218**

### Wreck Beach

Embark on a maritime treasure hunt amid the golden sands of Victoria's treacherous Shipwreck Coast.

**P194**

### Minyon Falls Loop

Drop into a shady rainforest, where a swimming hole awaits at the base of this stunning hinterland waterfall.

**P52**

### Motor Car Falls

Escape the Kakadu crowds with this remote woodland walk leading to a hidden cascade.

**P94**

### Jerusalem Bay Track

Escape Sydney's bustle on a northbound train to the riverside bushland of Ku-ring-gai National Park.

**P30**

Wreck Beach (p194)

**TOP TIP**
The Australian Walking Track Grading System measures trail difficulty nationwide. Assess the trail's grade and your abilities before hiking.

Motor Car Falls (p94)

# When to Go

Australia flaunts its continental variety across the seasons, delivering sunlit landscapes, snowshoe shuffles and sweat-dripping saunas depending on where your feet land.

Australia presents a year-round climatic carousel, so you'll need to pair your walk with the season for the most favourable walking conditions. In the mainland's southeast, Victoria, southern New South Wales and coastal South Australia deliver warm, dry summers, cool, wet winters and mild shoulder months. Tasmania follows suit, although winter (June to August) and spring (September to November) can bring erratic, chilly temperatures. Meanwhile, winters north of Brisbane and the inland deserts of South Australia, the Northern Territory and Western Australia deliver dreamy sunlit days and cold nights; however, summer (December to February) quickly stifles, with conditions easing into

## ⓘ I LIVE HERE

### A WIDE OPEN SKY

**Emily Dallas Scott** hikes, rides, slow jogs, camps, writes and does social worky things on Kaurna Country, in Adelaide, SA. @dallasfly

South Australia provides a spectacular array of bushwalking, best explored between April and November (outside Fire Danger Season). My top hiking places include Adnyamathanha Country, covering the Flinders Ranges, where spring's wildflowers bloom, baby emus shuffle among the scrub, and I can disappear into its ancient ochre gorges. The stars shine brighter here, in a sky at its largest, and I feel Earth's magnificence. Then there's Peramangk Country, covering the Adelaide Hills, where winter offers misty serenity with undulating paths through yucca, gum and pine forests, with views over Kaurna Country (Adelaide) and the ocean.

Cradle Mountain-Lake St Clair National Park (p202)

## Weather Watch (Sydney)

| JANUARY | FEBRUARY | MARCH | APRIL | MAY | JUNE |
|---|---|---|---|---|---|
| Average daytime max: **26°C** | Average daytime max: **26°C** | Average daytime max: **25°C** | Average daytime max: **23°C** | Average daytime max: **20°C** | Average daytime max: **17°C** |
| Days of rainfall: **9** | Days of rainfall: **9** | Days of rainfall: **10** | Days of rainfall: **9** | Days of rainfall: **9** | Days of rainfall: **9** |

Sculpture by the Sea

autumn (March to May). Heading west, Perth and its southern districts experience hot Mediterranean summers, pleasant shoulder seasons and increased rainfall over winter.

## Accommodation

Summer's peak school holiday months (December to January) drive up accommodation rates. Consider shoulder months March, April (excluding Easter), October and November as budget-conscious alternatives for milder weather and fewer crowds.

### THE OZONE HOLE MYTH

Despite common misconceptions, the Antarctic ozone hole – which lets through the sun's harmful UV radiation unchecked – doesn't reach Australia. Nevertheless, the country grapples with high rates of skin cancer, although the numbers are declining thanks to sunsmart campaigns. Apply (and reapply) water-resistant SPF30+ sunscreen, and wear a hat, sunglasses and protective clothing on the trail.

### BIG FESTIVALS

For over three decades, **WOMADelaide** has hosted euphoric long weekends fueled by global headliners and niche acts in Adelaide's Botanic Park, showcasing international music, arts and dance performances. **March**

As summer's scorch fades, Alice Springs radiates over 10 nights at **Parrtjima – A Festival in Light**. Light exhibitions illuminate the outback canvas, while performances, workshops and screenings celebrate Aboriginal culture. **April**

### LOCAL EVENTS

Sydney's spring heralds the arrival of **Sculpture by the Sea** on the Bondi to Tamarama Coastal Walk, featuring over 100 captivating artworks scattered along the 2km cliff-edge route. **October–November**

Explore Australia's coastline at a supported **Coastrek** event while championing a charitable cause. Multiple trail distances span Sydney's Northern Beaches, the Sunshine Coast, the Mornington and Fleurieu Peninsulas, Margaret River and Canberra's lakefront. **Various months**

| JULY | AUGUST | SEPTEMBER | OCTOBER | NOVEMBER | DECEMBER |
|---|---|---|---|---|---|
| Average daytime max: **16°C** | Average daytime max: **18°C** | Average daytime max: **20°C** | Average daytime max: **22°C** | Average daytime max: **24°C** | Average daytime max: **25°C** |
| Days of rainfall: **7** | Days of rainfall: **7** | Days of rainfall: **7** | Days of rainfall: **8** | Days of rainfall: **8** | Days of rainfall: **8** |

# Get Prepared for Australia

Useful things to load in your bag, your ears and your brain

## Clothing

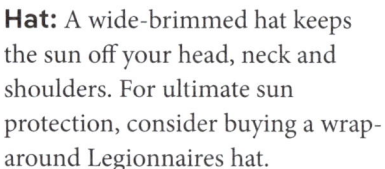

**Hat:** A wide-brimmed hat keeps the sun off your head, neck and shoulders. For ultimate sun protection, consider buying a wrap-around Legionnaires hat.

**Sunglasses:** Opt for high-coverage sunglasses that meet the UV protection Australian standard.

**Shirt:** Wear a long-sleeved collared shirt with a high UV protection rating to shield against the Australian sun. The moisture-wicking, odour-free qualities of merino wool are unrivalled, but so is the price tag. Synthetics such as polyester are an affordable alternative.

**Head net:** A face-covering mesh net shielding your eyes, mouth and ears from irritating insects; indispensable kit for remote fly-riddled trails.

**Jacket:** Stash a lightweight, windproof, rain-resistant (ideally waterproof) outer layer in your backpack. Pack a matching pair of waterproof overtrousers if the radar looks bleak.

**Socks:** Invest in breathable midweight wool-synthetic blends to counteract dreaded blisters. Additionally, lightweight sock liners can effectively wick moisture from your feet.

**Footwear:** Lightweight, worn-in hiking boots or durable trail runners are suited to most Australian day walks. Consider high-profile boots for extra ankle support on rugged multiday adventures.

**Gaiters:** These ankle-hugging spats guard against sand, insects and water infiltrating your shoes. Heavier-duty versions protect against nips from ticks, leeches and snakes.

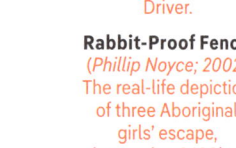

### WATCH

**Tracks**
(*John Curran; 2013*) A camel-supported solo trek 2700km across Australia's western deserts, starring Mia Wasikowska and Adam Driver.

**Rabbit-Proof Fence**
(*Phillip Noyce; 2002*) The real-life depiction of three Aboriginal girls' escape, journeying 2400km along Australia's continent-splitting fence.

**The Dry**
(*Robert Connolly; 2020*) Tense murder-mystery capturing the desolate and desperate landscapes of a drought-ravaged outback town.

Kakadu National Park (p94)

## Words

**Billabong:** A stagnant or slow-moving body of water, typically a small lake or river cutoff.

**Buckley's chance:** Little to no chance of success.

**Bush:** An all-encompassing word for Australia's rural, undeveloped areas, including forests, native landscapes and outback regions.

**Bushbashing:** Forging a path through thick scrub.

**Bushwalking:** An interchangeable term for hiking or walking through a spectrum of natural environments.

**Chockers:** Full or crowded.

**Crook:** Feeling unwell or angry.

**Dunny:** A restroom or outhouse.

**Esky:** A portable cooler or insulated box used to keep food cold.

**Hard yakka:** Physically challenging work.

**Swag:** A hardy canvas bedroll containing various bedding used for sleeping outdoors.

**Tucker:** Food.

**Woop Woop:** A remote or distant location.

### LISTEN

**Conversations**
(*Various, 2006–ongoing*) The ABC's extensive back catalogue of remarkable Australian stories – the perfect podcast companion for Aussie bushwalks.

**King Stingray**
(*King Stingray; 2022*) Fusing surf-rock, psych and traditional Aboriginal Songlines, this infectious debut album radiates energising, soulful harmonies.

**Songs from the South**
(*Paul Kelly; 1997*) Paul Kelly's melodious, toe-tapping greatest hits album leafs through Australia's national song sheet.

### READ

**Dark Emu**
(*Bruce Pascoe; 2014*) Pascoe reframes Australia's portrayal of its First Nations people, challenging the colonial narrative.

**From Snow to Ash**
(*Anthony Sharwood; 2020*) A classic self-discovery long-distance hiking novel detailing Victoria's sublime High Country bushscapes.

**Kindred: A Cradle Mountain Love Story**
(*Kate Legge; 2019*) Retracing the hard-fought origins of Tasmania's third-oldest national park.

# EXPLORE

Mt Feathertop (p172)

# Contents

**SYDNEY & AROUND** 21

**BYRON BAY TO THE SUNSHINE COAST** 39

**THE DAINTREE & THE FAR NORTH** 57

**THE OUTBACK** 75

**THE KIMBERLEY & PILBARA** 101

**SOUTHWEST FORESTS TO THE SEA** 123

**FLINDERS TO FLEURIEU** 141

**GRAMPIANS TO THE HIGH COUNTRY** 163

**THE PROM TO THE GREAT OCEAN ROAD** 181

**TASMANIA'S HIGHLANDS & COASTLINES** 199

Bondi Beach, Sydney (p32)

# Sydney & Around

**01  Prince Henry Cliff Walk**
Incredible Blue Mountains views from the escarpment. **p24**

**02  Wattamolla to Otford**
Wild beauty, isolated beaches and comfortable boardwalk hiking. **p26**

**03  Bouddi Coastal Walk**
Coastal moors, stunning swimming spots and a shipwreck. **p28**

**04  Jerusalem Bay Track**
Easy-access wilderness on a section of the Great North Walk. **p30**

**05  Bondi to Coogee Clifftop Walk**
Pick your favourite beach along Sydney's iconic coast. **p32**

# Explore
# Sydney & Around

Teeming with more natural beauty than any big city deserves, Sydney boasts the world-famous harbour, bush-lined rivers, tranquil lagoons and surf-smashed coast, all of which are threaded with fantastic opportunities to stretch the legs. And just outside the city limits there are national parks in every direction, including west to the Blue Mountains World Heritage Area, and south to the world's second-oldest national park.

## Sydney

With fantastic day walks through the waterfront suburbs and in the bushland areas that dot the urban sprawl, plus excellent transport links throughout the region, it makes sense to base yourself in Sydney. There are places to stay for every budget and taste, not to mention a thriving dining and arts scene to keep you entertained when the sun goes down.

## Katoomba

Katoomba, 1½ hours' drive from Sydney (two hours on the train), is the hub for walks in the Blue Mountains and also has great accommodation options, from hostels to B&Bs and luxury hotels, as well as anything else you may need to stock up for (or to celebrate after) your walks.

 **When to Go**

Summer (December to February) can be brutal, with temperatures often tipping over 40°C, and getting hotter every year. It's also bushfire season, and coincides with school holidays, which puts the squeeze on facilities. Make sure you have plenty of water and sun protection if you walk at this time, and check for any safety warnings before heading out. Autumn (March to May) is the wettest time in the region.

Better options are winter and spring (June to November), with crisp sunny days that get slowly warmer as summer approaches.

 **Where to Stay**

In Sydney, Central Station is the main hub for trains to regional areas and buses throughout the city. If you want easy connections look for something nearby, such as in Surry Hills. **Little Albion** (littlealbion.com.au) and **Big Hostel** (bighostel.com) are both walking distance from Central. The camping ground at **Lane Cove National Park** (lanecoveholidaypark.com.au) puts bushwalks, including the Great North Walk, on your doorstep.

In Katoomba, top picks include **No 14 guesthouse** (14lovelst.com) and the **Carrington** (thecarrington.com.au).

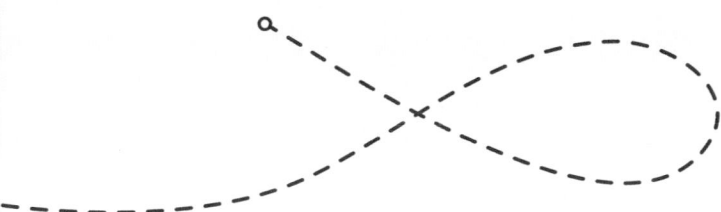

##  What's On

**Sydney Festival** (sydneyfestival.org.au; ◷Jan) Sydney's premier arts and culture festival showcases three weeks of music, theatre and visual art.

**Sydney Gay & Lesbian Mardi Gras** (mardigras.org.au; ◷Feb/Mar) A two-week cultural and entertainment festival celebrating all things queer.

**Blue Mountains Music Festival** (bmff.org.au; ◷Mar) International folk, blues and roots music comes to Katoomba.

**Vivid Sydney** (vividsydney.com; ◷May/Jun) Light installations, performances and public talks.

**Sculpture by the Sea** (sculpturebythesea.com; ◷Oct) The world's largest free sculpture exhibition is held on the Bondi to Coogee Clifftop Walk.

##  Transport

It's helpful to have your own wheels to access trailheads, but many walks are accessible using public transport (and the odd taxi). In fact, for one-way walks, it's often less complicated to use public transport.

If you want to hire a car, the big players have airport desks and city offices (mostly around William St, Darlinghurst). If you take a small car for a few days, you can hope to find deals for around the $30 a day.

All trains in Sydney and throughout the region connect to Central Station in the centre of town. Many buses also connect from here, with bus services on the north shore of the harbour connecting with Wynyard train station, two stops along from Central. The Manly Ferry connects with Circular Quay, one more train stop again from Wynyard.

## Resources

**National Parks & Wildlife Service** (nationalparks.nsw.gov.au) Maps, camping bookings, information and crucial safety warnings.

**Transport NSW** (transportnsw.info) Very useful door-to-door trip planner for using public transport.

**Sydney Coast Walks** (sydneycoastwalks.com.au) Inspiring blog with practical information.

**Wild Walks** (wildwalks.com) NSW-based online walking guide with detailed maps and trail notes.

**Best Sydney Walks** (bestsydneywalks.com) Walking blog with top picks and inspiration.

# 01

# Prince Henry Cliff Walk

| DURATION | DIFFICULTY | DISTANCE | START/END |
|---|---|---|---|
| 3½hrs one-way | Easy | 7km | Echo Point/ Gordon Falls Reserve |
| **TERRAIN** | | Bush track, some steps & mud | |

The suburban streets of quaint Katoomba give way to a colossal escarpment overlooking valleys and ranges that stretch to the horizon. This beautiful walk wraps you around the cliff edge to nearby Leura, past stunning waterfalls, bird-filled bushland and a series of breathtaking lookouts hanging over the void. This area is the traditional land of the Gundungurra and Darug peoples.

Begin in Katoomba at **Echo Point**, where the **Three Sisters** (pictured) rock formation enjoys an incredible view across the **Jamison Valley**. Watch mists swirl in this vast cauldron in winter; in summer the air shimmers with eucalyptus oil rising from millions of trees – it lends a blue haze to the forests and gives the mountains their name. Take the arched entrance between the visitor centre and the toilets and follow the signs along the trail. About 1.5km along you'll come to **Honeymoon Point**, a narrow tongue of rock looking over the valley. Continue upwards as views from the lookouts get better and better and you begin to gaze out along the valley. The path joins the road briefly, passing **Solitary Restaurant**.

A little further along the track splits. Take the high road on the clifftop, or the low road to the base of **Leura Cascades**, which is well worth it for the beautiful **viewing platform** at the end of the falls, as they wrap around a wall of rock before tumbling over the escarpment at **Bridal Veil Falls**. Back at the top, don't miss the unsigned detour to the right to **Bridal Veil View**, especially if there's been recent rain. Continue on up a steep climb to breathtaking **Tarpeian Rock**, and on to **Olympian Rock** with their perfect views of **Mt Solitary**; you'll definitely want to get that pano shot here. Finally, wrap around to **Gordon Falls Reserve**, via a number of amazing viewpoints.

# 02

# Wattamolla to Otford

| DURATION | DIFFICULTY | DISTANCE | START/END |
|---|---|---|---|
| 6 ½ hrs one-way | Moderate | 18km | Wattamolla/ Otford station |

| TERRAIN | Boardwalk, steep steps, rough track |
|---|---|

This classic walk, part of the famous Coast Track, serves up clifftop wilderness, palm jungles and sometimes an upside-down waterfall. It's in Royal National Park in Dharawal Country, on Sydney's southern doorstep. Boardwalks and evenly spaced steps installed along much of the track mean you can enjoy the incredible views without watching your footing.

## Getting Here
Park Connections (parkconnections.com.au) runs buses from Sutherland train station to Wattamolla.

## Starting Point
Wattamolla is popular for family day trips, with picnic tables, barbecues and toilets. There are five parking areas; the trail starts from the most southern (topmost) parking area.

**01** Beautiful **Wattamolla** has a **waterfall**, **lagoon** and **sheltered beach** if you want a pre-walk swim. Once on the trail you'll soon find yourself out on the open clifftops, gasping at the views. The trail leads down to rocky little **Curracurrang Cove** then up and over a set of stepping stones, after which Curracurrong comes into view.

**02** **Curracurrong (Eagle Rock)** looks spectacularly out to sea with its hooked beak. Royal National Park is home to Australia's two largest raptors – the **wedge-tailed eagle** and the **white-bellied sea eagle**. Nearby, the **Curracurrong Falls** drop straight off the cliff into the ocean;

## Tailor Your Trail

Shorten this walk by starting or stopping at Garie Beach (7.6km south of Wattamolla, 10km north of Otford). Park Connections buses run to/from Sutherland station.

Lengthen the walk by doing the full 26km **Coast Track** from Bundeena to Otford. Bundeena (8km north of Wattamolla) is linked by ferries to Cronulla (on Sydney's train network); the wharf is 1.5km from the Coast Track trailhead. A Park Connections bus stops at Sutherland train station, Bundeena Wharf and the Coast Track trailhead. Most people do the full Coast Walk over two days, camping at North Era, which has nothing but a pit toilet and an incredible beachfront location.

TRAVELLING ABOUT/SHUTTERSTOCK ©

on super-windy days the water is blown back up from the waves, seeming to flow upwards.

**03** Continue through bush regrown after a 2018 fire, until you reach steep steps down to **Garie Beach** (pictured), with toilets and sometimes a surf patrol.

**04** Climb the steep stairs to **Thelma Head**, your halfway point. Pass through the community of **South Era**.

**05** The **Burning Palms** beach is the access point for the notorious **Figure 8 Pools**. Though popular thanks to Instagram, this rock pool is extremely dangerous at high tide – there have been deaths. See nationalparks.nsw.gov.au/figure8pools.

**06** Climb over the grassy headland and descend to **Palm Jungle**, where you step among the giant cabbage palms, and it feels like a wild rumpus might begin. From here there's a steep climb through Sydney red gums (*Angophora costata*) and gymea lilies up to **Garrawarra Ridge**, where the track flattens out. Turn left at the fire trail for the 2km to the lookout.

**07** **Otford lookout** offers grand views of the coast. Cross the road here, head 30m south and turn right onto Fanshawe Rd. You may be sceptical, but this rough track will lead you down to **Otford station**, with trains to Sydney.

 ## Take a Break

The only refreshments available on the track are at the **Garie Beach Surf Life Saving Club**, which has ice creams and drinks.

# 03

# Bouddi Coastal Walk

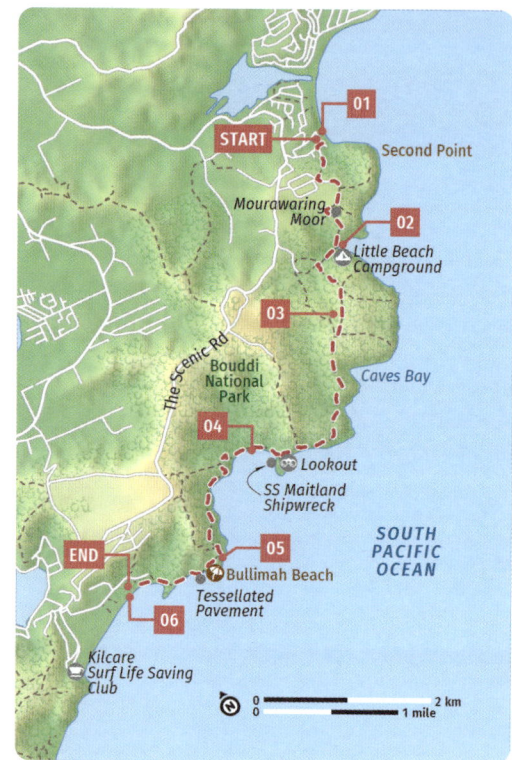

| DURATION | DIFFICULTY | DISTANCE | START/END |
|---|---|---|---|
| 4hrs one-way | Moderate | 8.5km | Macmasters Beach/Putty Beach |

| TERRAIN | Steep steps, rough track & fire trail |
|---|---|

Breathtaking coastal views, tessellating rocks, a shipwreck and the chance to spot whales make this a standout day walk. This walk links a string of beaches surrounded by Bouddi National Park (pictured) wilderness, in a well-to-do corner of the Central Coast, 90 minutes' drive north of Sydney. This is the traditional country of the Guringai and Darkinjung peoples.

## Getting Here

If possible, bring two cars and leave one at each end of the trail; public transport is scarce in this area. Otherwise take a taxi or rideshare back to your car, or to/from Woy Woy train station.

## Starting Point

You can start from either end; both have car parks, toilets, showers and cafe-restaurants.

**01** Stunning **Macmasters Beach** nestles between **Tudibaring Head** in the north and **Second Point** in the south. Access the walk via the steps painted yellow at the back of the car park behind the beach, which lead you up to Macmaster Pde. Turn left and continue to the end, where you pick up a short bush trail to Beach View Esplanade (you could also park here). Turn left and follow the trail to the end, and then a little way down the driveway of No 10, where you'll see the Bouddi National Park sign. Follow the **Mourawaring Moor** fire trail until it ends at a shady foot track into the bush.

**02** A steep trail takes you down to pretty **Little Beach**, 1.8km from Macmasters, a surf spot with a camping ground, barbecues and toilets surrounded by **littoral rainforest**. Stop for a dip, or follow the road up behind the beach until you reach a signed track to the left.

## Whale Watching

Sydney is prime whale-watching territory. Over 30,000 whales travel between Antarctica and the Pacific along the 'Humpback Highway' every year. Southern right whales also take this route, along with blue whales, orcas, minkes, sperm whales and dozens of other species. The season runs from May to November, with the best time around winter solstice (June/July), when the whales head north, swimming close to shore to avoid the southbound eastern Australian current a few kilometres offshore. From September they head south again, but ride the current so it's harder to spot them.

**Best for**

**A POST-WALK DRINK**

**03** Head steeply upwards to join the **Bombi Moors** fire trail; **native flowers** bloom here in spring. A few fire trails peel off, but stay on the signed route. Around 1km from Little Beach the route becomes a foot track again up and down steep gullies, passing **Caves Bay**, then opening out to sea views along the coast: a great photo stop is the little **wooden bridge**. Continue 600m, past a **lookout** on the left, to the steep steps down to the beach.

**04** At **Maitland Bay**, an idyllic arc of golden sand is lapped by turquoise waters. At the eastern edge a few rusty remains litter the rocks from the tragic 1898 **shipwreck** of the SS *Maitland*, which claimed 24 lives and gave the bay its name. Pick up the paved trail at the far end of the beach. Take a left at the signed track, which hugs the coast via rough tracks, boardwalks and bridges.

**05** At **Gerrin Point Lookout** you can look back over Maitland Bay, and out to the ocean to spot whales in season. Back on the trail, a right branch heads to **Bullimah Beach**, 120m off the main route. The unusual **tessellated pavement** in the sandstone, which looks like brownies sliced up in a tin, is explained on an information board.

**06** It's another 700m to **Putty Beach**, a popular swimming spot with a camping ground.

 **Take a Break**

On the opposite side of Putty Beach from the trailhead (about 1.5km), the **Kilcare Surf Life Saving Club** has a cafe.

# 04

# Jerusalem Bay Track

| DURATION | DIFFICULTY | DISTANCE | START/END |
|---|---|---|---|
| 5hrs one-way | Hard | 12km | Cowan/ Brooklyn |

| TERRAIN | Rough, steep track & fire trail |
|---|---|

A stunning slice of the Great North Walk, this track offers red-gum-studded bush with water views, a thigh-burning climb or two and the chance of a swim at pretty Jerusalem Bay. Best of all, you can easily take the train from Sydney. This walk is in Ku-ring-gai National Park, in Darramuragal and Darug Country.

## Getting Here
This trail begins and ends at train stations on the same line, Cowan and Hawkesbury River, which are linked to Sydney's Central Station.

## Starting Point
There's not much at little Cowan but a train station and a car park. Make sure you're in one of the four rear train carriages, as it's a short platform.

**01** If you're coming by train from Sydney to **Cowan station**, cross over the tracks (eastward) and head 100m north to find the signposted start of the walk. A **footbridge** takes you over the busy Pacific Motorway, after which you head steeply downhill. Follow the red Great North Walk (GNW) arrows, which guide you all the way along this walk.

**02** Head down through thick bush to step across **Cowan Creek** (pictured) on a rocky platform. The creek quickly widens as you follow it to beautiful Jerusalem Bay. The headland has a gorgeous view and is a great spot for lunch, but if you feel like a swim go a little further on to where the track touches the water (but watch for oysters).

**03** From **Jerusalem Bay** the most challenging part of the track begins with a very steep climb; latticed grips cut into the rock help secure your footing. There are two benches, one around a third of the way up and another at

## Great North Walk

Completed in 1988, the **Great North Walk** links Sydney to Newcastle with over 260km (16 days) of amazing bushwalking; this track offers just a taste of it. You can tackle the walk in many different stages. If you'd like to extend this section, the GNW continues from Brooklyn via a ferry (book ahead) or water taxi to Patonga and on over scenic Mt Wondabyne to Wondabyne train station (20km). In the other direction, the trail runs from Cowan station down to Berowra Waters (7km).

The walk is well signposted, and there are camping options along the track. If camping's not your cup of tea, you can book 'inn to inn' accommodation for most walk stages. See thegreatnorthwalk.com.

**Best for**

SOLITUDE

the top, where you can wait for any stragglers. Descend again to cross **Campbell's Creek**, then climb up until you reach a set of rungs helping you over a large boulder; beyond it you'll find a green log box.

**04** Fill in your details at the **log box** and check out the other walkers sharing the trail. You'll now take the fire management trail all the way to Brooklyn (6km away), roughly following the telephone lines. Stay on the main trail at any branches, these are service roads for the phone towers. You'll soon glimpse the water to your right – the **arched bridge** carries the train line north from Long Island, not far from where you're headed.

**05** Where the trail bends sharply to the right, an unsigned rock platform offers great **views over Long Island** and the waterways around it. Continue down to Brooklyn Dam, which is prettily sprinkled with yellow water lilies.

**06** At **Brooklyn Dam** you can take a shortcut through the camping area (to the left just before you reach the water) or follow the trail about 500m around the dam. The final 2km ends with an extremely steep descent on a concrete road, which delivers you to a residential street in **Brooklyn**. Turn left at George St to bend 300m around to the pub, or turn right if you'd rather a 1.3km stroll along the waterfront. You can't miss **Hawkesbury River train station**, which connects to Cowan station and Sydney.

 **Take a Break**

The **Anglers Rest Hotel** (anglersresthotel.com.au) is a welcome sight with a bar, a restaurant and accommodation.

# 05

# Bondi to Coogee Clifftop Walk

**Best for**

**A COOLING SWIM**

| DURATION | DIFFICULTY | DISTANCE | START/END |
|---|---|---|---|
| 2½hrs one-way | Easy | 6km | Bondi/Coogee |

| TERRAIN | Paved, some steep steps |
|---|---|

A must-do on any trip to Sydney, the Bondi to Coogee Clifftop Walk takes you on a stroll straight into the city's laid-back lifestyle. Join the dog-walkers, runners, pram-pushers and beach-hoppers, clad only in bikinis and budgie smugglers, for this coast-hugging walk, where you can take your pick from a string of fabulous places to jump in the ocean. Slather yourself in sunscreen for this one – there's very little shade on the trail – and don't forget your swimmers.

## Getting Here

Many buses head to Bondi and Coogee Beaches; the regular No 362 links the two. Parking is tricky and mostly time limited – try the back streets. You can walk the track in either direction.

## Starting Point

There are facilities aplenty at Bondi and Coogee Beaches, including cafes, bars, toilets, drinking fountains and showers.

**01** The walk starts at the south end of **Bondi Beach**, one of Australia's most iconic sites. It's the closest ocean beach to the city and is a genuinely world-class stretch of sand with great waves, ocean pools at either end and a holiday atmosphere. Thousands of unfortunates have to be rescued from the surf each year (enough to make a TV show about it), so don't become a statistic – swim between the flags.

**02** When you're ready to walk, head up to Notts Ave, which runs behind the legendary **Bondi Icebergs** (pictured) ocean pool at the south end of the beach. The pool started as a swimming club in 1929 for local surf life-savers wanting to keep up their fitness over winter. To become a member you must swim on three Sundays out of four through winter for five years. At the end of Notts Ave, take the steps down along the shore. You pass beautifully eroded sandstone as you head around to **Mackenzies Point**, where there's a circular lookout with **great views back over Bondi Beach**.

**03** About 50m further along look out on your left for the **Aboriginal rock engraving** of a small fish inside a large sea creature (it can't be a whale because it has gills). This is an important Bidjigal and Gadigal site. Continue around rocky **Mackenzies Bay** and **Tamarama Point** to the creamy yellow Tamarama Surf Life Saving Club.

**04** At **Tamarama**, the long, narrow run of sand meets a beach with notoriously rough surf and rips. Marked on early maps as 'Gamma Gamma' (which may be an Aboriginal word for 'storm'), Tamarama is also known as 'Glamarama' for its high concentration of ritzy residents. The beach is backed by a park and the trail swings around it, or you can cut across the beach and up behind the **cafe**. Continue on the footpath along Tamarama Marine Dr until you reach Bronte, and take the steps down towards the beach.

**05** **Bronte Beach** lays claim to having the oldest surf life-saving club in the world (1903), which you pass just before reaching the beach. Contrary to popular belief, Bronte is named after Lord Nelson, who doubled as the Duke of Bronte (a place in Sicily), and not the famous literary sisters. Behind the popular stretch of sand is a **large park** dotted with sheltered picnic tables. The sweet **Bronte Train** has chugged around its tiny track with little kids aboard since 1947; it runs from 11am to sunset on weekends. The **Bronte Baths** ocean pool lies in the south corner of the beach, but the trail heads up the steps before the pool to Calga Pl.

## Detour: Bronte Gully

A surprising find behind Bronte Beach is a lovely spring-fed waterfall in a patch of natural bushland. To find it, head inland through the park from Bronte Beach, dodging Frisbees and cricket matches, past the kids' playground and continue on as the park becomes a foot track. The vegetation here is thick enough to hide the surrounding houses. About 500m from the beach you'll find the pretty falls, which tumble from a permanent spring, probably with a dog or two in the pool taking a swim.

The council rehabilitated the creek after decades of neglect in 2011, pulling 20 bags of garbage from the site.

**06** Follow the road around the cliff edge and through a **rock cutting** that was built around 1910 for the long-gone Bronte tram. At the end of the cutting turn left onto the footpath and head through Calga Reserve past **Oushi Kokei (Twice Twist Bands)**, a granite sculpture by Japanese artist Keizo Ushio on permanent display since it featured in Sculpture by the Sea in 2012.

**07** Ahead, **Waverley Cemetery** has gorgeous **views out to sea**. It was opened in 1877, and notable Australians such as the poets Henry Lawson and Dorothea Mackellar and Olympic swimming legend Fanny Durack are buried here among lovely old Victorian and Edwardian memorials; the cemetery is still taking new residents. The walk heads down the wooden steps and onto a boardwalk between the cemetery and the cliff edge, but you can meander through the graves if you prefer.

**08** At the corner of Boundary and Ocean Sts, stick to the coast to head down past the **Clovelly Bowling Club**. This sunbaked square of clifftop grass is a lawn-bowls club offering sensational ocean views and a hipster scene on weekends. Book in advance if you want a game, or just drop in for a beer in the down-to-earth bar.

**09** Continue along Burrows Park around to **Clovelly Beach**, a sheltered swimming spot with concrete platforms along each side covered in sunbaked bodies, plus an ocean pool. The concrete surrounds were built during the 1930s depression to create work for unemployed men. The same scheme planned to build a causeway across the entrance to the bay, but a huge storm in 1938 put a stop to that; the remains of the causeway works can still be seen at low tide. Make your way to the other side of the beach and up around the surf life-saving club to take the footpath between the car park and the rock shelf. You'll shortly find yourself on the trail down to the next bay.

**10** Rocky **Gordon's Bay** is short on sand, but still popular with bathers who stretch out on the rocks lining the shore. The trail heads up steep steps on the north side of the bay and continues on boardwalks. The bright green plants with diamond-shaped leaves growing along the trail are warrigal greens – a native, antioxidant-rich, spinach-style plant that James Cook took aboard the *Endeavour* in Sydney to ward off scurvy. Right now these greens are having something of a moment, as Sydney chefs fall in love with native flavours. However, *warrigal* means 'dog' in the local Darug and Dharawal languages; bear this in mind if you're tempted to sample the greens along this popular dog-walking route.

**11** Round the bay past the racks of dinghies pulled up on the Gordon's Bay shore and follow the path up to Major St and the top of the hill; take the sandy walking track that branches to the left at the edge of the park. This short detour

## Sculpture by the Sea

In October/November the 2km section of this walk between Bondi and Tamarama becomes an open-air gallery for **Sculpture by the Sea** (sculpturebythesea.com), when more than 100 artists display their creations alongside Mother Nature's efforts. It's great for art buffs, though not so great if you dislike crowds – half a million people walk the trail during the three-week run. Opened in 1997, the free exhibition features sculptures large and small, serious and humorous, with plenty of chances to interact with the works.

around the headland takes you through scrub and across pink, gold and white sandstone, then delivers you back to the path. Ahead, the **Bali Bombing Memorial** (pictured) stands at Dolphins Point. The three interconnecting loops commemorate the 2002 Bali bombings, when 202 people, including 88 Australians, were killed in a terrorist attack at Kuta Beach. Dolphins Point is named in memory of the six Coogee Dolphins footballers who were killed in the blast. Nearby, crucifixes, rosaries and other offerings mark the spot where the **Virgin Mary** appeared on sunny afternoons in 2003. Sceptics claimed it was an optical illusion – judge for yourself online.

**12** From here the golden arc of Coogee Beach comes into view. **Giles Baths**, accessed from a trail near the Bali Memorial or along the rock platform from the beach, is a 'bogey hole' (natural rock pool). Oscar Giles ran a health centre here from 1928, popular with celebrities, offering remedies such as electricity treatments, hydrotherapy and sweat therapies for weight loss, where people sat in heated boxes with their heads poking out the top.

**13** **Coogee** (locals pronounce the 'oo' as in the word 'took') has a deep sweep of sand and plenty of green space for barbecues. This is the perfect spot for a post-walk swim. If surf and sand aren't your thing, there are (another) three popular ocean pools nearby – **Ross Jones Memorial Pool** at the far end of the beach; women-only **McIvers Baths** up on the headland, which dates from 1886; and open-to-everyone **Wylie's Baths** next door.

 **Take a Break**

With numerous indoor and outdoor bars and restaurants, and a large kids' play area, the cavernous **Coogee Pavilion** (merivale.com.au/coogeepavilion) complex packs them in, especially at weekends. It's a few steps from the end of the walk.

# Also Try...

## SPIT TO MANLY

| DURATION | DIFFICULTY | DISTANCE |
|---|---|---|
| 4hrs one-way | Moderate | 10km |

This wonderful harbourside walk offers pristine bushland, Aboriginal rock carvings, swimming beaches and a stickybeak at some of Sydney's most affluent suburbs.

Take a bus from either Wynyard in the city or Manly Ferry Wharf to the Spit Bridge. The walk (pictured) wraps around the foreshore past harbour beaches, through suburban streets and into 2km of wilderness in Sydney Harbour National Park. You can detour south 400m to cute little Grotto Point Lighthouse, an active beacon. Not far past the turn-off are engravings of kangaroos, boomerangs, a whale and lots of fish, believed to be in Kuring-gai Country. These ceremonial grounds command a fine view straight out to the ocean between North and South Heads. Continue on, passing rocky shorelines and parkland, until you reach Manly with its restaurants, bars and the ferry back to town.

## GRAND CANYON WALK

| DURATION | DIFFICULTY | DISTANCE |
|---|---|---|
| 3½hrs return | Moderate | 6.3km |

Though hard hit by the devastating bushfires of 2019, the Grand Canyon Walk remains a Blue Mountains classic for its steep descent to the canyon floor, weaving behind waterfalls, and now also offers the chance to see the amazing powers of the Australian bush to regenerate.

The trailhead is at Evans Lookout in Blackheath, a breathtaking viewpoint across the Grose Valley. It loops back via the Neates Glen car park; the last section of the walk is on the road but you can take this less-interesting section first by parking at Neates Glen. Steep steps, some dating from 1907, take you in and out of the canyon, making it a hot walk in summer, but the canyon is shaded by its tall cliffs and there's a chance for a swim if you follow a short detour upstream at the bottom of the canyon.

ALEXROCH/SHUTTERSTOCK ©

## LANE COVE RIVER LOOP

| DURATION | DIFF | DISTANCE |
|---|---|---|
| 5hrs return | Easy | 9.5km |

Follow the Lane Cove River through natural bushland just 12km north of the Harbour Bridge, where you can enjoy frog song, birdlife and lovely spots to picnic.

Park near the Fullers Rd entry of Lane Cove National Park (or catch the bus from Chatswood train station) and follow the Riverside Walking Track for 5.2km on the south side of the river, cross De Burghs Bridge with the busy A3 highway, and join the trail on the other side of the river, which is part of the Great North Walk heading all the way to Newcastle.

## WEST HEAD LOOP

| DURATION | DIFF | DISTANCE |
|---|---|---|
| 5hrs return | Hard | 8.5km |

With twinkling water views to Barrenjoey Lighthouse through red gums in sandstone-studded bush, this walk from a car-free community is a stunner.

The walk starts at Great Mackerel Beach, which is only accessible by boat (including a ferry from Palm Beach). The trail hugs the steep shore of Pittwater on Sydney's northern fringe, past isolated beaches and historic gun emplacements installed during WWII. The track loops back to the ferry via the beautiful West Head Lookout (pictured) and superb Garrigal rock-art sites.

## NARRABEEN LAGOON TRAIL

| DURATION | DIFF | DISTANCE |
|---|---|---|
| 2½hrs return | Easy | 8.6km |

This wheelchair-, pram- and bike-friendly trail is a lovely lagoon loop in the Northern Beaches.

You'll pass grassy picnic spots, kids' playgrounds and sheltered lagoon beaches, and stroll through natural bushland. It's a great place to spot birds – there are 190 species in the area, including black swans, pelicans, cormorants and great egrets – or to learn to ride a bike. Jamieson Park Paddle rents bikes and kayaks. Buses from Wynyard (1¼ hours) stop near the bridge over the lagoon on Pittwater Rd.

**Byron Bay**

# Byron Bay to the Sunshine Coast

**06** **Tibrogargan & Trachyte Circuits**
Loop around ancient volcanic peaks in the Glass House Mountains. **p42**

**07** **Mt Mitchell**
Ascend this conical peak for great valley views from the top. **p44**

**08** **Mapleton Falls to Gheerulla Falls**
A ridge, woodland and valley hike between two splendid waterfalls. **p46**

**09** **Cape Byron**
A beautiful walk to the lighthouse on the eastern tip of the continent. **p50**

**10** **Minyon Falls Loop**
Experience spectacular Minyon Falls from the top and the bottom. **p52**

# *Explore*
# Byron Bay to the Sunshine Coast

Southern Queensland and the north of New South Wales (NSW) is a hiker's smorgasbord of wave-pounded coastal walks, rainforest and highland forest rambles, waterfall encounters and even some demanding peak scrambles. These trails are justifiably popular, but if you avoid weekends and school holidays, it's still possible to enjoy some solitude.

## Brisbane

Flanked by Moreton Bay with its low-lying sandy isles, the capital of Queensland is a happening place with a lively dining and nightlife scene, as befitting an Australian state capital, and a picturesque setting on the Brisbane River. The Glass House Mountains are an hour's drive north, while Mt Mitchell and the Main Range are just over an hour to the southwest, making it a decent base for bushwalking.

## Byron Bay

Picturesquely situated at the end of a long bay, Byron Bay has a hippie past that's still present in the form of alternative therapies and New Age bookstores, alongside a thriving surfer culture and an increasing number of chic boutiques, snazzy restaurants and craft-beer joints. Byron Bay is within walking distance of windswept Cape Byron, and it's half an hour's drive from the town to the Minyon Falls trailhead.

## Noosa

If you're keen on bushwalking in Mapleton National Park, glitzy Noosa – the Sunshine Coast's most popular resort – is less than 40 minutes' drive away. During your downtime, you can hit Noosa's fearsome waves and mix it up with some world-class dining and working on your tan. You can also stretch your legs in Noosa National Park, with its beautiful coastal walks and koala-spotting opportunities.

## When to Go

The cooler and drier months (May to September) are the best time for hiking in south Queensland and the north of NSW, when the days are warm and balmy without being scorching. Tropical cyclone season (November to April) sometimes brings torrential rains even this far south, while the shoulder months (October, November, March and April) are typically pretty dry with plenty of daylight, and minus the peak-season crowds.

##  Where to Stay

Accommodation in NSW and Queensland has something for every budget, from basic camping grounds and caravan parks to motels, international chain hotels, hostels and boutique hotels in cities, beachside resorts and even luxury wilderness camps in or near national parks. Figure out where you want to hike and base yourself near your chosen

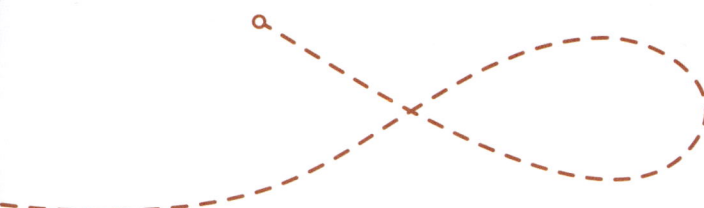

trailhead. Book accommodation in popular destinations and inside national parks well ahead (particularly during school holidays) and be prepared for soaring peak-season prices. See visitnsw.com/accommodation and discoverqueensland.com.au/accommodation for helpful listings.

##  What's On

**Noosa Festival of Surfing** (noosafestivalofsurfing.com; ⊙Feb or Mar) A week of wave-riding action with a huge range of competition divisions and live music.

**Byron Bay Bluesfest** (bluesfest.com.au) Held over the Easter long weekend, this popular festival attracts high-calibre international performers and local heavyweights.

**Bleach** (bleachfestival.com.au; ⊙Apr) Art shows, contemporary dance, music of all genres, theatre and other performances are held over 12 days on the Gold Coast.

**Splendour in the Grass** (splendourinthegrass.com; ⊙late Jul) This huge three-day Byron Bay festival features big-name artists such as Lorde, The Cure and LCD Soundsystem.

**The Curated Plate** (thecuratedplate.com.au/sunshine-coast; ⊙Aug) This fortnight-long food festival celebrates the Sunshine Coast's flourishing food scene.

**Bigsound Festival** (bigsound.org.au; ⊙Sep) Huge new Brisbane music festival held over four nights, featuring dozens of musicians and 18 venues.

**Brisbane Festival** (brisbanefestival.com.au; ⊙Sep) One of Australia's largest arts festivals, with three weeks of concerts, plays, dance and fringe events.

**Coolangatta Gold** (sls.com.au/coolangattagold) This is an epic gruelling test of surf life-saving endurance: a 23km surf-ski paddle, a 3.5km swim, a 6.1km board leg and two beach runs add up to an arduous 41.8km.

##  Transport

Brisbane is the regional hub for domestic flights from other state capitals and towns, as well as nonstop international flights to New Zealand, North America and Asia, while Byron Bay's closest airport in Ballina is served by flights from Melbourne and Sydney. Noosa is a couple of hours' drive north of Brisbane, linked to the city by numerous bus services.

## Resources

**Queensland Parks & Wildlife Service** (parks.des.qld.gov.au) Queensland's parks, nature reserves, trails and accommodation.

**NSW National Parks** (nationalparks.nsw.gov.au) Your one-stop shop for info on NSW parks, trails and accommodation bookings.

**Bureau of Meteorology** (bom.gov.au) Check the forecast before you set off.

**Queensland** (queensland.com) Extensive outdoor activities section under 'Things To Do'.

**Visit NSW** (visitnsw.com) Find NSW's outdoor activities under 'Adventure & Sport' and 'Nature & Parks'.

**Australian Fires** Useful bushfire app that shows up-to-date locations and severity of local bushfires.

**Bushwalking NSW** (bushwalkingnsw.com) Detailed walking trail info on 27 NSW national parks.

**QORF** (qorf.org.au/resources/places-to-go-master/multi-use-trails) Extensive info on Queensland's trails, from Great Walks to regional day hikes.

# 06

# Tibrogargan & Trachyte Circuits

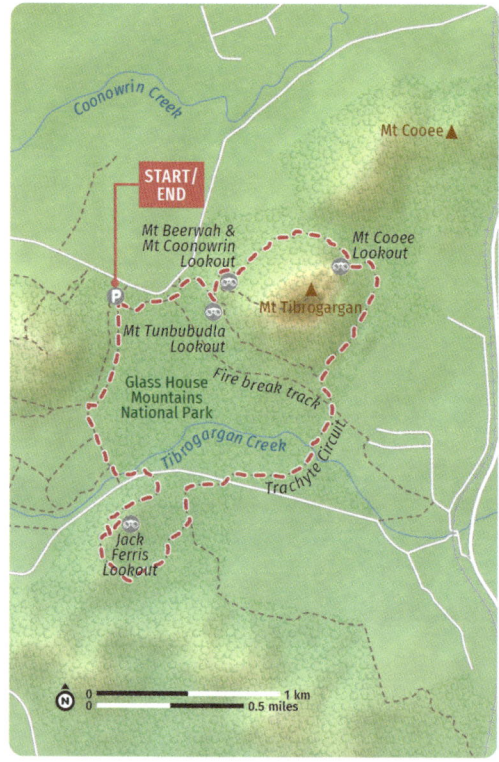

| DURATION | DIFFICULTY | DISTANCE | START/END |
|---|---|---|---|
| 3-4hrs return | Moderate | 7.3km | Mt Tibrogargan car park |

| TERRAIN | Forest trail with some steps & gentle inclines; little shade |
|---|---|

The Glass House Mountains (pictured) are ancient volcanic peaks, rising from dense woodland and steeped in Aboriginal history. This family-friendly loop allows you to contemplate Mt Tibrogargan from all angles and observe the ancient landscape from a lookout on Trachyte Ridge.

From the car park, the level trail runs through a casuarina grove, reaching a **viewpoint** some 400m later. Here you can see the two conical peaks of Mt Tunbubudla, known as 'The Twins' (or 'the breasts'!), before coming to a junction in the trail. Resume your clockwise circuit around Mt Tibrogargan, the stone monolith rising steeply out of verdant greenery.

As you go up some steps, you reach another **lookout**, with the distinctive cone of Mt Beerwah and the forbidden stone pillar of Mt Coonowrin dominating the thickly forested valley. The trail winds gently through thickets of paperbark, eucalyptus and casuarina trees. Ten minutes further into the walk, another **lookout point** shows off forest-covered Mt Cooee, where a warrior rested on his Dreaming journey, according to Jinibara folklore.

Another 15 minutes' walk takes you around the far side of Mt Tibrogargan. At the next turnoff, follow the Trachyte Circuit. Meandering through open woodlands and past spear-topped grass trees, the trail crosses a creek and a fire-maintenance road, before passing the trailhead for the challenging Yul-yan-man track. Look out for the yellow blossoms of the **candlestick banksia flowers** that attract rainbow lorikeets. Around 1km further along the trail, take the turnoff for the Jack Ferris Lookout for **stellar views of Mt Tibrogargan**. From the lookout, it's another 30 minutes back to the trailhead, with glimpses of Mt Tibberoowuccum en route.

# 07

# Mt Mitchell

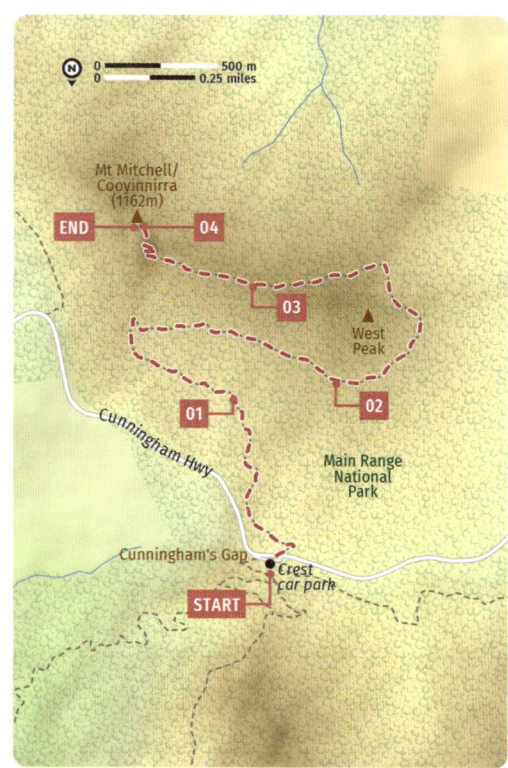

| DURATION | DIFFICULTY | DISTANCE | START/END |
|---|---|---|---|
| 3-4hrs return | Moderate | 10.2km | Crest car park, Cunningham's Gap |

| TERRAIN | Rugged track through forest & up a mountain ridge; some steep sections |
|---|---|

Enjoy unparalleled views of the Main Range, the Moogerah Peaks and Mt Barney from the knife-edge ridge of Mt Mitchell's summit. The hike is an occasionally steep, energetic leg-stretcher that takes you from rainforest and through grass-tree-filled woodland to an exposed bluff covered in montane heath. Only attempt this ascent if you're of above-average fitness, prepare for all weather eventualities and take plenty of water with you.

## Getting Here

From Brisbane take Cunningham Hwy towards Cunningham's Gap for 110km. At the top of Cunningham's Gap turn right into the Crest car park.

## Starting Point

The Mt Mitchell trailhead is on the opposite side of the highway from the Crest car park. Take extreme care when crossing, as it's a very busy road.

**01** Starting across the road from the Crest car park, the first part of the trail climbs steadily through **subtropical rainforest** of twisted vines and giant buttress roots, winding around moss-covered boulders and strangler figs. You'll need to scramble over fallen logs. This is arguably the most scenic day hike in the Main Range National Park, and the trail is home to rare, threatened and endemic reptiles and mammals, such as Fleay's barred frog, the spotted-tailed quoll and the Hastings River mouse.

**02** Just over 2km into the hike, as you pass the elevation of 1000m, there are noticeable changes in vegetation around you. The canopy opens up as you venture through **eucalyptus and**

## Scenic Rim Trail

Stretching from the trailhead in the Laidley Valley to Cunningham's Gap, the **Scenic Rim Trail** is a challenging four-day, 38km adventure. It follows a rugged track that combines new and existing walking trails through the mountains of Main Range National Park, at the northern tip of the Gondwana Rainforests of Australia World Heritage Area, and it will be possible to combine ascents of Mt Mitchell with multiday treks. Three camping areas designated exclusively for the Scenic Rim Trail will be available for independent hikers. For camping permits and route information visit parks.des.qld.gov.au/parks/main-range/scenic-rim-trail.html.

grass-tree woodland that covers the mountain's exposed ridges. Look out for rare birds, such as the Albert's lyrebird, eastern bristlebird and black-breasted button quail. At around the 3km mark, the trail levels out, and you get a breather for around 1km or so before tackling the steepest section.

**03** The final part of the hike feels interminable, as the trail corkscrews steeply up the exposed north flank of Mt Mitchell. Weather can be quite changeable up here, so make sure you have windproof and rainproof gear and be prepared for sudden onsets of rain and fog and windy conditions. Keep an eye out for **peregrine falcons** (pictured) circling the peaks overhead.

**04** When you find yourself on **West Peak** (1162m), make your way onto the saddle between the peaks, and scramble onto the knife-edge ridge above a sheer cliff on **East Peak** (1175m), known as Cooyinnirra to the original owners of this land. You'll be rewarded with **exceptional panoramic views across the Scenic Rim** – Fassifern and Millar Vale Creek Valleys, and Mts Maroon, Lindesay, Barney and Ballow in the Main Range escarpment.

 **Take a Break**

There are very few in terms of facilities in the immediate vicinity of the Mt Mitchell trailhead, so your best bet is to head back to Brisbane. In the city, treat yourself to a meal at the gastronomic carnival that is **Eat Street Northshore** (eatstreetmarkets.com). Brisbane's riverside village of shipping-containers-turned-kitchens serves everything from freshly shucked oysters to Japanese *yakisoba*, grilled meats, Sicilian cannoli and craft brews, with a backdrop of live music.

# 08
# Mapleton Falls to Gheerulla Falls

| DURATION | DIFFICULTY | DISTANCE | START/END |
|---|---|---|---|
| 7-9hrs return | Moderate | 17km | Mapleton Falls car park |

| TERRAIN | Partially shaded forest trail with some steep sections & stairs |
|---|---|

Bookended by two sets of waterfalls, this hike combines valley, mountain and forest scenery. An enjoyable tramp through eucalyptus groves and rainforest, this is the most varied day section of the Sunshine Coast Great Walk in terms of scenery and is accessible enough for families (with shortcuts for tired legs) while being suitably challenging. And if this isn't enough of a challenge, there are a number of ways that you can extend this walk.

## Getting Here
From Mapleton township turn west onto Obi Obi road and then turn right into Mapleton Falls Rd; it's a 4km drive. Mapleton is 118km north of Brisbane and 51km southwest of Noosa.

## Starting Point
The hike starts at the Mapleton Falls lookout. There is limited parking in the small car park next to the falls, so it's best to park further down the road.

**01** From the Mapleton Falls (pictured) day area, take the short boardwalk to the **vertigo-inducing viewpoint**, some 150m above the valley floor and overlooking the waters of **Pencil Creek** cascading 120m down the escarpment. The falls are at their most impressive during the summer wet season. Particularly during August and September, you may spot Australian peregrine falcons, which roost near the cliff edges of the falls. Spend a few minutes contemplating the **impressive views** of the Obi Obi Gorge and scenic Mary River Valley to the west before returning to the main trail. Make sure you have ample drinking water (there are no places to fill up along the trail), sunscreen and insect repellent, and consider using leech socks if hiking during wet weather.

**02** As you pass the picnic tables, the main trail merges seamlessly with the **Wompoo Circuit**. Take the left fork in the trail (follow the 'Great Walk' signs) and keep to the mix of dirt track, boardwalk and steps though a combination of dense eucalyptus forest and thickets of piccabeen palm trees near the creek. Look out for the **giant strangler fig** with its impressive buttress roots. As you're walking, listen out for the distinctive, haunting 'wallock-a-woo' and 'book-a-roo' calls of the endemic wompoo fruit doves after which this section of the trail is named.

**03** Shortly after the trail crosses a creek, you'll come to the **Peregrine Lookout** on your left. The viewpoint overlooking the valley is only a few metres away, with appealing vistas of greenery-covered rolling hills below.

**04** When the Wompoo Circuit trail splits in two, take the left fork. The dirt track becomes the unpaved Daymar Rd after some 200m, and you pass by some houses and reach Delicia Rd after another 300m. Make sure to follow the 'Great Walk' trail signs once you cross Delicia Rd to avoid going off along one of the fire trails instead of the main track.

**05** Less than 10 minutes down the track, you come across the shelter marking the Delicia Rd entrance to the Great Walk, complete with detailed information boards. Here the Great Walk continues along the **Linda Garrett Circuit** that passes through rainforest and a grove of piccabeen palms just before the trail splits. Take the left fork through wet eucalypt forest, dominated by blackbutt, turpentine, flooded gum and brush box

### Detour: Kondalilla Falls Circuit

Just 6km down the road from Mapleton, Kondalilla National Park offers a great half-day walk (4.7km, 2½ hours) to a viewpoint overlooking **Kondalilla Falls** (pictured p48), which is particularly impressive during the wet season. From the Kondalilla picnic area, take the mostly level Picnic Creek Circuit trail through dry eucalyptus forest and grass-tree groves until you reach the rock pools at the top of the falls. From here, the Kondalilla Falls Circuit snakes past exposed rocky bluffs, with numerous switchbacks, before descending steeply into the rainforest gorge, with great views of the cascading waters and the pool from the lookout. Your leg muscles will get a workout on the stairs up and down the escarpment.

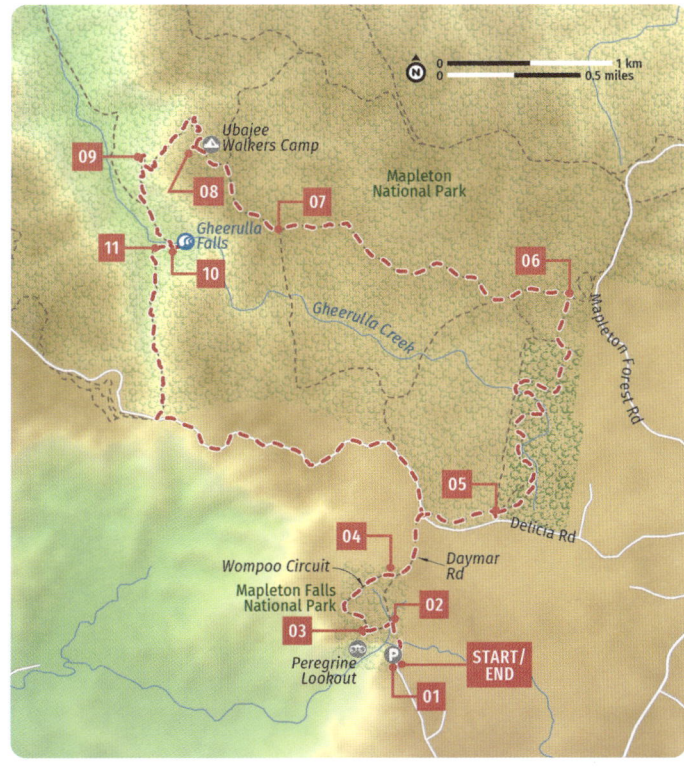

trees. Shortly before the trail reaches the rest area overlooking **Gheerulla Creek**, you'll spot a giant tree stump with centuries-old axe cuts. As you follow the creek, look carefully and you may spot the ground-dwelling great barred frog, its colouring blending in with that of the rotting vegetation.

**06** The next section of the Great Walk joins the firebreak system and becomes a multiuse track known as **Leafy Lane**. Departing from the Leafy Lane trailhead is the pretty, 400m-long Pilularis Walk that loops through an understorey of rainforest shrubs and ferns beneath a eucalyptus canopy.

**07** Back on Leafy Lane, follow the 'Great Walk' signs and be aware that you'll be sharing 2km with people on horseback and mountain bikes; take care not to tread in manure. It's a breezy ramble through open eucalyptus forest and even on sunny days there's plenty of shade, but you'll still be grateful you brought all that water along. After 2km you come to a fork in the trail; the Great Walk departs the multiuse trail along the left branch. This narrow hiking track leads to the **Ubajee Walkers' Camp**, one of the three basic camping grounds along the Great Walk, complete with wooden platforms and shaded by blackbutt forest. Here you'll find some toilets and it's a good place to break for lunch.

**08** Some 150m beyond the Ubajee Walkers' Camp, on the left, is the **Ubajee Viewpoint**, overlooking the forested hills of the Gheerulla Valley.

## Sunshine Coast Hinterland Great Walk

Have four days to spare? Then why not tackle the 58km-long **Sunshine Coast Hinterland Great Walk**? It passes through Kondalilla, Mapleton Falls and Mapleton National Parks and spans the mountains and forests of the Blackall Range, plus a whole range of ecosystems – from subtropical rainforest to open eucalyptus groves, with wonderful views over valleys, gorges and waterfalls en route.

This trail has multiple access points – the townships of Montville, Flaxton, Mapleton and Gheerulla. Walkers can choose between tackling the entire walk, camping overnight in the three remote walkers' camps, or opting for day walks and half-day walks, staying in holiday accommodation in the nearby townships.

If camping, book well in advance (qpws.usedirect.com/qpws) due to high demand.

**09** Pick up the trail and follow the signs for 'Thilba Thalba', descending along a steep series of switchbacks until the track hits an old logging road. At the trail junction, ignore the Great Walk continuing uphill and over a ridge to Thilba Thalba and turn left instead, following the signpost for the **Gheerulla Falls** along the narrow trail that runs parallel to the Gheerulla Creek, with gentle inclines.

**10** Another 500m along the trail, there's another junction. The left fork leads you to the falls themselves. As you're guaranteed to be pretty grimy and sweaty by then, it's worth descending the steps to the **pool below the cascades**, as it's deep enough for a relaxing soak. Contemplate the canopy above you as you float in the cool water.

**11** You then have two choices. You can either retrace your steps along the 8.5km trail you've just walked or you can take the shortcut from the junction that meanders through the valley alongside Gheerulla Creek, rejoining Delicia Rd near the exit from the Wompoo Trail. The shortcut is rather less scenic, but it shaves 4km off your return.

##  Take a Break

The walk's proximity to urban life is a boon. Of the three nearby townships, attractive little Mapleton is your best bet for post-hike refreshments due to sheer variety. The **Mapleton Tavern** (mapletontavern.com.au) – a favourite with bushwalkers – serves Aussie seafood platters and steaks with a side of valley views from its shady verandah.

# 09

# Cape Byron

| DURATION | DIFFICULTY | DISTANCE | START/END |
|---|---|---|---|
| 2hrs return | Moderate | 3.7km | Captain Cook Lookout |

| TERRAIN | Mostly paved; sandy sections, steps |
|---|---|

This stunning walk meanders through rainforest, wraps around ocean-pounded cliffs and swings by beautiful stretches of sand, all fairly close to central Byron Bay. Along the way you'll take in the most easterly point of mainland Australia, a photogenic lighthouse and multiple inviting beaches (definitely bring your swimmers). You may spot surfers, hang-gliders and ocean kayakers and, if you're lucky, dolphins and whales (June to November) – as well as plenty of bush turkeys.

## Getting Here

The track is a pleasant 1.5km walk from the centre of Byron; or park at Captain Cook Lookout or Palm Valley, or the lighthouse.

## Starting Point

You can start anywhere on the loop but a good place is Captain Cook Lookout, right on the beach, with toilets, showers and a water fountain.

**01** From **Captain Cook Lookout** follow the boardwalk along the road offering great views over the beach. Turn left 500m along at Brooke Dr for your first taste of rainforest before emerging at **Palm Valley**. There's a cafe and picnic tables here, but swing down to the beach where you'll see the steps up to Fisherman's Lookout.

**02** Keep your eyes peeled for dolphins from scenic **Fisherman's Lookout** overlooking **the Pass**, a famous right-hand point break. Retrace your steps to the car park to find the paved trail heading upwards into the scrub. You'll soon emerge on the windy cliffside overlooking the ocean. Stunning views accompany you as you round the headland and descend to Wategos Beach, 650m from Fisherman's Lookout.

## Detour: Little Wategos Beach

Australia's **most easterly beach** is only accessible on foot or by water, and it's well worth taking the short but steep 100m detour off the main trail. Far less crowded than Byron's other beaches, this secluded patch of sand feels like a private paradise. Take care swimming – currents can be strong.

This area is sacred to the Arakwal people, who know Cape Byron as Walgun. The place where the lighthouse now stands was a men's ceremonial ground, and there's a 1500-year-old pipi midden nearby, one of the largest and oldest in northern NSW. Find out more at arakwal.com.au.

**Best for**

A POST-WALK DRINK

**03** One of Byron's most beloved beaches, **Wategos Beach** is a great place to stop for a dip. Afterwards, head along the path beside the road for about 100m before it veers left into the bush and upwards onto the headland. It's 300m to the turnoff to Little Wategos Beach, after which the steps get serious till you reach the lookout.

**04** Time to get busy with your camera – this lookout is at the **easternmost point of the continent** and you might fancy you see the curve of the Earth in the ocean horizon.

Next, continue upwards to the pretty white sentinel keeping watch over the cape.

**05** The **Cape Byron Lighthouse** (pictured), built in 1901, is Australia's most powerful shipping beacon. From here wind down the path along the road with superb views over **Tallow Beach** until the walking trail leaves the road.

**06** You're now on the **Tallow Ridge Track**, following the spine of the headland. You pass a **hang-gliding launch site**, after which the track reverts to dirt and meanders through 850m of **peaceful, bird-filled rainforest**; this section is far less popular than the headland track. When you reach Lee Lane, turn left down the hill to find yourself back at Captain Cook Lookout, where a cool dip in the ocean awaits.

 **Take a Break**

Expect excellent Mediterranean-influenced dishes at exclusive little **Rae's Dining Room** (raes.com.au) overlooking Wategos Beach.

# 10
# Minyon Falls Loop

| DURATION | DIFFICULTY | DISTANCE | START/END |
|---|---|---|---|
| 4½hrs return | Moderate | 7.5km | Minyon Falls Lookout |

| TERRAIN | Maintained bush track; steep steps |
|---|---|

From the top of spectacular Minyon Falls (pictured), you traverse the rim of the escarpment, and descend through rainforest to the bottom of the falls. At the base you can scramble over boulders for a swim in the plunge pool, before making your way back out of the valley on the palm-shaded track. This is the traditional country of the Bundjalung people.

## Getting Here
The falls are only 24km southwest of Mullumbimby in Nightcap National Park, but the twisting roads around here mean it will take a good 40 minutes to drive.

## Starting Point
Most people start the loop at the Minyon Falls Lookout, but some start at Minyon Grass and complete the less-interesting road section first. Both are well signposted and have car parks, information boards, barbecues, picnic tables and toilets.

**01** At **Minyon Falls Lookout**, pause for a peek down into the valley where you're headed. The falls are spectacular when they're flowing, but can stop entirely in dry spells. Follow the track west for 200m until it branches left over Repentance Creek via a series of stepping stones (continuing on would take you to the Rummery Park camping ground). No access is permitted between the stepping stones and the edge of the falls.

**02** Cross the **stepping stones** and head up along the lip of the escarpment through blackbutt and gum forest, with **stunning views** back over the falls, and east across the rainforested valley. On a clear day you can see all the way to the coast.

## Detour: Swimming Hole

It can be easy to miss, but make sure you take the 100m detour after the creek crossing at the bottom of the cliff to the base of the falls. The route is a fairly challenging scramble over boulders and takes a bit of detective work to follow; orange arrows show the way. The plunge pool is a great place to cool off under the shower of Minyon Falls as it tumbles over columnar cliffs – just be aware that small twigs and rocks falling from the top can quickly become harmful projectiles; it's more of an issue after recent rain.

**Best for**

**SOLITUDE**

**03** The trail takes a **sharp switchback turn** to the left after about 1.5km, which marks the beginning of your steep descent into the valley. The vegetation changes dramatically as you slip into the shade surrounded by palms, ferns, Tarzan-worthy vines and magnificently tangled strangler figs. Fallen palm fronds litter the trail and the forest is pierced by blades of sunlight cutting through the canopy.

**04** You reach **Repentance Creek** again just when you've worked up a sweat. Cross it by clambering over the rocks. On the far side, signs show the way to the detour to the **swimming hole at the base of the falls**. When you're ready to get back on the track, you'll follow the creek for a while before climbing ever more steeply upwards, through a series of zigzags, until you reach **Minyon Grass picnic area** and **lookout**. The walk from the pool to the picnic ground is about 2km.

**05** From Minyon Grass, the final 1.5km stage of the walk is mostly uphill along the dirt road to the **Minyon Falls car park**, where you complete the loop. Stay on the main road when the Eastern Boundary Trail branches right. Though this road passes through pleasant-enough forest, it is the least interesting stage of the walk. For this reason, some people park at Minyon Grass picnic area and complete this stage first.

## Take a Break

The lovely town of Mullumbimby is a great place to head for a post-walk meal or drink. With its penchant for the individual and unusual, it's not surprising to find a fantastic Yemenite restaurant here: **Ya'man** (yamanmullumbimby.com.au).

# Also Try...

LARISSA DENING/SHUTTERSTOCK ©

## Double Island Point Walk

| DURATION | DIFFICULTY | DISTANCE |
|---|---|---|
| 9-11hrs return | Hard | 30km |

Hike through forest and along giant sand dunes, then refresh yourself with a dip in the tranquil lagoon before enjoying wonderful lighthouse views on this day-long walk.

Starting from Rainbow Beach, just north of Noosa, this largely flat but very long walk (set off early to make the most of the cooler hours) explores Cooloola's scenic coast and follows the old lighthouse telegraph line through blackbutt groves and along the high coastal dunes. Once you reach the beach at Double Island Point, the calm waters of the lagoon make for good swimming (unlike much of the coast, which is battered by the long, rolling waves). Watch the surfers play in the frothing sea before taking the one steep section of the trail to the lighthouse. Have a picnic lunch here against a backdrop of sweeping ocean and coastal views before retracing your steps.

## Protesters Falls Walking Track

| DURATION | DIFFICULTY | DISTANCE |
|---|---|---|
| 40mins return | Easy | 1.5km |

This short but important walk pays homage to the protesters who saved this rainforest from the logger's axe.

The 1979 Terania Creek Battle was a six-week confrontation between environmentalists, police and loggers. The human blockades against the bulldozers were the first time people put their bodies on the line to defend an Australian rainforest, and the action is credited with inspiring forest protests globally. The protest led to the 1982 'Rainforest Decision', which halted logging in most NSW rainforest. Terania Creek is now part of the World Heritage–listed Nightcap National Park, north of Lismore. The forest is home to 260 species of endangered plants and animals, including the remarkable pouched frog, whose males nurture their tadpoles to maturity in two 'hip pockets'. The peaceful walk starts on a brief boardwalk, crosses the creek and ends at the beautiful falls (pictured) and plunge pool.

PAINTINGS/SHUTTERSTOCK ©

## West Canungra Creek Circuit

| DURATION | DIFF | DISTANCE |
|---|---|---|
| 5½-6hrs return | Moderate | 14km |

Explore ancient forests, marvel at waterfalls and enjoy spectacular views in the World Heritage-listed Lamington National Park (pictured).

Take the trail down past the cascading Darraboola Falls through rainforest and groves of towering red cedars. Be careful crossing the creeks after it's been raining. Look out for monitor lizards and snakes basking in patches of sunlight. The trail takes you to the tranquil waters of Yerralahla and West Canungra Creek, where the bright blue Lamington spiny crayfish make a surprising amount of noise.

## Witches Chase Track & Witches Falls Circuit

| DURATION | DIFF | DISTANCE |
|---|---|---|
| 2-3hrs return | Moderate | 6.2km |

Trek through palm groves and past towering boulders and centuries-old cedar trees in the Tamborine National Park.

From the picnic area, the 3.6km Witches Falls Circuit trail descends through rainforest punctuated by buttress-like roots of strangler figs. It arrives at the lookout platform beside Witches Falls, where the waterfall flows into a pool over basalt cliffs. Branching off the Witches Falls Circuit, the Witches Chase Track meanders along the cliff to Witches Chase.

## Booyong Walking Track

| DURATION | DIFF | DISTANCE |
|---|---|---|
| 5-6hrs one-way | Moderate | 9km |

A lush and shady rainforest retreat filled with birds, reptiles, butterflies and majestic stands of buttressed booyong trees.

The walk is in Border Ranges National Park, 30km north of Kyogle, in the Byron Bay hinterland. You'll scramble over the occasional fallen log and across crystal-clear mountain streams (swimmable after recent rain). The track links two camping grounds – Sheepstation Creek and Forest Tops. Start at Forest Tops for a mostly downhill walk, or shorten the trek by taking the Rosewood Loop (6km) from Sheepstation Creek.

Cape Tribulation (p66)

# The Daintree & the Far North

**11 Mossman Gorge**
Navigate trails and boardwalks through the rainforest and along Mossman River. **p60**

**12 Pine Grove & Broken River**
Hike amid pines and ancient cedars, and spot platypuses in the creeks. **p62**

**13 Best of Great Keppel Island**
Explore the island from mountain peak to sublime beaches. **p64**

**14 Mt Sorrow Ridge**
Look out over the Daintree from Cape Tribulation's most challenging trail. **p66**

**15 Carnarvon Gorge**
Spot centuries-old Aboriginal art and lots of wildlife in this ancient gorge. **p68**

# Explore
# The Daintree & the Far North

Northern Queensland welcomes visitors with a wildly varied kaleidoscope of landscapes: tangled, lush vegetation and waterfalls in the world's oldest rainforest; ancient canyons with hidden Aboriginal art; highland and lowland forest; arid islands with white-sand beaches... Though some trails are well-trodden, you may have the rest entirely to yourself.

## Cairns

The gateway to the Great Barrier Reef and the rainforest in Queensland's far north, tropical Cairns is an amiable town, abuzz with seafront bars and restaurants, and packed with outdoor-adventure companies. It makes an excellent jumping-off point for hikes in the Daintree; Mossman Gorge is an easy hour's drive, while Cape Tribulation is less than two hours by car and ferry.

## Mackay

Sitting between a marina and the mangroves, the regional hub of Mackay is the perfect base for walks in the Eungella and Cape Hillsborough National Parks, and is just over an hour's drive from both. The town is also a day's drive from Cairns and its surrounding wealth of wilderness. Mackay's broad streets, lined with art-deco architecture, are fun to explore, excellent food is to be found all over the compact centre and the bars get lively after dark.

## Rockhampton

If you're planning on bushwalking in Carnarvon National Park or on Great Keppel Island, Queensland's beef capital – with Wild West–style architecture, a tranquil riverside location and a great dining scene – makes for a handy stopover. Learn about the cultural significance of Aboriginal rock paintings at the Dreamtime Cultural Centre before hitting Carnarvon Gorge, a 400km drive away, or head for the nearby coast, a mere half-hour's drive, to catch a boat to Great Keppel from Yeppoon.

## When to Go

The cooler, drier months (May to September) are the best time to hit the trail in Queensland. Tropical cyclone season (November to March) often brings torrential rains and can cut off access to parts of national parks, as well as making trails impassable. The shoulder months (April and October) mean fewer hikers on trails and mild weather. Hiking during the hottest months (December to February) means having the trails largely to yourself.

## Where to Stay

Accommodation in Queensland runs the gamut from basic camping grounds and caravan parks to motels, international

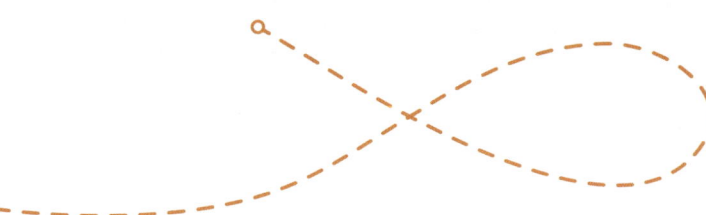

chain hotels, boho boutique joints, backpacker hostels in cities, beachside resorts and even luxury wilderness camps in Carnarvon National Park. Your best option is to base yourself in a town or national park near your desired trailhead. Book accommodation inside national parks well ahead.

## What's On

**Wintermoon Music Festival** (wintermoonfestival.com; May) On the edge of Eungella National Park, 70km north of Mackay, Wintermoon is a folk- and world-music fest.

**Port Douglas Carnivale** (carnivale.com.au; May) Port is packed for this 10-day festival, which includes a colourful street parade featuring live music and lashings of good food and wine.

**Laura Aboriginal Festival** (Jun) Sleepy Laura, 330km north of Cairns, hosts the largest traditional Aboriginal gathering in Australia, with dance, song and ceremony.

**Mackay Festival of Arts** (themecc.com.au/mackayfestivals; Jul) This 10-day extravaganza features everything from comedy, music and cabaret to food and wine.

**Australian Festival of Chamber Music** (afcm.com.au; Aug) Townsville hosts this internationally renowned festival at various venues across the city.

**Cairns Festival** (cairns.qld.gov.au/festival; late Aug) This two-week art-and-culture fest delivers a stellar program of music, theatre, dance, comedy, film and Aboriginal art.

**NRL Grand Final** (nrl.com.au; Sep) The Grand Final is the end of the annual National Rugby League competition, and is best celebrated with passionate locals.

## Transport

Cairns receives daily domestic flights from all major Australian cities (barring Canberra and Hobart), as well as many international flights, while Mackay is connected by air to Brisbane, Townsville and Rockhampton. You'll need your own wheels to access the trailheads, as there's no public transport, and bear in mind that the ferry to Cape Tribulation (for the Mt Sorrow Ridge Walk) gets very busy during peak months.

## Resources

**Queensland Parks & Wildlife Service** (parks.des.qld.gov.au) Info on Queensland's parks, nature reserves, trails and accommodation. Check out the 10 Great Walks of Queensland.

**Bureau of Meteorology** (bom.gov.au/qld) Check the forecast before you set off.

**Queensland Uncovered** (blog.queensland.com/2019/11/25/great-walks-hiking-trails-in-queensland) Get inspired before lacing up your hiking boots.

**Queensland** (queensland.com) Extensive outdoor activities section under 'Things To Do'.

**Australian Fires/QLD Fires** Useful bushfire app that shows up-to-date locations and severity of local bushfires.

**QORF** (qorf.org.au/resources/places-to-go-master/multi-use-trails) Extensive info on Queensland's trails, from Great Walks to regional day hikes.

# 11

# Mossman Gorge

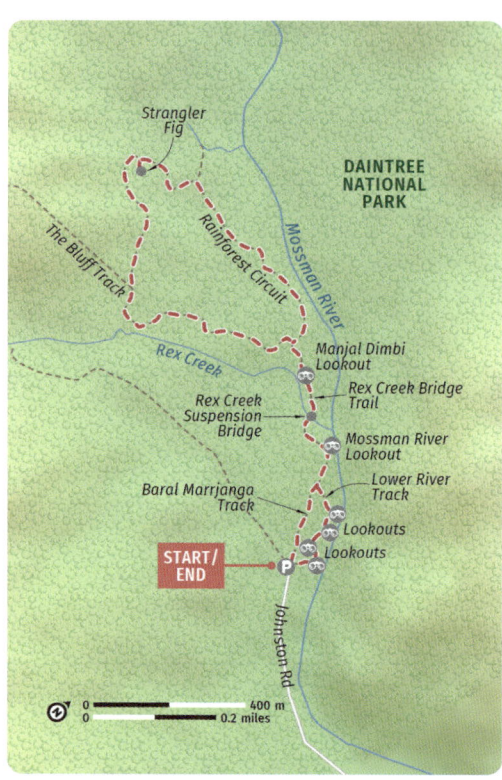

| DURATION | DIFFICULTY | DISTANCE | START/END |
|---|---|---|---|
| 2hrs return | Moderate | 3.5km | Mossman Gorge car park |

| TERRAIN | Mostly level trail, some steps |
|---|---|

Explore mighty buttress roots, rainforest canopy and the banks of Mossman River. Part of Daintree National Park, Mossman Gorge (pictured) offers four short walks, and your visit can be enhanced by doing a Kuku-Yalanji Dreamtime Gorge Walk with an Aboriginal guide.

To reach the trailheads, take a shuttle from the Mossman Visitor Centre. From the car park, the **Baral Manjara trail** (270m), consisting of elevated boardwalks, takes you through the lower rainforest canopy to a lookout point offering **terrific views of the mountains** beyond the Mossman River.

Baral Manjara then joins the short **Rex Creek Bridge trail** (230m), with a gently swaying suspension bridge across the eponymous creek.

Branching off from the Rex Creek Bridge trail is the longest of the four trails on offer: the **Rainforest Circuit** (2.4km). Head deeper into the rainforest and breathe in the smell of rotting vegetation on the forest floor as you find yourself dwarfed by ribboning, buttress-like roots. Witness the creeping vines, including the strangler fig that wraps its tendrils around its host tree and eventually chokes off its supply of nutrients, and wander beneath huge jungle ferns. From a **lookout point** near the beginning of the track, admire views of **Manjal Dimbi** (Mt Demi). Deeper in the rainforest, the track surface becomes rough and uneven with some steps, so wear shoes with good grip. Heavy rains can make the circuit temporarily impassable.

On your way back, take the **Lower River track** (300m), an easy ramble that runs parallel to the Baral Manjara trail and offers **views of the Mossman River** before depositing you back in the car park.

# 12

# Pine Grove & Broken River

| DURATION | DIFFICULTY | DISTANCE | START/END |
|---|---|---|---|
| 4½–6hrs one-way | Moderate | 12–13km | Pine Grove/ Broken River |

| TERRAIN | Forest trail, some steep sections & stairs |
|---|---|

Traverse spectacular highland and lowland scenery in search of Australia's most beguiling mammal. The Pine Grove–Broken River stretch of the Mackay Highlands Great Walk is the preferred day hike for those who don't have five days to spare for the 56km trek in its entirety, and it's easy to see why: it takes you from mighty cedars and pines and epic cliff views to rainforest creeks where platypuses play and giant monitor lizards bask in the sun.

## Getting Here

From Mackay it's an 82km drive west along the Eungella–Mackay road to Eungella, with a section of steep hairpin bends. There is no public transport.

## Starting Point

The trailhead starts at the Pine Grove car park in Eungella, just south of the main road junction and the Eungella General Store.

**01** The Pine Grove car park trailhead leads you into one of Queensland's most ecologically diverse national parks, with over 860 plant species and **ample wildlife-spotting opportunities**. Look up; the smell and the clamour may alert you to the presence of a colony of flying foxes even before you see them. As the trail meanders gently between pines, you catch a glimpse of the valley below.

**02** After 1km the trail splits. Follow the gentle inclines of **Cedar Grove Track** as it snakes around the mighty buttress roots of tulip oaks and towering red cedars, descending along some steps. One of the highlights here is the **Tree Arch** – a vast tulip oak choked by strangler fig vines with a human-sized hole between the roots.

## The Elusive Platypus

Most days of the year, you can be pretty sure of seeing a platypus (pictured) or two in the Broken River at the two **platypus-viewing platforms** and under the bridge. Broken River is reputedly one of the most reliable spots on Earth to catch these meek monotremes at play and we can vouch for it – few people leave disappointed. The best times are around sunrise and also in the afternoons, from around 3pm till dusk. You must remain patient, silent and still and watch out for tell-tale ripples, which announce the emergence of these 30cm-long mammals. Platypus activity is at its peak from May to August, when the females are fattening themselves up in preparation for gestating their young.

**Best for**

**WILDLIFE**

**03** Less than 3km later, you emerge at the **Sky Window picnic area**. The Sky Window trail is a 250m-long loop. Interpretive signs along the trail tell the story of the Wirri people, and the two lookouts offer **dramatic views** of the Pioneer Valley below.

**04** Sky Window is the beginning of the 8km **Clark Range Track** – the most demanding part of the day hike due to some steep sections and stairs. You pass through a grove of Alexandra and piccabeen palms before the trail descends to the **Broken River**. Viewpoints along the way provide glimpses of the farmland below, and you may hear the metallic-sounding 'tinks' of the tiny Eungella tinker frogs.

**05** The track crosses the Broken River and joins the **Granite Bend Circuit**, a mostly level, pleasant loop that traverses lowland rainforest and interlinks with the **Rainforest Discovery Circuit**, taking you to the Broken River picnic area. Following the riverbank, you may spot skinks and giant monitor lizards basking in patches of sunlight. Watch out for ripples and bubbles on the creek surface, alerting you to the presence of eels, river turtles and platypuses.

 **Take a Break**

A good spot for lunch or a break before you wander off in search of the eponymous riverbank-dwelling creatures, **Platypus Lodge Restaurant** is an appealing spot with outdoor seating next to the information centre. Treat yourself to good coffee, cakes and a few Aussie standards, like shepherd's pie. Nearby is a trail leading off to one of the platypus-watching platforms.

# 13

# Best of Great Keppel Island

| DURATION | DIFFICULTY | DISTANCE | START/END |
|---|---|---|---|
| 8-9hrs return | Moderate | 19-22km | Fisherman's Beach |

| TERRAIN | Moderately steep, partially sandy trail; little shade |
|---|---|

This walk takes in the best of Great Keppel, from the island's highest viewpoint to its most spectacular beaches. The largest of the Keppel Bay Islands, Great Keppel offers challenging bushwalking, terrific snorkelling and some of Queensland's best beaches, reachable via an easy-to-follow network of trails that criss-crosses the island's rugged terrain.

## Getting Here
Great Keppel Island is reached via regular 30-minute ferry trips from Yeppoon's Keppel Bay Marina on the mainland with **Keppel Konnections** (keppelkonnections.com.au) and **Freedom Fast Cats** (freedomfastcats.com).

## Starting Point
The trail starts just off Fisherman's Beach, the island's main white-sand beach, where ferries land and where most of the accommodation is located.

**01** The trail starts at the **Fisherman's Beach boardwalk**. Emerging at the unpaved road, take the **1st Lookout** trail through the bush and then ascend the partially paved road. It takes 30 minutes to reach the lookout shelter, with views of Fisherman's Beach.

**02** After a five-minute walk beyond the 1st Lookout, the trail divides. Take the right-hand trail, climbing the hillside. The 2km ascent takes 30 to 45 minutes, with viewpoints revealing **offshore islets** and a **turquoise sea**. Mt Wyndham is the highest point on the island (178m), with unobstructed vistas of Long Beach.

## Detour: Wreck Beach

It's a hot, shadeless and sandy 30-minute walk to **Wreck Beach**, but worth it for the best snorkelling on Great Keppel Island. At the north end of the beach there are some wonderful soft corals and brain corals, an abundance of reef fish, clownfish darting in and out of anemones, the occasional turtle and lots of live spider conchs. From Butterfish Bay, take the trail around the right side of the big sand dune and retrace your steps afterwards. Alternatively, instead of retracing your steps via Butterfish Bay, turn left before reaching the sand dune and follow another trail up a steep ridge, passing the turnoff to the lighthouse and descending steeply to the wetlands to rejoin the main trail.

**03** Retrace your steps to the fork, taking the dirt road down to the mangrove-fringed wetlands. Turn right, and continue beneath the sparse shade of eucalyptus trees until you reach the **Old Homestead**.

**04** Cross the pasture, pressing on though the eucalyptus grove as the trail zigzags up a hillock before descending to the **Second Beach**, separated from **Svendsen's Beach** by a promontory.

**05** From Svendsen's Beach eco-camp, it takes 15 minutes to reach Butterfish Bay. The trail climbs steeply up through woodland before skirting a sheer drop into the deep blue. Pause here on a makeshift 'bench' before scrambling down to the sandy crescent of **Butterfish Bay**.

**06** It takes two hours to retrace your steps to the 1st Lookout. Descend the potholed road and then follow the mostly shade-free trail for 2km to **Long Beach** (pictured), one of Queensland's loveliest beaches, with teal waters and squeaky white sand. Naturists can sun their buns at the north end.

**07** Take the wooden stairs at the south end of the beach and cross over to **Monkey Beach**, past a large shell midden. There's good snorkelling at the reef here.

**08** From the far end of Monkey Beach, it's a steep scramble up to the densely wooded promontory. The trail passes the turnoff to the **Shelving Beach** cove before descending to Fisherman's Beach.

 **Take a Break**

On your way back from Butterfish Bay, you can ask the owners of the eco-camp at **Svendsen's Beach** whether you can use their shady waterfront picnic area to relax and refuel. Alternatively, head for **Second Beach**, just south of Svendsen's Beach, where you can snorkel around the coral bommie (reef) and spot small eels.

# 14

# Mt Sorrow Ridge

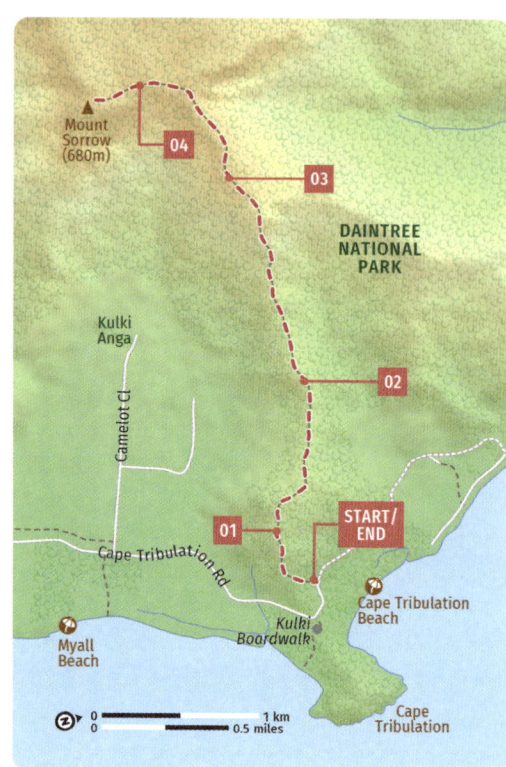

| DURATION | DIFFICULTY | DISTANCE | START/END |
|---|---|---|---|
| 6hrs return | Hard | 7km | 150m north of Kulki day-use area |

| TERRAIN | Steep rainforest trail, some log scrambling |
|---|---|

Cape Tribulation's toughest trail takes you up rainforest-clad mountain slopes to a spectacular vista. This remote, strenuous hike to the 680m viewpoint is for fit, experienced bushwalkers only, and your reward – apart from a tremendous sense of achievement – is an in-depth exploration of the world's oldest rainforest.

## Getting Here

Drive the Captain Cook Hwy for 104km north of Cairns, then take the ferry across Daintree River to Cape Tribulation. It's another 36km along a narrow, winding road to the trailhead.

## Starting Point

The trail is signposted off the main road opposite a gravel pull-off area, 150m north of the Kulki day-use area by the Kulki boardwalk, where there is ample parking.

**01** Set off well before 10am to make use of the cooler hours and give yourself plenty of daylight. The first kilometre or so of the trail climbs steadily up through a **lowland rainforest valley**, weaving its way around giant trees with large buttress roots and strangler figs winding their tendrils around host trees, with a canopy of greenery overhead and giant fan-palm leaves shading your way. You'll find yourself clambering over several fallen trees.

**02** The trail is well-marked with kilometre posts to indicate the distance. Shortly after 1km, you reach a **mini-summit**, with a short

## Dangerous Critters

The Daintree rainforest is home to the southern cassowary, Australia's second-largest flightless bird, with glossy black plumage, drooping red wattles and a crested head. Practically unchanged since the Gondwanan period, cassowaries wandered the land with the dinosaurs some 60 million years ago.

If you see one, never approach or feed it. Males defend their chicks aggressively and can inflict serious injuries by kicking with their razor-sharp claws. Back away slowly and, ideally, put a tree between the two of you.

There are venomous snakes in the Daintree too, such as the taipan, the Eastern brown, the death adder and the red-bellied black. Give them a wide berth.

**Best for**

**AMAZING VIEWS**

descent along the undulating trail that has you leaping over more logs. Just when you think the going is getting easier, the trail climbs again before dipping once more to the 2km post. Keep an eye out for the **large white flowers** growing on the trunk of the *Ryparosa kurrangii*, an endemic plant restricted to the compact area between Cape Tribulation and the Daintree River.

**03** The section between the 2km and 3km marks is the steepest and most challenging part of the trail. Even narrower in places than before, it's bisected by tree roots (which you may grab to pull yourself up in places). Along this ridge ascent, vines and giant buttresses give way to the slow-growing orania palm and other vegetation stunted due to wind shearing. If you're lucky, you may spot **Boyd's forest dragons** (pictured) perching on trees near the trail.

**04** The final 500m stretch to the lookout traverses open forest and the canopy opens up noticeably as you approach the summit. From this 680m vantage point, there are **all-encompassing views** of the Daintree coastline and Cape Tribulation township to the southeast. You may also spot **Snapper Island** and shadows of the individual reefs that make up the **Great Barrier Reef** in the teal water along the coastline. Spangled drongos and topknot pigeons make their way past the lookout platform, and there are also plenty of butterflies here. Leave the lookout at 2pm at the latest to give yourself enough daylight time for the descent.

### Take a Break

There are no day-use areas along the Mt Sorrow Ridge trail, but it's a good idea to take a breather around the 2km mark before making a push for the summit along the steepest section of the trail.

# 15

# Carnarvon Gorge

| DURATION | DIFFICULTY | DISTANCE | START/END |
|---|---|---|---|
| 7-8hrs return | Moderate | 21km | Carnarvon Gorge Visitor Centre |

| TERRAIN | Partly shaded, gentle inclines, some stairs |
|---|---|

See the highlights of the Carnarvon Great Walk in one day – from millennia-old Aboriginal rock paintings to cave gardens and waterfalls. Even if you don't have time to trek the whole CGW, some of its best features are found along this 10km stretch of Carnarvon Gorge and its side canyons.

## Getting Here
Carnarvon National Park is some 440km southwest of Gladstone along Rte 60 and Carnarvon Hwy, via Rolleston and a narrow 40km-long paved road from the turnoff.

## Starting Point
The entrance to Carnarvon Gorge is next to the Carnarvon Gorge Visitor Centre, near the seasonally open camping ground. The car park is a five-minute walk away.

**01** Starting from the **Carnarvon Gorge Visitor Centre**, cross Carnarvon Creek and proceed along the well-marked dirt track that rises gently though groves of gum and eucalyptus trees. The trail runs parallel to the north bank of Carnarvon Creek for some 3km until you reach a turnoff that takes you to the other side.

**02** Hop from stone to stone to get across the shallow creek and then follow the dirt trail as it ascends and descends among moss-covered boulders and gnarled tree roots to a short boardwalk with a bench to rest on, and a **viewing platform** overlooking an icy pool, fed by a small stream. The rock walls here are covered in different types of moss, nourished by the water seeping through porous rock and trickling down the rock face, hence its name: **Moss Garden**.

**03** Retrace your steps across the creek to the turnoff and continue along the main trail that traces the floor of the gorge, with sheer sandstone cliffs soaring on either side, topped with sparse vegetation. You'll have to cross the creek again twice before you reach the next turnoff, 1km ahead; luckily, the water isn't deep and there are **stepping stones** (pictured) here to help you across. There's some seating at the turnoff in case you need to rest your legs.

**04** At the turnoff, hop across the creek again and follow a side gorge along a rocky, uneven trail for some 350m until you reach some vertical metal ladders. Climb up the ladders to the crack in the sheer cliff. At the top of the ladders there's a narrow, partially flooded **passageway** with more stepping stones to help you cross it, and another small metal ladder for you to climb at the end. You emerge in a remarkably tranquil hidden garden, surrounded by sheer sandstone walls. The **Amphitheatre** is a natural phenomenon, caused by the gradual erosion of a massive chunk of sandstone by rainfall over hundreds of years, and a place of quiet contemplation (with a handy bench for resting).

**05** Scramble back down the ladders, cross the creek again, and carry on along the main trail that remains flat and shady as it hugs the creek bank. The gorge begins to open up, with wide creek flats covered with blady grass and copses of eucalyptus trees and tall **Carnarvon fan palms** reaching for the sky against the backdrop of yellow-and-brown cliffs. The main trail crosses the creek yet again and you shortly reach the turnoff for one of the gorge's biggest attractions.

## Carnarvon Great Walk

Carnarvon National Park's tour de force is the 87km-long, six- to seven-day **Carnarvon Great Walk** – one of Australia's best multiday hikes – a loop that links Carnarvon Gorge with Mt Moffat. It's hiked clockwise from the Big Bend camping ground, traversing the gorge and ascending to woodland plateaus and the top of Carnarvon Gorge, before descending to the mouth of the gorge via the Boolimba Bluff viewpoint. It's a serious expedition, and only to be undertaken by experienced bushwalkers during the cooler, drier months (April and October). Water is available at camping grounds, but you must bring all other supplies with you. The trail is closed for maintenance from November till March. See parks.des.qld.gov.au/parks/carnarvon-great-walk for details.

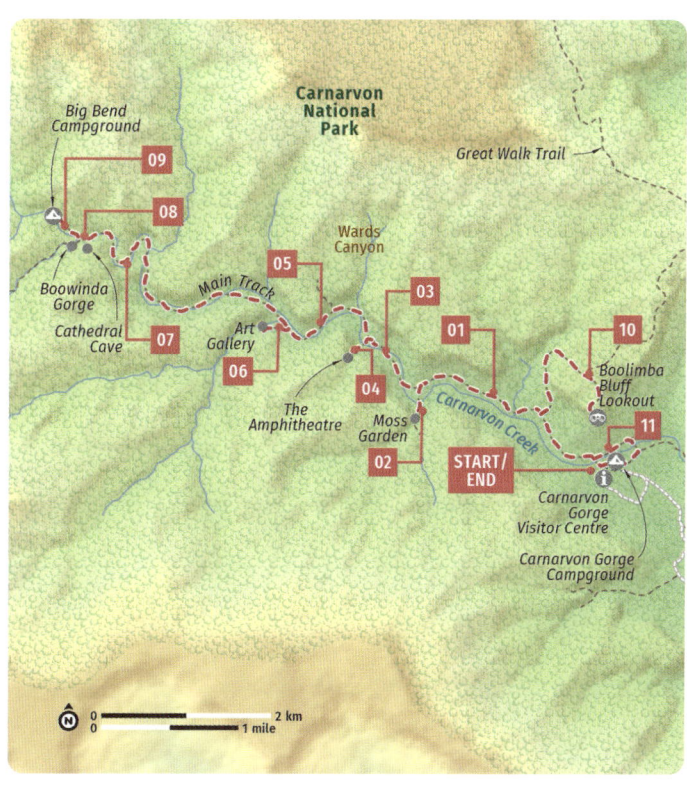

**06** A 340m trail climbs up gradually between boulders until you reach the **Art Gallery**, an impressive Aboriginal art site believed to have been in use for around 3650 years. Human habitation in the gorge goes back way further – some 19,500 years – but this site has particular spiritual and social significance for the Bidjara and Karingbal peoples. The stencilling techniques used here are among the most sophisticated of their kind in the world and the images on the rock face include human handprints, emu footprints, and large stencilled boomerangs resembling the number 7, used in war rather than the more gently curved boomerangs used for hunting. Emu egg stencils tell the tale of the totem animal of these Aboriginal groups. Freehand-style painted nets indicate that this was a final resting place of ancestors, while the multitude of carved stone vulvas – symbols of fertility – point to rituals and ceremonies performed here by women.

**07** Like the Art Gallery, **Cathedral Cave** (pictured) is a hugely important Aboriginal art site in the gorge, and the setting is particularly impressive: a short flight of stairs leads up from the main trail to the boardwalk spanning the length of a vast rock overhang and a rest area. Here you'll find numerous examples of stencil art and rock carvings going back many centuries. While it has a number of motifs in common with the Art Gallery – handprints, emu footprints, shell pendant stencils and boomerangs – look out for a stencil of a rifle and a hand-drawn evil spirit, attacked by a multitude of boomerangs. There are also several instances of multiple boomerangs stencilled on the wall; some hunters would employ that technique because they believed that by doing so, they amplified their hunting prowess. Also depicted is a large red oval stencil of a heavy war shield – the only such stencil of its kind in the Carnarvons. The multitude of net motifs drawn on the wall suggests that this was also a burial place, as bodies were traditionally wrapped in nets made of tree bark. The stretch of trail leading here from the Art Gallery meanders almost 4km through undergrowth, crossing the shallow creek eight times and rambling along the rocks of a dried-up riverbed.

**08** From Cathedral Cave it's a mere 550m to Big Bend, the furthest point of your walk. The trail is quite faint as it winds its way through the undergrowth before descending to the creek bank, 100m upstream from the cave, where you can rock-hop your way across the water. Make a note of where you've come out on the creek bank, as the trail can be a little tricky to pick up on the way back. Just before you cross the creek, you pass the entrance to the narrow **Boowinda Gorge**. There is no defined trail leading into this sculpted side-gorge, but you can meander along the uneven rocky floor, as its beautiful rock formations are well worth exploring, particularly for the first kilometre or so.

## Stories Set in Stone

A place of great spiritual significance to the Bidjara and Karingbal peoples, Carnarvon Gorge has two spectacular rock-art sites. Centuries' worth of stories have been recorded on the walls of the **Art Gallery** and **Cathedral Cave** using three methods: engraving, free-hand painting using pigment, and stencilling: blowing a finely ground mixture of powdered pigment and water around an object held against a porous, rocky canvas.

At the Art Gallery, look out for the carving of the Mundagurra Rainbow Serpent, who appears in creation stories all over Australia. Stencils of *che-ka-ra* oval decorative shell pendants point to ancient trade routes that stretched as far as northern Queensland, while the stencil of a rifle at Cathedral Cave confirms contact with Europeans.

**09** Once you've crossed the creek, it's an easy ramble through a patch of blady grass before you have to cross the water one last time, navigating your way along the rock-strewn shore. On the opposite side of the creek is the small, shaded **Big Bend camping ground** – it's very basic, with an outdoor privy, a picnic table and views of the creek and cliffs. If you haven't had lunch yet, this is a great place for a break before retracing your steps.

**10** Just over 1km from the visitor centre is the turn-off for **Boolimba Bluff**. How tired are you feeling? If you've just got your second wind, it's worth scrambling the 2km up the steps and steep sections to the rim of the gorge to watch the sun set over the 'Roof of Queensland' (give yourself two to three hours for this endeavour). If you're about to keel over at the very thought, it's best to leave it for another day; some trekkers hike this trail in the wee hours of the morning in order to watch the sunrise.

**11** You've come to the final creek crossing and can see the visitor centre beyond. Just before the crossing is the start of a short **nature trail loop** that brings you to the camping ground near the visitor centre. You're likely to have spotted wallabies and kangaroos during your hike through the gorge, but if you haven't, have a rest and return later in the day to stroll this level, easy trail where you're guaranteed wildlife sightings – **swamp wallabies** during the day and **yellow-bellied gliders**, **possums** and **bats** after dark.

 **Take a Break**

Roughly halfway along the Carnarvon Gorge stretch between the visitor centre and Big Bend, **Wards Canyon** makes for a cool rest stop on a hot day. A flight of steps leads some 200m up into a little side gorge, where a small waterfall trickles down the rock wall. It's shady here, thanks to the world's largest fern (*Angiopteris evecta*) that has strong links to the ancient flora of Gondwanan origin.

# Also Try...

SELLONLINEMARKETING/GETTY IMAGES ©

## Cape Hillsborough

| DURATION | DIFFICULTY | DISTANCE |
|---|---|---|
| 3hrs return | Moderate | 6.4km |

Some 50km northwest of Mackay, two short walking trails explore the furthest corners of the easternmost promontory of Cape Hillsborough National Park (pictured), taking in medicinal plants used by the Yuibeira people for millennia, an ancient stone fish trap and rugged, pine-clad cliffs.

Reachable via Seaforth Rd and Cape Hillsborough Rd, which branch off Bruce Hwy north of Mackay, the trailheads for both trails begin near the picnic area on the narrow isthmus. The Yuibeira Plant Trail (1.5km return) is an easy interpretive trail with multiple information boards that teach you about endemic medicinal plants. It meanders past a centuries-old fish trap. The steep and rocky Andrews Point Track (2.8km return) leads you to the opposite end of the promontory via a vine forest home to 150 bird species and along pine-studded cliffs. At low tide you can cross over to and explore nearby Wedge Island.

## Manjal Jimalji (Devil's Thumb)

| DURATION | DIFFICULTY | DISTANCE |
|---|---|---|
| 8hrs return | Hard | 10.6km |

Reaching a 1172m viewpoint, the significant Aboriginal site of Manjal Jimalji is a challenging trail that takes you through lowland and upland rainforest. It has an incredible range of birdlife and offers amazing views of the surrounding mountain ranges from the viewpoint.

Accessed via the unsealed Whyanbeel Rd, 17km north of Mossman (and 80km north of Cairns), this well-marked walking trail crosses Little Falls Creek and then climbs steeply up through lowland rainforest, where you may spot yellow-spotted honeyeaters and cassowaries. Above the altitude of 600m, the birdlife changes to golden bowerbirds and tooth-billed bowerbirds. At 3.7km, the trail reaches a natural clearing – the Coral Fern Patch. You need at least five hours of daylight to continue to Split Rock, where the last section of the trail to the viewpoint requires above-average fitness and scrambling skills. Bring plenty of water, a first-aid kit and communication equipment.

AUSTRALIANCAMERA/SHUTTERSTOCK ©

## Kahlpahlim Rock/ Ridge Circuit

| DURATION | DIFF | DISTANCE |
|---|---|---|
| 6-7hrs return | Hard | 12.3km |

The highest point in the Lamb Range in Dinden National Park (pictured), 60km southwest of Cairns, Kahlpahlim Rock (1300m) is reachable via two challenging trails that are walked as a circuit.

Both trails start from the Davies Creek road. From the first trailhead, take the Ridge Trail up through towering rose gum, turpentine and casuarina forests, then climb steeply along mostly open terrain to the 1km side track to Kahlpahlim Rock. These enormous granite boulders command a fine view over the surrounding landscape. Return via the steep but shaded Rock Trail.

## Finch Hatton Gorge

| DURATION | DIFF | DISTANCE |
|---|---|---|
| 3-4hrs return | Easy | 5.2km |

Some 70km west of Mackay along the Eungella–Mackay road, a turnoff leads to the rainforest-filled Finch Hatton Gorge, with tumbling waterfalls, swimming holes and platypuses in the creeks.

Araluen Falls are reached from the car park at the end of the road via a gorgeous 1.6km trail with mild inclines. Here you'll find a waterfall and deep swimming hole and see daredevils jumping and diving off the surrounding rocks. A further 1km takes you to the Wheel of Fire Falls, a series of cascades ending in another deep swimming hole.

## Wabunga Wayemba Rainforest Trail

| DURATION | DIFF | DISTANCE |
|---|---|---|
| 2hrs return | Moderate | 5.5km |

Around 130km southwest of Cairns, the longest trail in the Tully Falls National Park leads you through lush rainforest to a viewpoint overlooking a waterfall.

The Wabunga Wayemba track can be accessed from two trailheads on Tully Falls Rd. Halfway along the trail a steep side track involving numerous stone steps leads down to a lookout overlooking a waterfall on Charmillin Creek, where mountain water cascades over moss-coated rocks into a pool. If you're lucky you may spot cassowaries.

Standley Chasm (p88)

# The Outback

**16** **Valley of the Winds**
Wander awestruck beneath Kata Tjuta's sacred ancient domes. **p78**

**17** **Kings Canyon Rim**
Spectacular circuit above sheer cliffs encircling a deep gorge. **p80**

**18** **Mt Sonder**
Challenging peak-bagging in the remote West MacDonnell Ranges. **p84**

**19** **Ormiston Pound**
Cross a desert range to explore a narrow valley and gorge. **p86**

**20** **Above Standley Chasm**
Precipitous steps, fearsome pinnacles, narrow gorges. **p88**

**21** **Edith Falls & Sweetwater Pool**
Bring the bathers for this waterhole fiesta. **p90**

**22** **Motor Car Falls**
The road less travelled is open all year. **p94**

**23** **Florence Falls**
Nature at its most tropical not far from Darwin. **p96**

# Explore
# The Outback

From the spinifex, red dirt and ghost-gum-spotted ranges of the continent's ancient heart, through the sacred savannah Stone Country of Nitmiluk and Kakadu National Parks, to the languid tropical lushness of Litchfield, the outback is Australia at its rawest. Walking (indeed just travelling) here is one huge adventure and requires fitness, stamina and exceptional planning. Everything is brighter in the outback and the colours of the sky and land, and memories of its people, will be seared into your soul forever.

## Alice Springs

Love it or hate it, 'The Alice' is the only town of any size in central Australia, sitting almost halfway between Adelaide and Darwin. There's a good selection of accommodation and services; this is the place to rent, restock, repair, find information and enter/leave from.

Walkers will find **Lone Dingo** (lonedingo.com.au) has an excellent range of gear and advice while the **Bean Tree Cafe** (opbg.com.au/bean-tree-cafe) in the botanical gardens is a perfect wallaby-watching brunch spot.

## Darwin

Capital of the Top End, and with one tropical foot planted firmly in Asia, Darwin has all the resources needed to tackle any walk in the region. If you want a quick turnaround, Casuarina Mall, close to the airport, has supermarkets and a camping store and you can be on the road within an hour. Otherwise try exploring East Point and Bicentennial Park, grab a laksa from **Mindil Beach Market** (mindil.com.au), source maps and gear from the **NT General Store** (thentgeneralstore.com.au) and enjoy a sundowner at the **Trailer Boat Club**.

## Katherine

Once an outpost for the Overland Telegraph, modern Katherine, 300km south of Darwin, sits at the junction of the Stuart and Victoria Hwys and is the closest town to Nitmiluk National Park. The usual services are found here, and while there's some adequate accommodation most walkers will prefer to camp in the NP, either at **Nitmiluk Gorge** (30km from Katherine) or the beautiful **Edith Falls** (61km).

## Yulara

Almost 450km (five hours) closer to Kata Tjuta than Alice Springs and with cheaper flights than the latter, Yulara is an attractive alternative for time-poor walkers. While car-rental prices are comparative to Alice, expect higher prices for everything else. There's a limited range of dining, accommodation, tours and services, though you will find a handy supermarket, a fuel station, a mechanic and an ATM. Bring all your camping and walking gear. Yulara is also marginally closer to Kings Canyon on a good sealed road.

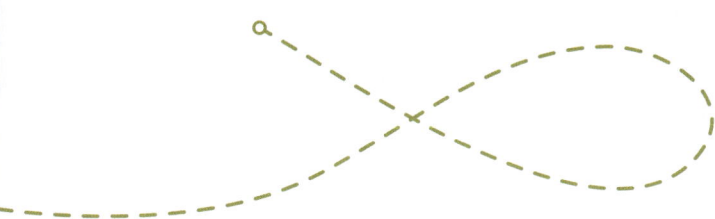

## Resources

**Parks Australia** (parksaustralia.gov.au) For Kakadu and Kata Tjuta information and permits.

**Parks and Wildlife** (nt.gov.au/leisure/parks-reserves) For all other NT parks.

**Northern Territory Tourism** (northernterritory.com) Official NT tourism website with background info and links.

**Lone Dingo** (lonedingo.com.au) The Centre's one-stop adventure shop.

**Visit Katherine** (visitkatherine.com.au) Katherine tourism site and booking engine.

**Larapinta Trail** (larapintatrail.com.au) Information and maps for Larapinta Trail sections.

## When to Go

The Dry (May–October) is the best time for walking; daytime temperatures are manageable, all parks are normally open and there are less bothersome insects. July and August is high season and nights are cold south of Katherine. The Wet (November–April) brings cyclones, road and track closures to the north (especially Kakadu), and insane temperatures, flies and deserted camping grounds to the Centre.

## Where to Stay

Dust off your tent and sleeping bag and embrace the '50 Million Star Hotel', as 'roofed' accommodation is generally prohibitively expensive and available only in hub towns, resorts or the odd pastoral station. All walks have a camping ground nearby, with facilities ranging from minimal (aka 'bush camping') to sites with toilets, showers and even swimming pools. The Milky Way has never looked brighter than from the Red Centre.

## What's On

**Parrtjima** (parrtjimaaustralia.com.au; Apr) Showcases Arrernte/Aranda culture around Alice Springs.

**Beer Can Regatta** (beercanregatta.org.au; Jul) Typically Territorian activity of drinking beer then trying to float away on the empties.

**Henley On Todd Regatta** (henleyontodd.com.au; Aug) Irreverent outback 'boating' festival on Alice's dry Todd River.

**Darwin Festival** (darwinfestival.org.au; Aug) Music and visual arts over two weeks.

**Alice Desert Festival** (desfest.com; Aug–Oct) Parades, music, film and comedy for six weeks.

## Transport

Distances are massive: the Territory is at least a three- to four-day drive from another capital city, so unless you're on a road trip, flying makes sense. Darwin, Alice Springs and Yulara (Ayers Rock Airport) are all well serviced by air from the rest of the country (and each other) and Darwin also has connections to Southeast Asia. Greyhound buses ply the Stuart Hwy between Darwin and Adelaide and AAT Kings runs transfers to Yulara and Kings Canyon. You will need to hire a car (or join a tour) to reach the trailheads, and vehicle rental (including campers) is available in all hubs (check vehicle conditions carefully). Off-season camper relocations are another option.

# 16

# Valley of the Winds

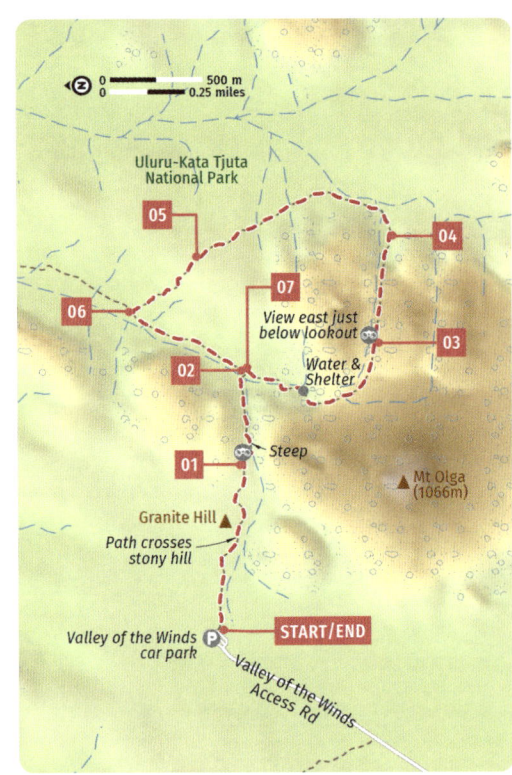

| DURATION | DIFFICULTY | DISTANCE | START/END |
|---|---|---|---|
| 2½-4hrs return | Moderate | 8km | Valley of the Winds car park |

| TERRAIN | | Rock, sand, steep sections |
|---|---|---|

In the red heart of Australia lies somewhere so sacred its stories cannot be revealed, yet respectful visitors are still welcome to this 'many headed place'. Ancient and enigmatic, the conglomerate domes of Kata Tjuta hold special significance to the Anangu people, and only initiated males may learn their tjukurpa (lore).

## Getting Here

Kata Tjuta is 59km from Yulara's Ayers Rock Airport (car rental and tours available). Otherwise by road it's six hours (489km) from Alice and 4½ hours (350km) from Kings Canyon; both have daily shuttle connections to Yulara.

## Starting Point

Take the signposted turn after the Uluru-Kata Tjuta park entrance station and drive 44km to the Valley of the Winds car park. Water is available but the closest toilets are back at the sunset viewing area (3km). Start early as the walk closes on high-temperature days.

**01** From the east side of the car park, follow the broad, shadeless track towards Kata Tjuta's signature **orange domes** (pictured). After 400m the track skirts a stony hill before climbing to **Karu Lookout** on a rocky saddle. The track closes here at 11am when forecasted temperatures are 36°C or above.

**02** Descend steep loose rocks and slabs to a track junction. Turn right (south) and within 200m there is a **water tank**. The valley's incredible towering orange walls almost block out the sun, which is not such a bad thing. Geologists say the

## Walpa Gorge

Nearby **Walpa Gorge** provides a gentler (though just as shadeless) experience. A 3km (one hour) return smoothed trail leads over a barren, rocky landscape into a deep cleft between two massive domes, terminating at a viewing platform. While nowhere near as scenic as the Valley of the Winds, the inner gorge is a sanctuary for rare plants, some of which are found nowhere else. Benches and interpretive panels line the trail.

When you're photographing the gorge, the Anangu ask that you capture both sides in the frame. The gorge car park is 1km past the Valley of the Winds turnoff, at the end of Kata Tjuta Rd.

36 domes of Kata Tjuta consist of a rough conglomerate of granite, basalt, sand and mud (hence their 'cheese grater' appearance). Unlike with the smoother sandstone of neighbouring Uluru, what caused the shaping of the domes is still open to conjecture; the Anangu have their own explanation.

**03** Follow the track onto smooth rock, then into shade as it swings east, climbing to **Karingana Lookout**, on a saddle between cliffs. The **views** back down the valley are worth the effort, though the lookout can be crowded; continue down the far side for less-cluttered vistas.

**04** Continue descending to the sandy valley floor, pausing several times to check the scenic rearward view of the pass until you reach a **large rock cairn**.

**05** Flattening, the track heads north across rocky, shadeless country populated by stunted mulga and spinifex until eventually climbing a **small hill offering good views** to the south and east.

**06** Descend to another **shelter** and water tank before the route turns south and follows a sandy dry creek bed to complete the circuit at the track junction below Karu Lookout.

**07** Retrace your steps up the steep path to the lookout then stroll gently downhill to the car park.

 **Take a Break**

**Curtin Springs** (curtinsprings.com), a classic outback cattle station, is the perfect place to break up the long drive from Yulara to the Stuart Hwy or Kings Canyon. Actually, it's the only place, but you can get a meal and a beer in the shady open-air restaurant, fuel up the car or just lie on the grass and listen to the birds in the aviary. Want to stay the night? No problem, unpowered sites are free, but you'll pay for showers.

# 17

# Kings Canyon Rim

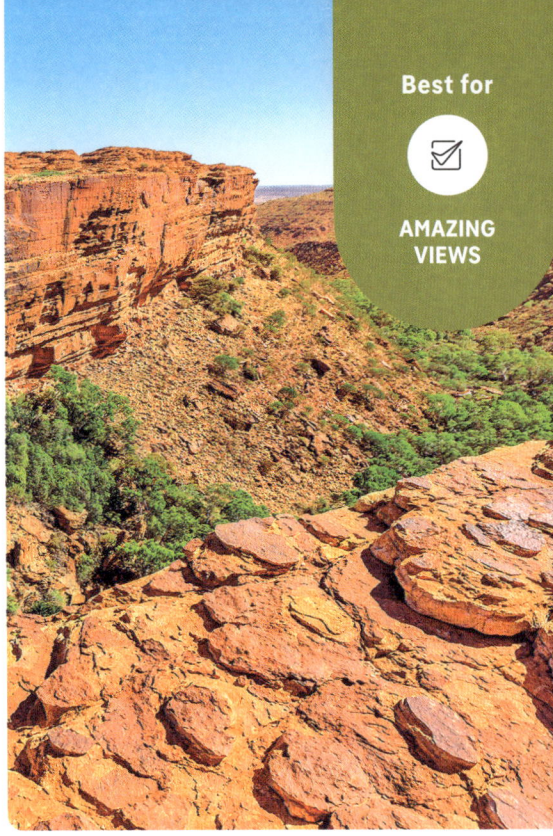

**Best for**

**AMAZING VIEWS**

| DURATION | DIFFICULTY | DISTANCE | START/END |
|---|---|---|---|
| 3-4hrs return | Moderate | 6.4km | Kings Canyon car park |

| TERRAIN | Rocky, steep stairs, cliff edges |
|---|---|

A literally breathtaking circuit around the sheer cliffs and sandstone domes of Watarrka National Park's remarkable Kings Canyon. In remote Martutjarra Luritja Country south of Alice Springs, a well-marked trail climbs steeply onto a rocky plateau then follows exposed clifftops past magnificent viewpoints as it circumnavigates the deep and incredibly photogenic canyon far below. Other than the initial climb and final descent, most of the route is easy walking.

## Getting Here

Kings Canyon (pictured) is roughly 300km from either Yulara (sealed road) or Alice Springs (sealed/unsealed) and is best visited with your own vehicle. AAT Kings (aatkings.com) runs day tours to Kings Canyon (and resort) from both towns. The canyon is 10km from the resort, which is also the closest accommodation.

## Starting Point

Head to the car park at the end of the access road (4km), beyond the picnic area (toilets, tables, water). Follow signs for the Rim Walk at the car park's eastern edge. Start as early as possible, bringing plenty of water and sunscreen. The Rim Walk is a one-way circuit and cannot be walked in the opposite direction.

**01** Do not be fooled by the initial 350m of wide, easy paved track leading away from the car park.

**02** Veer left at the track junction, pass through the fence (where the walk closes on extreme-temperature days) and start climbing steeply up hundreds of **spinifex-fringed stone steps**. In the

## Hot Weather Detours

The Rim Walk closes at 9am when the forecasted temperature is 36°C or above, so it's important to start early. A cooler, less-energetic alternative follows **Kings Creek** (45 minutes, 2.1km return; pictured p83) along the canyon floor, winding below shadowy gums and narrowing red walls before the trail terminates at a lookout.

Alternatively, fit, experienced hikers could consider walking to **Reedy Creek** on the **Giles Track** for a swim or even to camp overnight (2½ hours, 7km one way). The Giles Track links Kathleen Springs with Kings Canyon and is normally walked in one direction over two days (22km), although a return trip from Kings Canyon is certainly possible.

early morning most of this climb is shaded.

**03** Several **benched viewpoints** make pleasant rest stops. Notice the large fan-like **umbrella bushes** (*Acacia ligulata*) nearby, known locally as Watarrka, for which the park is named.

**04** The hardest section is over when the **trail crests the ridge**, flattening out and winding towards low cliffs.

**05** A short rocky scramble protected by a wire railing threads through **orange sandstone domes** onto the plateau.

**06** Negotiate a tight squeeze between domes.

**07** Follow the well-worn trail over smooth stone to several abrupt, **unfenced viewpoints** above plummeting cliffs. The **unimpeded vista** of both the canyon far below and the massive South Wall opposite are exceptional. Maintain a safe distance from the crumbling edge.

**08** Turn right at the marked track junction for Cotterills Lookout, named after an Englishman who pioneered tourism here in the early '60s. Jack Cotterill was the first to try to carve out a road to the canyon.

**09** Clamber over rocks and the odd, airy bridge for 300m to more **magnificent views** from a spur almost at the canyon head. Look directly down the whole canyon, marvelling at the sheerness and immensity of the much closer South Wall, not to mention the white streaks of guano, made over generations. Beware the cliff edges are severely undercut, something that becomes obvious later when looking back from the opposite side. Return to the main track.

**10** This rippled section of plateau was once an **ancient lake floor**. Follow the markers as the track heads between domes back towards the edge.

**11** Take the stairs down the cliff face, cross the wooden bridge spanning the **macrozamia-filled upper canyon**, and ascend the first set of stairs on the other side.

**12** Bypass the second set of stairs and head to the right, following the track under the cliffs to the **Garden of Eden**. The shady terminal pool and ghost gums make a pleasant lunch spot out of the sun's death rays.

**13** Return to the bypassed stairs and climb to the canyon rim for incredible views of the **'Lost City' beehive domes**. Scientists explain the domes as a result of weathering by wind and rain exploiting cracks in the sandstone over millions of years. The local Luritja people regard the domes as *kuninga* (quoll – a carnivorous marsupial) men, an important Dreaming site. The track is now hot and exposed to full sun as it climbs over small outcrops.

**14** Pass through a **bizarre one-way gate** and bridge over a narrow gap that terminates the shorter South Wall Walk.

**15** From the edge of the **South Wall** look back across the canyon to the sheer walls below Cotterills Lookout.

**16** Head away from the canyon as the trail winds slowly down through an area of many sandstone domes, before entering a **macrozamia-filled gully**.

**17** As the track swings west along a wide shelf, there's some **decent shade** under the south-facing cliffs on the right. Macrozamia and ghost gums line the shaded slope.

**18** Ignore the junction with the Giles Track that heads up onto the George Gill Range (leading to **Reedy Creek** and Kathleen Springs) and stay on the main trail.

**19** The flat top of **Kestrel Falls** has impressive views over the adjacent rocky valley. The falls are named for the nankeen kestrels nesting in the cliffs to the left, evidenced by more guano streaks.

**20** Cross another wide shelf then start a steep descent to **Kestrel Falls Lookout**, which offers a final **panorama** of the falls, sandstone cliffs and the fairly hostile-looking valley beneath them. The cliffs are the southern edge of the rugged **George Gill Range**, a remote area of deep, permanent rock holes and springs supporting a large and diverse range of endemic flora and fauna

**21** Enjoy the shade as the trail enters scrub, descending by rocky steps back to the car park.

## Dinosaur Plants

Looking like squat palms, **macrozamias** are actually cycads, an ancient plant type unchanged since the Triassic period (230 million years ago). Unlike palms (which flower), cycads bear cones. Of the 40 macrozamia species (all unique to Australia), *M. macdonnellii* is the only one found west of Queensland, in shaded gorges and south-facing slopes around the **MacDonnell Ranges**. The Watarrka macrozamias are the westernmost of all. Traditionally not favoured as bush tucker due to their toxicity, they are popular with gardeners due to their uncommon bluish tinge. Considered near-threatened (in part due to illegal predation by humans), they are one species likely to benefit from climate change, given that $CO_2$ levels were three times higher during their evolution. If they don't burn first.

 Take a Break

On any given afternoon, the lively **Thirsty Dingo Bar** (kingscanyonresort.com.au) is chock-full of package tourists, backpackers, grey nomads and every camper from Kings Canyon Resort. There's bar food, a bistro, live music and a nightly barbecue.

The family-run **Kings Creek Station** (kingscreekstation.com.au), 37km from Kings Canyon, serves up camel burgers, smoothies and icy beers during daylight hours, in an authentically outback setting.

# 18

# Mt Sonder

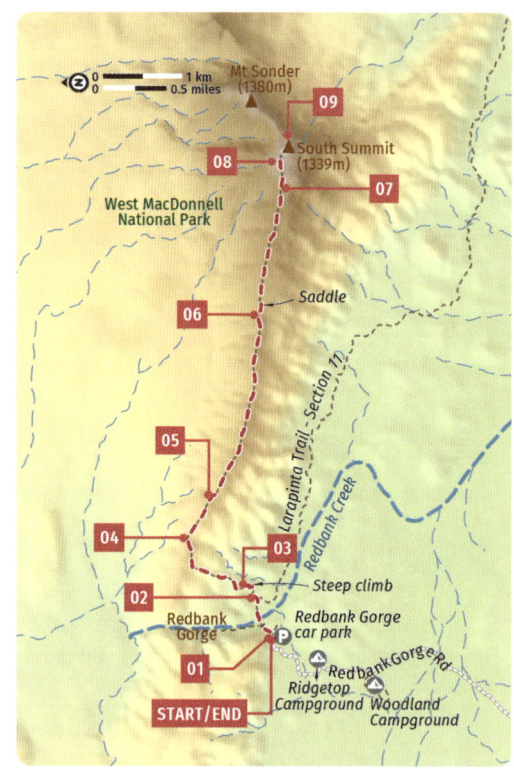

| DURATION | DIFFICULTY | DISTANCE | START/END |
|---|---|---|---|
| 5-6hrs return | Hard | 15.2km | Redbank Gorge car park |
| TERRAIN | | Steep, rocky, no shade | |

The remote western end of the MacDonnell Ranges (Tjoritja) is home to the Territory's loftiest peaks, and the most accessible and unmistakable is fourth-highest Mt Sonder (1380m; pictured). It is known as Rutjupma (also spelt Rwetyepme) to the local Aranda (Western Arrernte) people, and the strenuous track to its southern summit forms Section 12 of the long-distance Larapinta Trail.

## Getting Here

Redbank Gorge is 2¼ hours (156km) from Alice Springs on mostly sealed roads. From Kings Canyon via unsealed Mereenie Loop (3½ hours, 217km) you will need a 4WD and a permit from Kings Canyon Resort.

## Starting Point

Follow Redbank Gorge Rd to the terminal car park where there's toilets, shelter and water. Start early as the trail is mostly unshaded. Carry adequate water (at least 4L per person).

**01** Take the gorge walk northeast from the car park and within 50m, at the track junction, stay right for 'Larapinta Trail'.

**02** Cross the (usually dry) **Redbank Creek** and amble under **ghost gums** to the next junction (400m), turning left for Mt Sonder. Ignore the Parks sign claiming 'eight hours' – it should take only six hours.

**03** If you've left early enough, the sun should still be below the ridge as you climb steeply through light woodland onto a rocky, **spinifex-studded ridgetop** with good views south.

## Tjoritja High Peaks

These wild, remote peaks can be visited by experienced, self-sufficient parties skilled in off-track navigation and local conditions. Parks NT permits are mandatory.

**Mt Giles/Ltarkalibaka** (1389m) The NT's third-highest peak is a three-day round trip from Ormiston Gorge to the Chewings Range.

**Mt Zeil/Urlatherrke** (1531m) At the very end of the range, the NT's highest peak is a serious undertaking, scaled from the north in one long day.

**Mt Razorback/Ntwaperre** (1274m) Beyond Redbank Gorge, the NT's number-five peak is a rarely visited and true off-track adventure.

**04** The stony trail climbs more gently, with **increasingly impressive views** until finally you reach a saddle revealing country to the north.

**05** Climb the next knoll for 400m to **Mt Sonder Lookout**, where a sign identifies the high peaks visible in all directions, including your goal. From here it's simply a matter of following the well-marked track along the **narrow ridgetop** towards the summit.

**06** After 2.5km on the ridge, descend steeply towards a saddle and climb out the other side.

**07** Keep following the obvious path up the bare narrow ridge as the summit pyramid looms closer.

**08** Pass an automatic **weather station** en route to the summit dial.

**09** The dial lists Mt Sonder's elevation at 1380m, which is correct, but that isn't where you're standing. The elevation of the **South Summit** is 1339m. The true (or Northern) summit is the gnarly-looking, very rocky peak 750m away to the northeast across a deep chasm. Both Parks NT and the Aranda don't want you to go over there.

Retrace your outward route before the day heats up; there's no water until the tank near the car park.

 **Take a Break**

The only cafe at the western end of the MacDonnells, **Glen Helen Lodge** (glenhelenlodge.com.au) serves up cold drinks, pretty tasty pub fare and excellent air-con.

**Ellery Creek Big Hole** is probably the nicest swimming hole in the West Macs and the most reliable. It's the perfect place for a picnic lunch and a freezing dip to wash away the day's exertions.

# 19

# Ormiston Pound

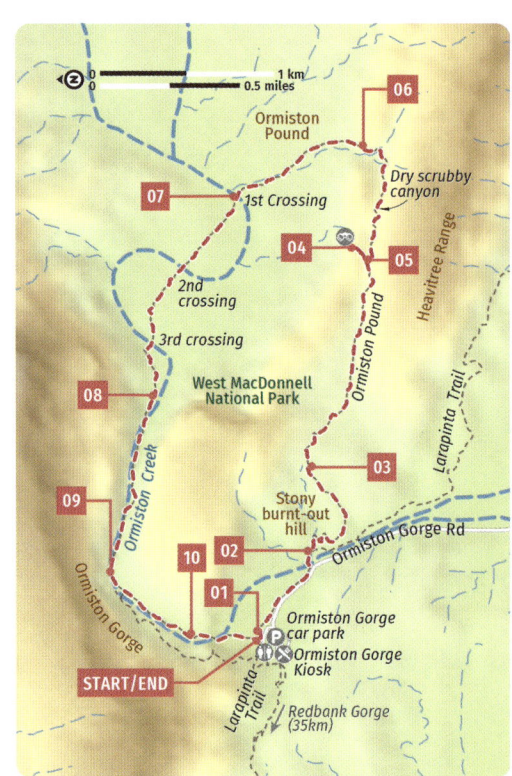

| DURATION | DIFFICULTY | DISTANCE | START/END |
|---|---|---|---|
| 2-3½hrs return | Moderate | 8.5km | Ormiston Gorge car park |
| TERRAIN | | Rocky, sandy, steep climb, hot | |

Channel your inner explorer by traversing the sun-blasted Heavitree Range into a wilderness valley enclosed on all sides by magnificent red walls. Once in the pound (pictured), cross creek after dry creek before entering the most magnificent gorge in Tjoritja (West MacDonnell Ranges), treading its sandy floor to the final payoff, a much-needed swimming hole. Phew!

## Getting Here

Ormiston is only 35km from Redbank Gorge on sealed roads (30 minutes) or by walking the Larapinta Trail (two days), so it can be bundled with Mt Sonder over a weekend. Otherwise it's a 135km (90-minute) drive from Alice Springs. Day tours and Larapinta Trail drop-offs (neither of which are cheap) from Alice are possible, though self-driving, as always, is the best option.

## Starting Point

A sealed access road runs 7km from Namatjira Dr to the Ormiston Gorge car park, where there's a handy kiosk, picnic tables, toilets and water. All walks depart from a shelter on the northern side.

**01** Head east following the **Pound Walk** (orange arrows). This first section runs parallel to the access road and coincides with Section 9 of the Larapinta Trail (blue arrows).

**02** After crossing the usually dry Ormiston Creek, leave the Larapinta at a track junction, following the Pound Walk left as it climbs steeply around a **stony, burnt hill**.

**03** The angle lessens as you wind up a hot, desolate valley towards a **secluded pass**, the low point in the range. The unshaded route is littered with rocks and burnt, stunted trees.

## Larapinta Trail

The Larapinta is the NT's premier long-distance walking trail, stretching 230km from **Alice Springs** to **Redbank Gorge** following the ridgelines of the **Heavitree** and **Chewings** Ranges of Tjoritja (the West MacDonnells). The well-marked trail comprises 12 sections (the last a return climb of **Mt Sonder**) and links the ranges' various attractions like **Simpson Gap**, **Standley Chasm** and **Ormiston Gorge**. Most end-to-end walkers take 17 to 20 days, arranging food drops at various camp sites, though it's also possible to just walk a couple of sections. The walk is very popular during the winter months and several companies in Alice offer trail transfers and food drop-offs.

**04** At the small saddle there's an unmarked track junction and possibly some shade nearby. Follow the left-hand track for 100m until you reach a rock ledge with **magnificent views** of the entire pound – **Bowmans Gap**, the whole **West Wall** and elusive **Mt Giles** are all visible.

**05** Back at the saddle, take the other track as it descends slowly east through a **dry, scrubby canyon**.

**06** A final cresting of the last ridge and the track spills down onto the **pound floor**.

**07** Distant Ormiston Gorge grows larger as you make the **first of three crossings** of the dry creek snaking towards it.

**08** Once in the gorge, the trail mostly disappears (as a final sign warns) so just walk wherever's shaded as the gorge floor alternates between rocks and sand.

**09** As the gorge narrows, the tall orange quartzite walls and scattered ghost gums provide welcome shade. Follow the sandy gorge for 1km to a sharp left bend.

**10** Now running southwest, the route passes several small skanky pools before arriving at a more inviting **swimming hole**, only 300m from the car park. Definitely jump in!

 **Take a Break**

**Ormiston Gorge Kiosk** in the gorge car park dispenses hot and cold drinks, various snacks and also basic supplies like sunscreen and insect repellent.

# 20

# Above Standley Chasm

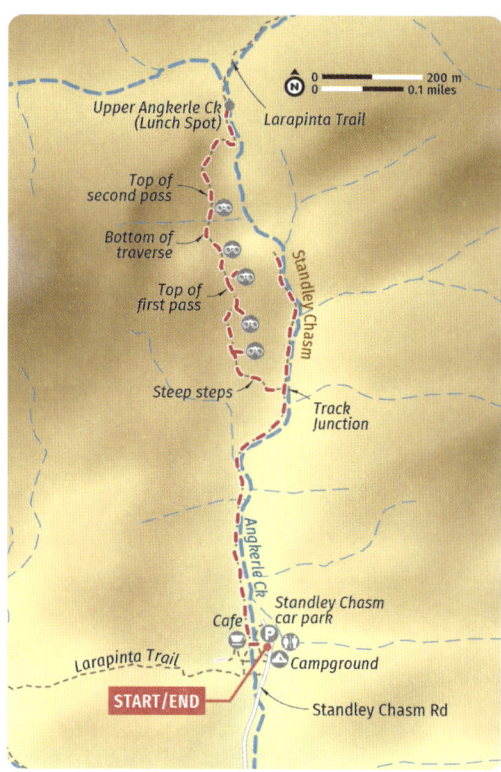

| DURATION | DIFFICULTY | DISTANCE | START/END |
|---|---|---|---|
| 2-3hrs return | Moderate | 3.4km | Standley Chasm Cafe |

| TERRAIN | Paved path, steep steps, loose rocks |
|---|---|

Venture off the tourist trail and reach for the sky on this intimidating climb over 1000 stone steps. From airy ledges you'll view the jagged, crumbling peaks above Angkerle Atwatye, 'the place where the water moves between'.

At the cafe, pay your entrance fee then follow the smooth, shady path alongside **spring-fed Angkerle Creek**, passing by lush ferns, palms and eucalypts. This section is suitable for strollers and wheelchairs; interpretive panels are spaced along the route.

After 500m there's a track junction with a set of steep rocky steps off to the left, Stage 3 of the 230km **Larapinta Trail** (pictured). Continue straight for another 200m to the **Chasm**, a narrow gap between towering orange quartzite cliffs. The Chasm floor is usually dry as the creek runs underground here, and it's possible to walk to the far end (but no further).

Return to the track junction and climb the steps up a steep gully showing evidence of recent bushfires. Keep an eye out for unmarked tracks on the right leading to rocky outcrops, where each **view of the surrounding peaks and gorges** is increasingly more magnificent.

At the top of a pass the track descends steeply, hugging the cliff face, before traversing, then climbing again to another saddle.

Finally descend to **upper Angkerle Creek**, whose dry bed shaded by ghost gums and cycads makes a **pleasant picnic spot**. This is the turn-around point for day walkers.

Reclimb the 1000 steps and reward yourself with an ice cream at the **lovely, breezy cafe**.

# 21

# Edith Falls & Sweetwater Pool

**Best for**

☑

**A COOLING SWIM**

| DURATION | DIFFICULTY | DISTANCE | START/END |
|---|---|---|---|
| 3½-5hrs | Moderate | 10km | Edith Falls car park |

| TERRAIN | Mostly sandy, some steep steps |
|---|---|

Pack the bathers and sunscreen for this relaxed outing to a selection of stunning waterholes in Jawoyn Country. The well-marked trail never strays far from serene, pandanus-lined swimming holes, picturesque plunge pools and several magnificent waterfalls, strung out like pearls along the Edith River in Nitmiluk National Park near Katherine. This is a walk on which to take your time and savour each new location. It's suitable for families.

## Getting Here

The turnoff for Edith Falls (pictured) is 274km (three hours) south of Darwin on the Stuart Hwy, 42km before the town of Katherine. Do not head to the Nitmiluk Visitor Centre at Katherine Gorge. Katherine is serviced by Greyhound bus from Darwin, Alice Springs and Broome. Rental cars and local transport to the falls can be arranged in the town (try travelnorth.com.au).

## Starting Point

Edith Falls (Leliyn) is 19km from the Stuart Hwy on a sealed road. The walk starts at the stairs near the car-park entrance. Drinking water, toilets and a small cafe are nearby.

**01** Climb the stone steps and follow the well-marked path to the top of the escarpment, where it then leads southeast to a signed track junction, 600m from the car park.

**02** Turn left (east) towards the Sweetwater and Long Hole pools and follow the now narrower path across **Stone Country**, keeping an eye out for the blue marker arrows. Undergrowth fires are common so the arrows may be high up on

# Jatbula Trail

The 62km **Jatbula Trail** (named after Jawoyn elder and land rights warrior Peter Jatbula) follows the escarpment rim from Katherine Gorge to Edith Falls. Its difficulty is overstated – the walking is mostly flat and mundane on ex-station roads; it's the dramatic camp sites alongside towering waterfalls, rugged gorges or luxuriously shaded swimming holes that are the attraction. Strictly regulated, the walk is designed for a midday arrival at each night's camp site, leaving the hottest part of the day for swimming and relaxing. Most people take four to six days to complete the trail, and you're obliged to stay in specific camp sites. Bookings are mandatory (parksandwildlife.nt.gov.au).

tree trunks, suspended by wire from overhanging branches or topping steel pickets. You'll notice the bright-green post-fire regrowth and plentiful birdlife, which is some of the most varied in the Territory, including the outrageously coloured Gouldian finch (*Erythrura gouldiae*) and the striking red-backed fairy-wren (*Malurus melanocephalus*).

**03** The undulating path turns south and heads into more open country near the **Edith River**. Along with 17 Mile Creek and the Katherine, King and Fergusson Rivers, the Edith rises in Arnhem Land and cuts a narrow swathe across the sandstone Nitmiluk escarpment before draining into the northwest-flowing Daly River.

**04** Heading east again, a break in the riverside pandanus (*Pandanus aquaticus*) reveals the beautiful **Long Hole Pool**, fringed by water lilies. If you're already hot and bothered, a dip here should do the trick.

**05** Otherwise, continue on for another 150m, leave the track at the Park sign and head for the obvious **sandy beach** by an inviting **rock hole** just past the stoney shallows at the head of Long Hole Pool. Definitely make time for a swim here.

**06** Regain the sandy track and continue east through light savannah. This section of the track can be quite hot and although the track runs parallel to the river, you won't see it for the **dense riparian vegetation**. Path and river eventually diverge and soon you'll reach a (normally) **dry tributary**.

**07** Cross the creek and the track turns south again to rejoin the Edith at the aptly named **Sweetwater Pool** – a perfect place for a snack, and let's see, maybe another swim?

Choose from the large tree-lined pool or the small rock hole with mini waterfall at its head. Or choose to swim in both. It's also possible to camp overnight here (ask for a permit at the Leliyn Kiosk). If you do camp and hear a crazed, eerie cry at night, it's not the ghost of the billabong but a Bush Stone-curlew (*Burhinus grallarius*), a large, wandering nocturnal bird infamous for its otherworldly screeches.

**08** Retrace your outward path (this section comprises the last stage of the one-way 62km Jatbula Trail), back past Long Hole (another dip anyone?) to the track junction on the escarpment, this time taking the other fork for the Leliyn Trail to Upper Falls and Pool.

**09** Within 50m another track junction forks right to the overgrown **Leliyn Lookout**, where you might glimpse Middle Pool and a distant Upper Falls between the trees. A bench seat offers a rest opportunity, though there are better views to come, so return to the track junction and descend steeply to the rocks surrounding the Upper Pool and Falls.

**10** It must be time for another swim. Leave the track before it crosses to the other bank and scramble over rock slabs to find a good entry point. There's one above a narrow channel that leads into the **Upper Pool**, where, after drifting easily over shallow ledges, you can swim across deeper water to the falls.

**11** The track crosses to the far bank and climbs steeply, before traversing around a barren hill to a slabby saddle and another junction. The right-hand route climbs through boulders a short distance to **Bemang Lookout**, overlooking the exquisite **Middle Pool and Falls** (pictured). *Bemang* is the local name for the frill-necked lizard (*Chlamydosaurus kingii*) found across northern Australia, renowned for raising an evil-looking jagged frill around its face when threatened.

**12** Back on the main track, climb briefly through more Stone Country until a series of long, easy zigzags leads down off the escarpment through lightly wooded savannah to the bridge at the outlet of the **Lower Pool below Edith Falls**.

## Stone Country

The rocky escarpment at Nitmiluk is actually the southern edge of **Arnhem Land**, a vast high wilderness plateau full of jagged sandstone cliffs, crumbling hills, deep gorges, magnificent waterfalls and fragile ecosystems, stretching northeast through **Kakadu** to the **Gulf of Carpentaria**. Home to unique and endangered plants and animals, including the largest slice of the NT's remnant rainforest, the area is of special significance to the different Aboriginal groups who are its custodians. There are many sacred sites and rock-art areas scattered across the stark, sparsely populated landscape. It is recognised as a biodiversity hotspot, and many of the NT's largest river systems, including the Katherine, originate there. Nitmiluk's Traditional Owners, the Jawoyn people, look after Country that includes the southern section of Kakadu and Western Arnhem.

**13** Turn right after the bridge and there's a small pontoon for easy swimming access – yep, it's that time again. The barred and netted bridge also acts as a sturdy barrier against the ingress of large reptiles into the plunge pool – good to know. There's lots of nice grass and shady trees to **picnic** nearby, and there's no need to rush, as the car park and cafe are only 200m away.

**14** Several other swimming access tracks lead off the main path as you return to the car park, coming out next to the conveniently placed **kiosk** where, over an ice-cold beverage, you can reflect on the fact that *Nitmiluk* is Jawoyn for 'sound of the cicada'.

## Take a Break

The small **Edith Falls Kiosk** on the south side of the car park has a lovely, shady verandah, the perfect place to sample its excellent mango smoothies and toasted sandwiches. Just watch out for psycho birds who will steal unguarded food right off your plate. The shop doubles as the camping ground office, arranges camping permits for Sweetwater Pool and also sells local arts and crafts.

# 22

# Motor Car Falls

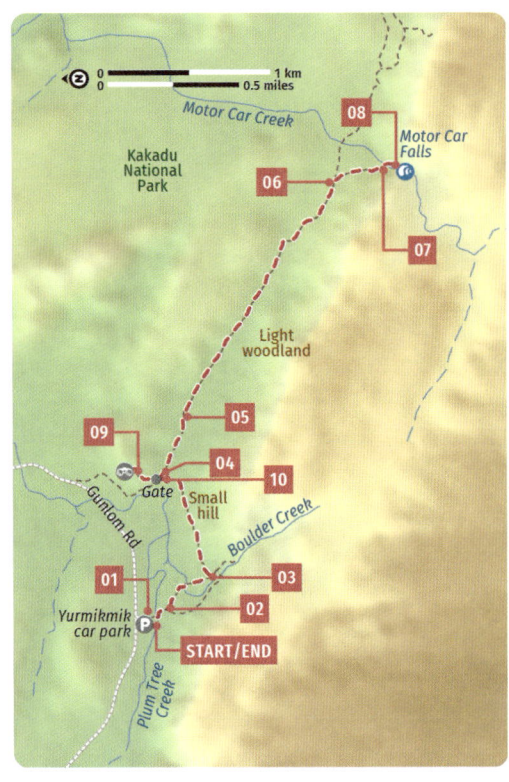

| DURATION | DIFFICULTY | DISTANCE | START/END |
|---|---|---|---|
| 3hrs return | Moderate | 8km | Yurmikmik car park |// 
| TERRAIN | | Mostly flat track, boulder-hopping | |

A relaxed walk to a stunning plunge pool and waterfall in a less-visited corner of Kakadu. Traversing wooded Jawoyn Country in the Mary River region, the mostly flat walk is accessible all year, though it's arguably even better in the Wet, when the falls are pumping.

## Getting Here

You will need your own vehicle. From Darwin it's 313km via Pine Creek and Mary River Roadhouse or 184km north from Katherine. Entry permits are mandatory for Kakadu: arrange this online before arrival.

## Starting Point

Turn off Kakadu Hwy 1.5km north of Mary River Ranger Station onto unsealed Gunlom Rd (usually OK for 2WD vehicles). Yurmikmik car park is 21km on the right – blink and you will miss it. There's an Emergency Call Device (ECD), picnic table and walks info.

**01** Walk south from the car park on a well-marked track, past the signs (noting any crocodile warnings) and across the (usually dry) creek.

**02** Veer left at the first track junction, then 400m from the car park turn left at the signpost, heading east away from Boulder Creek.

**03** The narrow track climbs, traverses the side of an open hill then drops down to cross a creek before rising briefly again to a large four-way track junction at a gate.

**04** Turn right, pass the gate and head southwest on a wide, smooth vehicle track providing easy walking as it leads up the lightly wooded valley.

## Freshies & Salties

Crocodiles in Australia come in two varieties:

**Freshwater** The smaller, less-troublesome species, freshies are found in almost every watercourse across the Top End. Generally shy and non-aggressive unless cornered, they can still give a nasty, infectious bite.

**Estuarine or Saltwater** Fearless killing machines, salties consider anything fair game. Growing up to 5m and with a broader, shorter snout, they are commonly found in coastal areas, though they can and do move inland. Don't take risks with salties; heed all signs and keep well away from riverbanks. If in doubt, do not swim.

**Best for**

**SOLITUDE**

**05** When the trail splits below a **small rise**, take either fork as they rejoin at the top.

**06** Reaching another track junction (2km from the gate), steer right (south) towards the **obvious gorge**.

**07** The marked path ends at a shady, **tree-fringed pool**.

**08** Cross the creek and scramble over slippery boulders upstream to a **second pool** and **waterfall** (pictured). Surrounded on three sides by sheer cliffs, this plunge pool is normally safe to swim in, but always check the current crocodile situation with park rangers beforehand and heed the sign at the track start. If in any doubt, do not enter the water!

**09** Retrace your outward route back to the gate. If time permits, turn right (north) and ascend the rocky ridge for 200m towards **Yurmikmik Lookout**, where you'll be rewarded with 360-degree views of your day's outing.

**10** Back at the four-way track junction ensure you return to **Yurmikmik car park** (not 'Motor Car Falls Car Park') by heading south, retracing your earlier route.

 **Take a Break**

Located 15km kilometres past Yurmikmik, **Gunlom** (Waterfall Creek) is the perfect picnic location, with plenty of shade, tables and toilets. A lovely plunge pool and waterfall are a short stroll from the car park and the well-maintained camping ground includes showers. But the real drawcard is the natural infinity pool perched on the clifftop above the falls, a 500m steep climb on a well-marked track. The view is simply sensational.

# 23

# Florence Falls

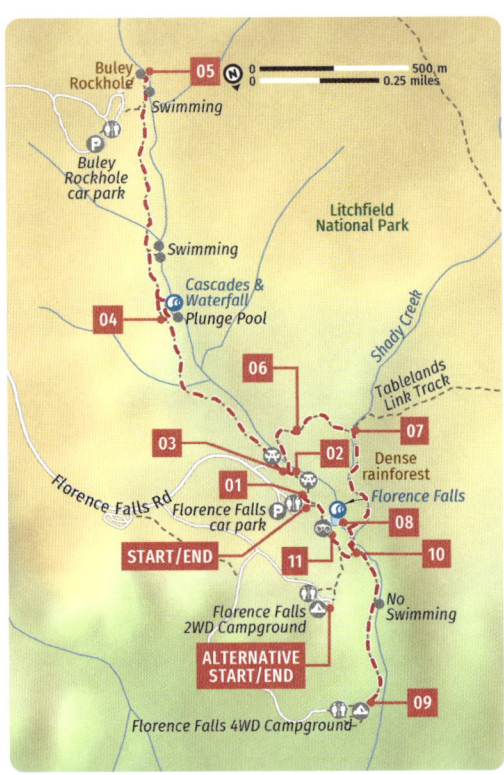

| DURATION | DIFFICULTY | DISTANCE | START/END |
|---|---|---|---|
| 2-3hrs return | Easy | 7km | Florence Falls car park |

| TERRAIN | Mostly paved track, some stairs |
|---|---|

Lap up tropical lushness in the rainforest and shady waterholes of Darwin's 'back yard' national park. Litchfield's proximity, picnic tables and paved walks make an easy family-friendly outing any time of year, though to escape the dry-season crowds, consider bush camping midweek. The falls are biggest during the Wet or early Dry, though too much water may close some areas.

## Getting Here
Florence Falls are 140km (1¾ hours) from Darwin via Batchelor on sealed roads. There is no public transport. Day tours from Darwin are plentiful, though hiring a car is cheaper.

## Starting Point
A well-paved track suitable for wheelchairs links the car parks and camping grounds as well as Buley Rockhole. This walk starts at Florence Falls car park.

**01** Follow Buley Rockhole signs onto the well-paved path running alongside **Florence Creek**. The dense rainforest foliage is alive with birds.

**02** Numerous small turnoffs on the right lead to creekside **picnic areas** and **swimming holes**.

**03** Pass a track junction to Shady Creek, which you will use later, and continue straight ahead for Buley.

**04** Around 700m past the signpost, an unmarked track on the right leads to a **large plunge pool** at the bottom of cascades. Follow a faint track that loops back to the main trail.

## Rainforest Birds

Litchfield's dense tropical rainforest supports a variety of birdlife:

**Figbird** A striking yellow-and-green bird with an unmissable red eye patch; feeds on fruit in the canopy.

**Rose-Crowned Fruit Dove** Medium-sized dove with large pink helmet and orange underbelly; perches on high branches.

**Rainbow Pitta** Small black-and-green bird with a vivid blue shoulder and chestnut head stripe; found rummaging through leaf litter.

**Rufous Fantail** Small fantail with chestnut markings on tail and head and a black-and-white chest; feeds on insects.

**05** **Buley Rockhole** (pictured) is a collection of photogenic plunge pools on a rocky section of the upper creek. Access tracks lead to a car park (toilets, barbecue).

**06** Return to the **Shady Creek track**, following it across Florence Creek and through dry **savannah woodland**.

**07** The habitat changes to wet **monsoon rainforest** at Shady Creek. A link track leads to the escarpment's **Tabletop Track** (39km, three days). Stay on the main track.

**08** The rainforest thickens, blocking out the sun as the path winds along the creek before arriving at the fig-lined plunge pool below **Florence Falls**.

**09** After a refreshing dip, continue on the track 100m to a bridge, crossing the creek to another track junction. Here you can stay low, following the creek to the **4WD camping ground** (2km return; toilets, barbecues, picnic tables), before returning the same way. You can't swim in Florence Creek below the plunge pool.

**10** The main track heads straight up a set of steep, steel stairs to the clifftop path, where you should turn right to return to Florence Falls car park. An access track heads left to the 2WD camp.

**11** Just near the car park, **Florence Falls Lookout** has an excellent view of the twin falls, plunge pool and rainforest canopy.

 **Take a Break**

Busy **Wangi Falls Cafe** (wangifallscafe.com.au) has a lovely shady verandah, cold drinks and just OK burgers and toasted sangers (sandwiches).

# Also Try...

O. ALAMANY & E. VICENS/GETTY IMAGES ©

## Kantju Gorge via Mala Walk

| DURATION | DIFFICULTY | DISTANCE |
|---|---|---|
| 1hr return | Easy | 2km |

Head around to the northern face of Uluru's sunburnt sandstone for a close-up inspection of Australia's most famous rock.

Part of the well-trodden Uluru base walk, this straightforward section passes a series of overhangs and caves, once vital shelter for the Mala (rufous hare-wallaby) people, forebears of the Anangu, the Traditional Owners. Explore ancient teaching and kitchen caverns, complete with traditional ochre rock paintings, before finishing at Kantju Gorge's dramatic cliffs (pictured). Time your walk after a downpour to witness the canyon's rivulet-etched escarpment transform into a surging waterfall. For a deeper understanding, join a free 90-minute ranger-guided stroll, leaving from the Mala car park each morning. But note that these tours can attract a crowd. Plan a sunset visit for a quieter ambience when the burnt-orange walls are at their most vivid.

## Barrk Sandstone

| DURATION | DIFFICULTY | DISTANCE |
|---|---|---|
| 5-6hrs return | Moderate | 12km |

A challenging and enthralling circuit linking two of Kakadu's most impressive rock-art sites.

Barrk is the local name for the male black wallaroo. The walk begins from Nourlangie Rock (Burrungkuy) car park and winds through the amazing art sites of Angbangbang before climbing up through lush monsoon thicket and a wet-season waterfall to the stone plateau of Burrungkuy. The marked trail weaves in and out of rocky outcrops before descending steeply to savannah woodland and the incredible Nanguluwur Gallery hidden under a long overhang. Images include hand prints, X-ray animals and a 'first contact' sailing ship. The trail then skirts around the base of the plateau through alternating sandstone and savannah rich in birdlife, crossing a final low ridge to arrive back at the car park. Start early and carry plenty of water.

JACK KINNY/SHUTTERSTOCK ©

## Butterfly Gorge

**DURATION** 6hrs return | **DIFF** Hard | **DISTANCE** 16.5km

Deep in the Stone Country of Katherine's Nitmiluk National Park lie hidden swimming holes, lofty viewpoints and rainforest-filled gorges.

This walk connects several 'Southern Walks' features around Katherine Gorge. From the visitor centre head to Baruwei Lookout above the Katherine River. Continue on signed trails to the Southern Rockhole (a shaded swimming hole), Pat's Lookout and Jedda's Rock (both above the river), then across exposed ridges to rainforest-filled Butterfly Gorge (pictured above). Return on the direct route. Note the trail is closed during summer.

## Chain of Ponds

**DURATION** 3hrs return | **DIFF** Moderate | **DISTANCE** 11.5km

East of Alice Springs, the less-visited East MacDonnell Ranges hold a few surprises, none more so than this excellent canyon at Trephina Gorge.

Start walking from the 2WD car park by the info shelter, soon joining a 4WD track for 4km to John Hayes Rock Hole. The trail then climbs a ridge to a modest lookout before turning into a sandy gorge that becomes rockier as you descend a series of seasonal pools and waterfalls back to the 4WD track. With a 4WD you can save the 8km road plod.

## Tabletop Circuit

**DURATION** 2-3 days | **DIFF** Moderate | **DISTANCE** 39km

Escape the crowds on this multiday circuit linking Litchfield's most popular attractions.

The route follows the hot, dry escarpment rim above the park's waterfalls, accessed from four separate link tracks – Florence, Wangi, Greenant and Walker. Most parties try to reach one of the three designated walker-only camp sites by midday, spending the rest of the day swimming. Carrying a topographic map is mandatory and this should be purchased prior to arrival. The walk is closed during the Wet, though permits may be arranged from Parks NT.

**Bungle Bungles (p112)**

# The Kimberley & Pilbara

**24 Emma Gorge**
The prettiest plunge pool in the Kimberley. **p104**

**25 Punamii-Unpuu/Mitchell Falls**
Remote walk to multitiered falls, taking in rock art, swimming holes and wildlife along the way. **p106**

**26 Bell Gorge**
Wash off the dust in this welcome oasis. **p110**

**27 Bungles Gorges**
Two of Purnululu's best. **p112**

**28 Mt Bruce**
Grab some altitude on WA's most impressive peak. **p114**

**29 Weano & Hancock Gorges**
Journey to the centre of the Earth in Karijini. **p116**

**30 Dales Gorge Circuit**
Family-friendly circuit linking several shady pools and a waterfall. **p118**

# Explore
# The Kimberley & Pilbara

Australia's last frontier, the vast, sparsely populated Kimberley is a wide, sun-baked land of boab-studded plains, hidden gorges, strong Aboriginal culture and minimal infrastructure. Travelling here isn't easy, but like all good adventures, the journey lingers long after the passage. Further south, but just as remote, the mine-pocked Pilbara contains the hidden gem of Karijini National Park. Walking through these spectacular landscapes, which resemble nowhere else in the country, will make for a truly memorable experience.

## Broome

The Yawuru Country of red pindan cliffs and turquoise ocean is every traveller's first glimpse of the Kimberley on flying into Broome, one of Australia's most remote towns, almost 2000km by road from Perth or Darwin. This is the place to rent a fully kitted 4WD to tackle the gorges on the Gibb River Road, and gather all your food and camping supplies. And with its many restaurants, bars, resorts and iconic Cable Beach, it's also a great place to unwind after a few weeks on the road. The laid-back vibe of 'Broome Time' is seductive, and some people find they never leave.

**Good Cartel** still does the best and earliest coffee in town, while **Matso's** (matsos.com.au) mango beer complements the climate perfectly.

## Kununurra

At the Kimberly's eastern edge in Miriwoong Country near the NT border, this relaxed town has useful services and transport connections, loads of accommodation, several stunning art galleries, car hire and some excellent food options.

For a lovely laid-back lunch, try the verandah at the lakeside **Pumphouse** (thepumphouserestaurant.com) before checking out the incredible local art scene at **Waringarri Arts Centre** (waringarriarts.com.au). See **Bushcamp Surplus** (facebook.com/BushcampSurplus) for all your camping needs.

## Tom Price

WA's highest town has a good **visitor centre** (tomprice.org.au), which can arrange tours of Karijini. The tidy mining town also has the closest fuel, supermarket, bank and takeaway food to the national park.

 ## When to Go

In the dry season (May to October) roads are open and daytime temperatures are milder. July and August is peak season.

In the summer (wet season), Karijini is still open but very hot, while the Kimberley gorges are inaccessible.

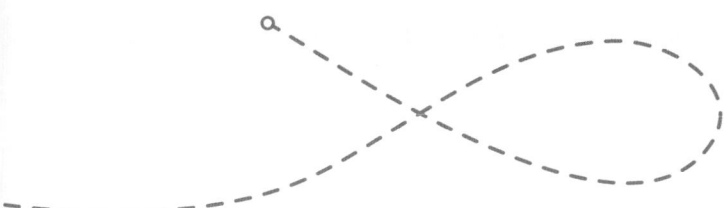

## Where to Stay

Broome accommodation is plentiful but not cheap. Camping is the best option for both the Kimberley (especially out on the Gibb) and Pilbara. Peaceful **Broome Bird Observatory** (broomebirdobservatory.com) on Roebuck Bay is a good choice for nature lovers, while **Beaches of Broome** (beachesofbroome.com.au) has reasonable rooms. Travellers passing through Kununurra prefer camping at **Hidden Valley** (hiddenvalleytouristpark.com), **Lakeside** (lakeside.com.au) or **Kimberleyland** (kimberleyland.com.au).

In Karijini you have two options, the **Eco Resort** (karijiniecoretreat.com.au), especially if you want to glamp, or the cheaper **Dales Gorge Campground**.

## What's On

**Staircase to the Moon** (visitbroome.com.au/info; Apr–Oct) Broome celebrates the full moon with evening markets, food and music.

**Ord Valley Muster** (ordvalleymuster.com.au; May) Kununurra rocks out with a 10-day festival of music, sports, art and charity events.

**Naidoc Week** (naidoc.org.au; Jun/Jul) A celebration of Aboriginal culture across various towns in the region.

**Nameless Jarndunmunha Festival** (namelessfestival.com.au; Aug) WA's highest town, Tom Price, downs tools for a weekend of music, food and mayhem.

**Shinju Matsuri/Pearl Festival** (shinjumatsuri.com.au; Aug/Sep) This weeklong love song to all things pearly in Broome includes parades, food, art and music.

## Transport

Broome and Kununurra receive daily flights from Perth and Darwin and seasonal direct flights from east-coast cities. A high-clearance 4WD is necessary for most Kimberly gorges and you can rent one in Broome, Darwin or Kununurra.

Paraburdoo (131km) is the closest airport to Karijini. Integrity Coaches drop off at Tom Price and Auski Roadhouse and transfers can be arranged with the Flying Sandgroper. Or you can drive from Perth in roughly two days (2WDs are OK).

## Resources

**Parks and Wildlife** (parks.dpaw.wa.gov.au) Information and permits for most WA parks (except Mitchell River).

**Wunambal Gaambera** (wunambalgaambera.org.au) Uunguu Visitor Passes for Mitchell Plateau/Ngauwudu.

**Tourism WA** (westernaustralia.com) Broader tourist information.

**Main Roads Western Australia** (mainroads.wa.gov.au) Road closures (also check local shire websites) and driving tips, contacts for the Gibb River Road.

**Hema Maps** (hemamaps.com) Best driving maps for the Kimberley.

**Integrity Coach Lines** (integritycoachlines.com.au) Buses for Karijini.

**Flying Sandgroper** (flyingsandgroper.com.au) Karijini transfers.

# 24

# Emma Gorge

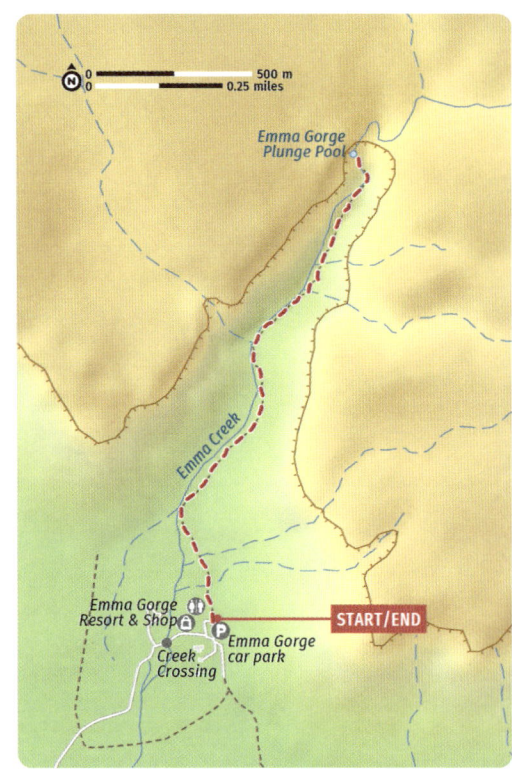

| DURATION | DIFFICULTY | DISTANCE | START/END |
|---|---|---|---|
| 2-3hrs return | Moderate | 4km | Emma Gorge Resort |

| TERRAIN | Marked trail, some steep sections |
|---|---|

A short, tropical stroll leads to the prettiest plunge pool in the Kimberley. It's an easy day trip from Kununurra (80km) on the sealed end of the Gibb River Road; leave 2WD vehicles at the water crossing just before the car park.

Head north from Emma Gorge Resort car park along the dry, open track that narrows, crossing typical **savannah woodland**.

Soon the **orange sandstone walls** of the gorge constrict, and the path, now **shaded by pandanus and livistona**, follows the outlet creek.

Watch closely for markers when the track climbs around rocks and other obstacles as the exact route may vary depending on prior bushfires and wet seasons.

At some point the path will cross the creek, usually more than once. The last crossing is marked by a **brilliant turquoise pool** (pictured) reflecting the sun.

Follow the route up past the pool on the left, where there's a short steep climb, before a more gentle, shady track to the edge of the plunge pool, an almost **perfectly circular swimming hole** surrounded by towering cliffs.

Paddle lazily out beneath the trickling falls, lying on your back, watching the droplets descend in dazzling slow motion.

Refreshed, retrace your route back to the car park and treat yourself to an ice cream from the resort shop.

# 25

# Punamii-Unpuu/ Mitchell Falls

**Best for**

☑

**WILDLIFE**

| DURATION | DIFFICULTY | DISTANCE | START/END |
|---|---|---|---|
| 3-5hrs return | Moderate | 8.6km | Mitchell Falls day-use area |

| TERRAIN | Marked trail, sandstone country |
|---|---|

A fabulous walk across far-flung Ngauwudu leads to majestic Punamii-Unpuu, the sacred home of Wunggurr, the Wunambal creation serpent. In the Kimberley's far north, isolated Ngauwudu (Mitchell Plateau), rich in Aboriginal culture, is an island of biodiversity, providing refuge for many endangered species. The Punamii-Unpuu trail in Mitchell River National Park traverses tropical savannah dotted with rock-art galleries, rainforest-fringed waterholes and deep sandstone gorges to the magnificent, multilayered Punamii-Unpuu/Mitchell Falls.

## Getting Here

To access Mitchell River National Park your choice is two days of rough 4WD-only roads (from Kununurra or Derby), initially along the Gibb River Road, or a charter flight (ex Kununurra, Derby or Drysdale River). All visitors to Ngauwudu (Mitchell Plateau) must purchase an online Uunguu Visitor Pass (UVP) prior to arrival.

Kalumburu Rd north from the Gibb River Road junction is usually in good condition until the Mitchell Plateau turnoff. The Port Warrender (Mitchell Plateau) Rd is rocky and can be heavily corrugated after the King Edward crossing, as it passes through extraordinary livistona (fan palm) forests. Check conditions at Drysdale River.

## Starting Point

The trail starts by the information shelter at the day-use area, where there's also toilets and drinking water. Start early to avoid the heat, to maximise your chances of seeing wildlife and to get in and out before the noisy tourist helicopters start turning up. Most people will complete the trail in three hours.

**01** Follow the white-topped trail markers (complete with Wandjina symbols) north past the info signs and cross pandanus-fringed **Mertens Creek**. The spiky pandanus (*Pandanus spiralis*, or screw pine) provides a safe habitat for small birds, and the ripe orange fruit, which you might find scattered on the track, is a favourite wildlife food source.

**02** The trail climbs then turns sharply west (left). Ignore a side track for the (very dry) **River View Trail** and continue following the white markers across rocky ground. Quite often this area shows evidence of bushfires and can either be brown and blackened or bursting with green regrowth.

**03** Alternating between rock and sand, the path winds over outcrops where it's possible (though highly unlikely) to spot the elusive **Black Grasswren**. This striated black and chestnut twitcher's holy grail hides in Ngauwudu's sandstone crevasses and has also been reported along the (just bypassed) River View Trail.

**04** After 500m, a side trail branching left leads to the top of **Little Mertens Falls** (Bunjani), where the force of the water over time has carved fantastic, smoothed shapes into the rock. In early morning, the **view from the edge of the falls** over the mirror-like surface of the tree-lined pool and surrounding canopy below is simply sublime.

**05** Return to the main trail, continuing for 150m as it descends a small cliff, then take the next, unmarked track on the left. This leads to several **rock-art galleries** featuring Gwion Gwion figures and local animals.

**06** Clamber down steeply to the edge of the leafy **plunge pool** below Little Mertens Falls. A swim here is recommended.

## Wandjina & Gwion Gwion

Considered powerful creator spirits by the Worrorra, Ngarinyin and Wunumbal peoples, Wandjina are unique to the Kimberley, adorning rock shelters and overhangs, usually near water. With large eyes, no mouth and straight lines radiating from their heads, they're sometimes called 'lightning men', thought to signify the coming of the Wet. Strict cultural laws govern who can paint Wandjina.

Gwion Gwion (also Gyorn Gyorn or 'Bradshaw' images) are long, thin, enigmatic figures depicting ancient ancestors in a unique style that predates Wandjina by thousands of years. See **Mowanjum Arts Centre** (mowanjumarts.com).

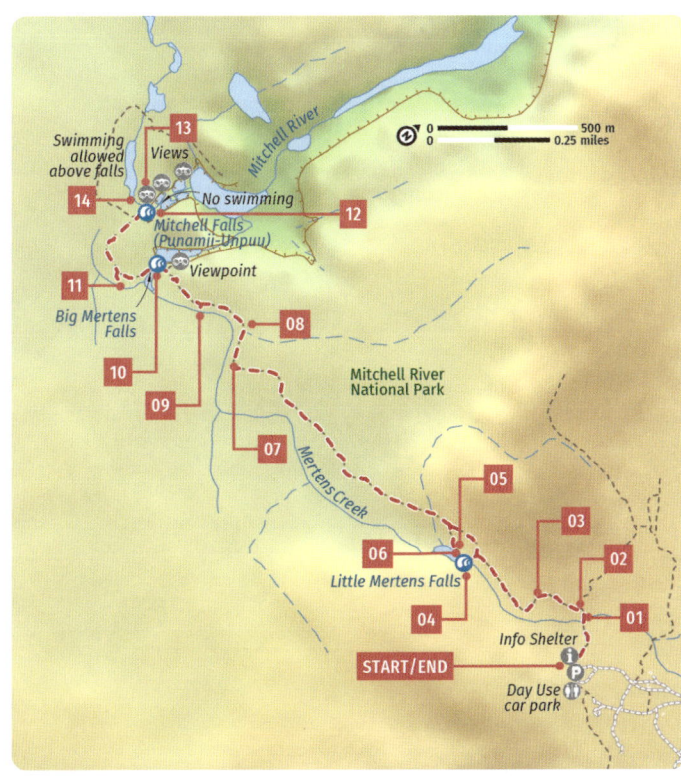

**07** After a steep climb back up to the main trail, head left across (possibly burnt) savannah and rock slabs. If you've started early enough, you might be lucky to spot a **monjon** when passing by sandstone outcrops. These tiny, shy rock wallabies are mostly nocturnal but are sometimes still active in the early morning. They are distinguished by a long, tufted tail.

**08** Descend towards the creek again, where the **lush rainforest** and native fig trees with their long aerial roots provide some welcome shade.

**09** When the track emerges from the rainforest onto rocks, you'll find another **rock-art gallery** under an overhang off to the left, this one depicting a **Gwion Gwion battle scene**.

**10** The huge, deep gorge containing **Big Mertens Falls** is up next, and impressive though it is, it's merely the curtain raiser for Punamii-Unpuu. **Peregrine falcons** (pictured) nest among the sheer sandstone walls and there's a pleasant *yawal* (billabong) opposite.

**11** Leave the falls and follow the trail above the **billabong** to a track junction where a side path drops down to a **rock lookout over the water**. The billabong is carpeted in *miiyani* (**water lilies**) and sometimes you'll see **brolga** here. The large grey crane with a distinctive red ear band is famous for its intricate courtship dance and is normally found in pairs by billabongs and wetlands across the Top End.

**12** Finally, the main trail drops down several rock terraces to arrive above the magnificent multitiered **Punamii-Unpuu/Mitchell Falls** (pictured p106). Unfortunately, unless you are here early in the season, these will only be a trickle in the Dry, but the view is still incredible.

**13** Experienced walkers can find more **extensive views** from the untracked plateau above the left side of the falls. Tread lightly here and keep away from crumbling edges. Under no circumstances try to descend to any of the pools beneath the falls, as these are sacred to the Wunambal people, and considered to be the resting place of the Wunggurr, the creation Rainbow Serpent.

**14** Swimming is permitted in the **upper billabong** west of the falls and you might see a **Mertens' water monitor** sunning itself nearby. These long, slender goannas have a flattened tail perfectly adapted for swimming. When you've finished, retrace your outward journey to the car park before the day heats up. Or if you're feeling flush, you can jump on a chopper for the five-minute trip.

## Bush Fires

Fires in the Kimberley fall into two categories:

**'Cool'** or early-season burn – purposely lit early in the Dry when temperatures are low and vegetation green. Following Aboriginal burning principles developed over thousands of years, these fires burn slowly, reducing the amount of fuel (undergrowth) for late-season burns while retaining important wildlife habitat and mature foliage.

**'Hot'** or late-season burn – the hottest, most destructive fires occur late in the Dry when temperatures are extreme, humidity low and the landscape is like a tinderbox. Often sparked by dry lightning preceding the coming Wet, these fires can be devastating to both wildlife and habitats in areas that haven't had a cool-season burn.

See klc.org.au/indigenous-fire-management.

It's a long way for a break, but you have to pass (or fuel up at) **Drysdale River Station** (drysdaleriver.com.au) anyway, so you might as well relax in the shady beer garden and tuck into its legendary burgers and icy cold lagers (if you're not the driver).

If you're heading east on the Gibb, then don't miss **Ellenbrae's** (ellenbraestation.com.au) famous Devonshire teas, the only scones this side of the asphalt.

# 26
# Bell Gorge

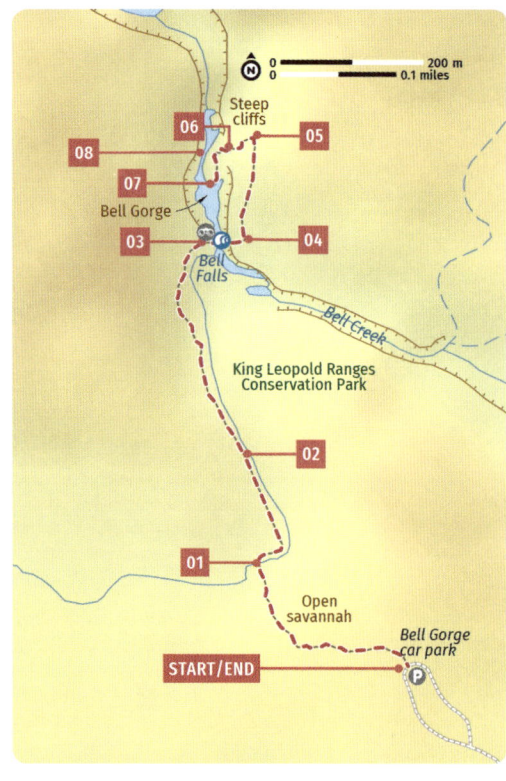

| DURATION | DIFFICULTY | DISTANCE | START/END |
|---|---|---|---|
| 2hrs return | Moderate | 5km | Bell Gorge car park |

| TERRAIN | Rocky, partly shaded, steep section |
|---|---|

Bathers are mandatory for this short, nature-packed trek to a magnificent cliff-ringed oasis of swimming holes and cascading falls. Descending through savannah to rainforest, the walk then crosses open sandstone slabs before a steep scramble down rock ledges brings you to the inviting water's edge, the perfect spot for soaking away the dust and corrugations of the Kimberley's infamous Gibb River Road.

## Getting Here

The turnoff to Bell Gorge is around 8km west of Imintji on the mostly unsealed Gibb River Road, some 218km (three hours) from Derby and almost 500km (seven hours) from Kununurra. You will need a high-clearance 4WD. Overland tour groups usually visit the gorge. Note the trail is closed during the wet season when roads are impassable.

## Starting Point

Bell Gorge car park is 29km from the Gibb on a rough unsealed road, 10km past Silent Grove camping ground, in the Wunaamin Conservation Park; entry fees apply. There are no toilets beyond Silent Grove. Bring a hat and plenty of water as sections of this walk are in full sun.

**01** Follow the track from the car park down a short, scrubby ridge before crossing a **small creek**.

**02** Enjoy the shade and birdsong of the lush creekside **rainforest** where you might spot a crimson finch or purple-crowned fairy wren hiding in the pandanus. Look on the path for nibbled orange pandanus fruit, a favourite of cockatoos.

## Wildlife

You might spot the following:

**Mertens' water monitor**
A medium-sized goanna found near water, commonly seen basking by the main pool.

**White-quilled rock pigeon**
A sandstone-coloured pigeon with distinctive white wing patches; makes a 'woodblock' sound when flying. Roosts in cliffs.

**Purple-crowned fairy wren**
Spectacular small bird, the males develop a bright purple 'crown' during mating season (September to October). Found in pandanus.

**Short-eared rock wallaby**
Blink and you'll miss these sure-footed marsupials bounding along knife-thin cliff ledges.

**Best for**

**A COOLING SWIM**

**03** Arrive at the rock slabs on top of **Bell Falls** (pictured). Peer over the edge of the falls to the spectacular plunge pool below. The **best views** of the falls are from further around the western (left) rim.

**04** Cross **Bell Creek** and follow the track markers up open rocky slabs. The sun is your enemy on this climb.

**05** Reach a high point above the pool with **good views** across the surrounding country.

**06** Descend a **steep, narrow gully**, eventually following wide rock ledges to the water below. This is the hardest section of the walk.

**07** A narrow finger of rock on the left offers shade. The **heart-shaped pool** is the perfect place to float on your back and stare up at the sheer red walls and deep blue sky. Take extra care when entering the water as the submerged rocks are very slippery. You may spot a **Mertens' water monitor** sunning itself nearby.

**08** If you have time, **explore the pools downstream** until you reach the top of more falls. Retrace your steps back to the car park.

 **Take a Break**

Only 8km from the Bell Gorge turnoff, and a long way from anywhere else, the tiny **Imintji Store** supplies the Kimberley essentials of diesel, insect repellent, wi-fi and ice cream. There's a few alfresco tables out back, perfect for checking emails and wolfing down a toastie and cappuccino. The nearby Arts Centre is worth a look, and a tidy, community-run camping ground is 500m back towards Derby.

# 27

# Bungles Gorges

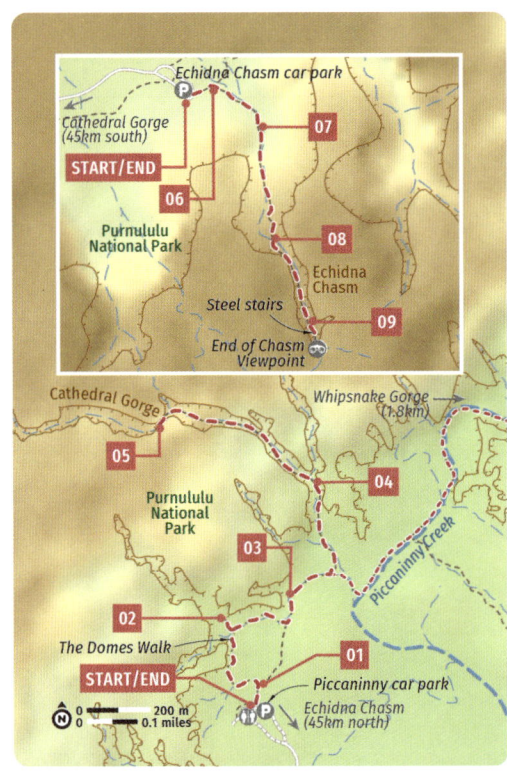

| DURATION | DIFFICULTY | DISTANCE | START/END |
|---|---|---|---|
| 2hrs return | Easy | 4.5km | Piccaninny/ Echidna car parks |
| **TERRAIN** | | Sand, rock, minimal shade | |

Easy walking will take you to two of the startling Bungle Bungles' most exceptional and accessible features. The gorges are located deep in the Kimberley's harsh interior, so you will need to be totally self-sufficient as the raw beauty and geological significance of Purnululu National Park is best experienced by camping overnight.

The walk's two gorges are at opposite ends of the range, connected by a 45km drive. Avoid the considerable heat by starting your walk as early as possible.

## Getting Here

The visitor centre is 52km (2½ hours) down a rough 4WD-only road from the Great Northern Highway, 108km north of Halls Creek. Leave 2WDs at the caravan park 1km from the highway and take a day tour. Alternatively, arrange a hike-and-fly package from Kununurra.

## Starting Point

Piccaninny (or Southern) car park is 27km from the visitor centre, with toilets and shaded picnic tables. The walk starts from the northern side.

**01** Head north along the sandy trail, turning left after 50m towards 'The Domes', pass another track junction, eventually arriving at a dead end.

**02** The Bungles' extraordinary orange-and-black 'beehives' **Domes** are a classic example of karst sandstone. The black bands indicate the presence of moisture-seeking cyanobacteria; the orange of rusting iron minerals.

## Whip Snake Gorge

For a less-touristed adventure, Whip Snake Gorge is a further 4.5km (one hour) one way from the Cathedral Gorge track junction.

A well-signposted route follows the wide, sandy bed of Piccaninny Creek for several kilometres past a wall of banded domes before heading north across flat rocky ground to the narrow gorge. Less dramatic than Cathedral, this quieter gorge has some interesting rock formations, a (usually dry) terminal pool and plenty of shade. You're more likely to see wildlife here.

Start early and carry plenty of water; while the walking is easy there's no shade until the gorge, and the reflected heat off the white sand of the creek bed could cook an egg.

JACK KINNY/SHUTTERSTOCK ©

**03** Return to the previous junction and turn left (east) to regain the main track, passing larger domes before entering a **dry creek bed**. Continue northeast on the opposite bank or stay in the creek.

**04** At the next track junction turn left and walk 300m towards Cathedral Gorge, where **massive rock walls** provide some welcome shade.

**05** Enter the gorge, cross the dry creek then climb a small steel ladder, following the path until a final corner reveals the **'Cathedral'** (pictured), a colossal orange rock amphitheatre and small terminal pool. Return to the car park and drive 45km to Echidna Chasm in the park's north.

**06** Following signs, turn right after 50m, to enter a **dry, rocky creek**.

**07** The hot creek slog is tempered by **livistona palms** and massive **conglomerate boulders** near the chasm.

**08** Enter the tight cleft of **Echidna Chasm**, which soon narrows even further. The sky is a thin slit several hundred metres above. Look for **microbats** perching high on the walls.

**09** The chasm opens into a **large chamber**, popular with photographers. Beyond, the route narrows, continuing briefly to a **final viewpoint**.

## Take a Break

**Kungkalanayi Lookout** on the low ridge running parallel with the west side of the Bungles is perfect for a sunset picnic. From the car park (toilets), climb steep steps for 200m to the ridge crest, then turn left or right to find the perfect bench to break out the hors d'oeuvres and pinot. The setting sun softens the surrounding hills and spinifex, while setting the long wall of Bungles ablaze.

# 28

# Mt Bruce

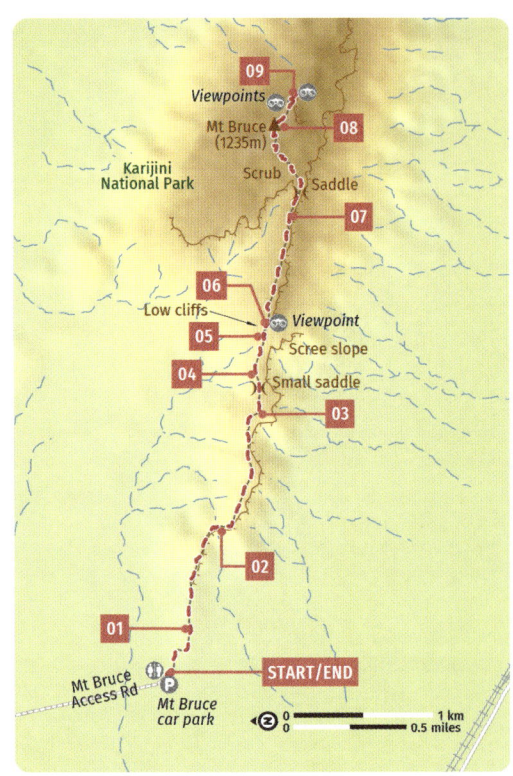

| DURATION | DIFFICULTY | DISTANCE | START/END |
|---|---|---|---|
| 4-5hrs return | Hard | 10km | Mt Bruce car park |

| TERRAIN | Steep, rocky, minimal shade |
|---|---|

Peak-baggers will relish this climb to the summit of one of WA's tallest, remotest and most spectacular mountains. Dominating the Karijini skyline, the state's second-highest peak, 1235m Mt Bruce (Punurrunha; pictured), in the Pilbara's iron-rich Hamersley Range, is a much more satisfying adventure than the marginally higher Meharry (1253m). A well-marked track leads up Mt Bruce's western flank to a broad summit with exceptional views.

## Getting Here
Karijini is a two-day drive from almost everywhere (2WDs are OK). Local tour company the Flying Sandgroper can arrange transfers with Integrity Coaches (Tom Price or Auski/Munjina) and Paraburdoo Airport (102km).

## Starting Point
Turn off Karijini Dr 51km from Tom Price (or 68km from the Great Northern Highway) onto Mt Bruce access road (almost opposite Karijini's western entrance). The car park is 3km (toilet, no water). Start at first light and carry plenty of water; temperatures can be extreme.

**01** Head up the spinifex-clad west ridge, cresting the first hill where **already impressive views** reveal the surrounding countryside.

**02** Watch for track markers as you climb some low stone slabs (hint: keep left when climbing; right on descent). You'll start to get **views of Marrandoo**, the huge mine to the south that's been excised from the national park.

## Hamersley Gorge

Popular with Tom Price locals, **Hamersley** is Karijini's 'forgotten gorge', tucked away in the park's far northwestern corner away from other attractions. On the southern branch of the Fortescue River, this wide, spectacular gorge is a prime example of geological uplift with folded fault lines running through the gorge walls, most impressive in the late-afternoon sun when they turn fiery red. A large, paperbark-edged swimming hole beckons invitingly. It's possible to continue swimming downstream some way; alternatively, walk upstream from the falls to discover hidden pools. Roughly 55km from Karijini's western entrance, there's a viewing deck and toilets at the car park.

MARKUS KAROLY/SHUTTERSTOCK ©

**03** Easy walking with **excellent views** along the long undulating ridge brings you to the top of a small hill with an interpretive panel for the **Honey Hakea** (corkwood) tree.

**04** Descend into a small saddle and climb steeply out the other side onto the next hill, where a panel describes the rare **Pebble-mound mouse**, whose 'pebble mounds' you may be able to spot.

**05** Follow the blue track markers closely up a scree slope, ignoring false leads, and head for the base of some low cliffs and possibly some welcome shade if you've started early enough.

**06** A fixed chain on the cliffs leads into a narrow, shady slot, a good place for a rest and a drink. Large arrows show the way up the slot onto the flat clifftop with more **stunning views**, including of most of the route already covered.

**07** Traverse the long ridge of angled rock slabs towards the summit spur, descending briefly into a flatish saddle, before scrambling steeply up rocks.

**08** Zigzag up through scrub to the broad summit plateau and massive **summit cairn**, with a nearby dial locating WA's highest peaks. The views, as you would expect, are exceptional.

**09** Explore the plateau for other **viewpoints** before retracing your outward route.

# 29

# Weano & Hancock Gorges

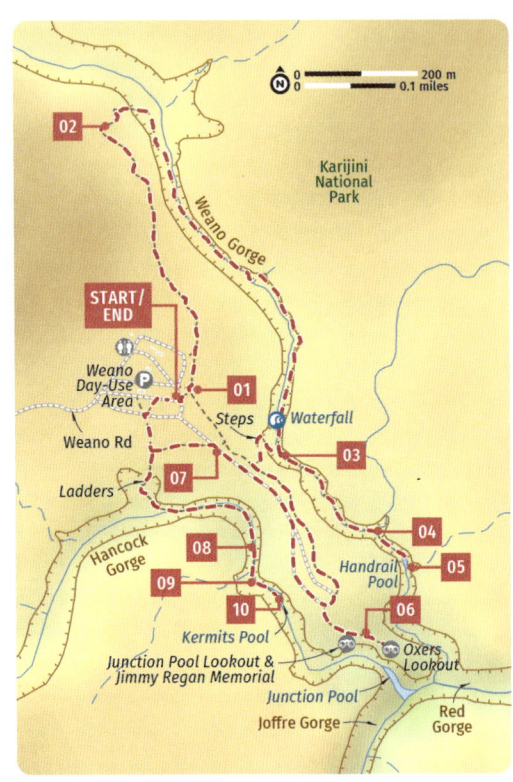

| DURATION | DIFFICULTY | DISTANCE | START/END |
|---|---|---|---|
| 2hrs return | Moderate | 4.3km | Weano day-use area |

| TERRAIN | | Slippery rocks, ladders |
|---|---|---|

Unleash your inner Jules Verne by descending into the bowels of the Earth in Karijini's incredible slot canyons. Beneath the rusting, sun-scorched Pilbara, water has carved another world of surrealistic passages and subterranean pools, so bring your swimmers and good grippy footwear that you're not afraid to get wet (cheap tennis shoes are perfect!). And remember, if it starts to rain, leave the gorge immediately, as flash floods have caused fatalities in the past.

## Getting Here

Karijini is a two-day drive from almost everywhere (2WDs are OK). Local tour company the Flying Sandgroper can arrange transfers with Integrity Coaches (Tom Price or Auski/Munjina) and Paraburdoo Airport.

## Starting Point

From Karijini's western entrance, follow Banjima Dr to the Eco Retreat turn, then unsealed Weano Rd another 10km to the day-use area. Locate the info shelter on the car park's eastern side.

**01** From the info shelter head north (left) towards **Upper Weano Gorge**, glimpsed far below.

**02** Descend into the upper gorge then turn downstream along a sandy track and/or rock ledges. Walk right, past a **small waterfall and pool**, perfect for a dip.

**03** Pass the steep direct-access steps beyond which the gorge narrows. Crisscross the stream. The **next pool** can be avoided by scrambling right.

## Gorge on the Wild Side

Beyond Handrail Pool, Weano Gorge becomes a restricted zone, not least because it ends in a 40m waterfall. Likewise Hancock Gorge beyond Kermits Pool, and the bottom of nearby Knox Gorge, are also restricted. These areas are easy to get trapped in and rescues are long and complicated. Spare a thought for Jimmy Regan, the SES volunteer whose memorial is by Junction Pool Lookout.

The easiest way to visit the restricted gorges is on a West Oz Active Adventure tour. Be prepared for a fantastic action-packed day of sliding over waterfalls, abseiling, climbing, swimming and floating around on inner tubes. All gear and lunch is supplied. Book through the Eco Retreat.

BEWLEY GEORGE SHAYLOR III/SHUTTERSTOCK ©

**04** Enter a narrow, slippery orange slot with a **small pool** in its middle. This is the Jules Verne bit!

**05** You're now inside the bowels of the Earth, and exquisite **Handrail Pool** is suitably named. Reverse down the handrail moving onto an obvious ledge. If the pool looks clean enjoy a well-earned swim in the freezing water!

**06** Return to the steps, climb steeply to the clifftop, turn left and follow the track to **two lookouts** above Junction Pool, some 100m below at the gorges' confluence.

**07** Follow the road, taking the first track signposted to **Hancock Gorge**, then descend steel ladders to the gorge floor.

**08** Head downstream. A **long deep pool** can be bypassed by a tight scramble along the steep, right wall. Or you could just swim it.

**09** The **Spider Walk** is another extremely narrow, smooth slippery slot, and you'll be making like a spider just to stay upright.

**10** Arrive at the sublime **Kermits Pool** (pictured) where filtered light casts an eerie green glow. If you're not wet already, now's the time. Return to the car park on the direct track above the ladders.

 **Take a Break**

If you're not avoiding the heat by soaking in a gorge, then you'll want to be under the fans at the open-air restaurant of **Karijini Eco Retreat** (karijiniecoretreat.com.au), the only dining option in the national park. Whether it's sophisticated salmon, a humble seared sanger or just a thirst-quenching sundowner on ice, you won't be disappointed. It's open all day; dinner bookings are essential.

# 30

# Dales Gorge Circuit

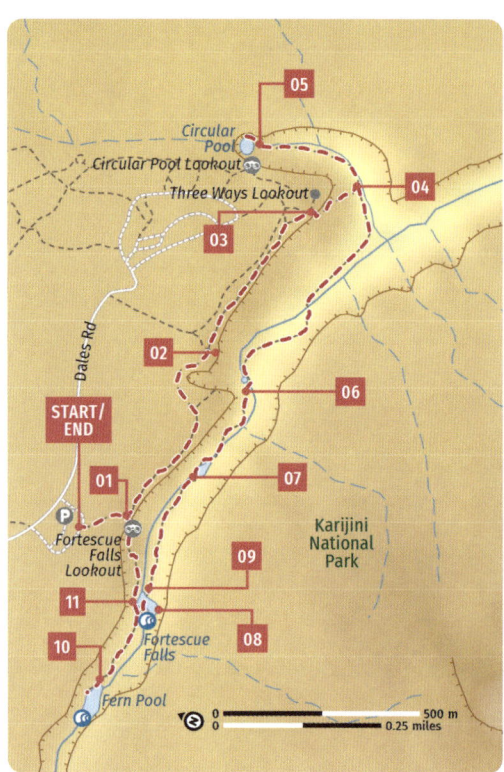

| DURATION | DIFFICULTY | DISTANCE | START/END |
|---|---|---|---|
| 2hrs return | Moderate | 4.5km | Fortescue Falls car park |

| TERRAIN | Stairs, rocky path, slippery rocks |
|---|---|

Escape the Karijini heat on this short, family-friendly circuit joining two lovely plunge pools. The walk initially skirts the gorge clifftops before dropping steeply to the first of two pools, then follows the open gorge upstream past more swimming opportunities to a waterfall and on to the second pool. The circuit can be walked in either direction, though going clockwise provides a shorter return from the last swimming hole.

## Getting Here

Karijini is a two-day drive from almost everywhere (2WDs are OK). Local tour company the Flying Sandgroper can arrange transfers with Integrity Coaches (Tom Price or Auski/Munjina) and Paraburdoo Airport.

## Starting Point

From Karijini's east entrance drive 8.5km to Dales Rd then follow that 9km to Fortesecue Falls car park, the first car park after the camping ground turnoff. Walks start from the southeast corner. Toilets are provided.

**01** From the car park walk 130m to the **cliff-side lookout** for a view of Fortescue Falls.

**02** Locate a track on your left just before the lookout and follow this east along the clifftops. There are **excellent views down the gorge** from several viewpoints, especially one by an **old ghost gum** (pictured), after the trail curves inland briefly to skirt a minor gully.

**03** Continue east along the clifftop trail towards **Three Ways Lookout**, where just before the lookout a set of stone steps descends steeply on the right.

## Karijini Trees

**Common Rock Fig** Found in the damper sections of shady gorges; its exposed roots hang down cliffs, searching for water.

**Snappy Gum** Striking white or pale smooth-barked eucalypt growing on ridgetops. Scattered along Weano Rd, they're particularly photogenic in low light.

**Silver Cadjeput** A large, droopy paperbark (melaleuca), liking the edges of open pools and rivers. They are common in all gorges and their bark has many traditional uses.

**Corkwood** Unique 'honey' hakea whose thick corklike bark is fire-resistant, and the nectar from its large yellow flowers is an important bush-tucker source.

**04** After a short, steep descent you'll reach a track junction on the gorge floor. Turn left and follow the yellow trail markers along rocky slabs, eventually crossing the creek.

**05** Ringed by red cliffs, **Circular Pool** is a lovely spot for contemplation and a quiet swim.

**06** Return to the track junction, then continue along the gorge. The route follows rock slabs, crossing the creek several times to some **small cascades** and a nearby rock arch.

**07** A **pool** beneath a shady paperbark calls invitingly for another much-needed swim.

**08** Continue upstream until you reach the pool at the base of **Fortescue Falls**. Go on, have another swim, though there's not much shade.

**09** Cross the stones at the pool's outlet and ascend the falls on the right side, following the markers. Beware of slippery rocks.

**10** Ignore the stairs to your right and follow the obvious path upstream through **shady rainforest** for 250m to the beautiful, native-fig-lined **Fern Pool**. With a small, permanent waterfall at its far end, this popular swimming hole is also sacred to the Banyjima people, and they ask visitors to act respectfully.

**11** Return to the stairs and climb steeply to the lookout and car park.

 **Take a Break**

For more lazy picnics by lovely deep swimming holes, try the Pilbara's 'other' national park, the lesser-known **Millstream-Chichester**, encompassing the shady billabongs of the Fortescue River, a mere 300km away. Turn left at Auski/Munjina.

# Also Try...

## Bigurda Trail

| DURATION | DIFFICULTY | DISTANCE |
|---|---|---|
| 2hrs one-way | Moderate | 8km |

An enjoyable winter stroll high above the Indian Ocean against a backdrop of migrating humpback whales.

Joining several of Kalbarri National Park's (pictured) coastal lookouts, the exposed trail winds along the treeless, crumbling clifftops between Eagle Gorge and Natural Bridge. Look down on massive fallen boulders and eroded sea stacks while searching the ocean for telltale whale spray and, if you're lucky, a full breach.

Walkable in any season, the totally shadeless trail is much more pleasant during the cooler months when whales are migrating and flies dormant. In hotter weather expect a flyblown death march, in which case start from the northern end with the wind behind you and find shade and water at Natural Bridge car park, unlike Eagle Gorge. You will need to arrange return transport, otherwise it's another shadeless 8km back the way you came.

## Sir John Gorge

| DURATION | DIFFICULTY | DISTANCE |
|---|---|---|
| 4-6hrs return | Moderate | 15km |

A sensational walk upstream along a remote gorge on the Kimberley's majestic Fitzroy River.

Located on the Kimberley's Mornington Wilderness Camp, the walk descends briefly from the car park past a large boab onto smooth red rock slabs beside the river. The unmarked route follows the slabs upstream, passing long pools terminating in gravel bars, staying high or low as conditions demand. Cross the river at a shallow section in the third pool, just after climbing and descending a small buttress, and before the obvious indentation of Tin Can Gully on the right bank. Keep walking beyond the gully to the fifth pool at a 90-degree bend in the river. Have a swim and some lunch, then return the way you came, recrossing the river, and picking up the car-park track at the big boab. You can also hire the canoes positioned by the first three pools.

PHILIP SCHUBERT/SHUTTERSTOCK ©

## Piccaninny Gorge

| DURATION | DIFF | DISTANCE |
|---|---|---|
| 2-3 days return | Hard | 30km |

An extended overnight walk far from the tourist crowds explores one of Purnululu's wilder gorges.

The large gorge system at the end of Piccaninny Creek (roughly 7km past the Whip Snake Gorge turnoff; pictured) provides experienced overnight walkers plenty of off-track exploration possibilities. Given the distance, most parties camp in the gorge for one or two nights. While early in the season some pools may still have water, you should carry all that you will need. Walkers must register with the rangers and carry an ELB (emergency locator beacon) or satellite phone. The trail is closed in the wet season.

## Tunnel Creek

| DURATION | DIFF | DISTANCE |
|---|---|---|
| 1½hrs return | Moderate | 2km |

A short, exhilarating adventure along an underground river in Bunuba Country.

From the car park off Fairfield-Leopold Downs Rd, a short walk and boulder scramble leads to a tall cave entrance. Ensure you have a good torch and footwear for the 750m pitch-black trek in and alongside the sandy creek as it winds through the limestone cave beneath the Kimberley's Napier Range, part of the ancient Devonian Reef. The cave was once a hideout for Jandamarra, a celebrated Bunuba guerilla fighter. Look out for bats. There's rock art near the far entrance.

## Mt Augustus (Burringurrah)

| DURATION | DIFF | DISTANCE |
|---|---|---|
| 4-6hrs return | Hard | 12km |

On Wajarri land in the sparsely populated Gascoyne region a massive inselberg (island mountain) rises 715m above the surrounding plains.

Twice as large as Uluru, Burringurrah is impressively remote, 355km from Meekatharra. Two trails lead up – the shorter Summit Trail stays on the spinifex-crusted ridge, climbing gently at first, then rising more steeply. The more sporting Gully Trail follows a scrubby dry creek before rejoining the other. Summit views are appropriately stunning.

Hamelin Bay (p134)

# Southwest Forests to the Sea

**31** **Bluff Knoll**
Wildflowers line the steep climb to the tallest peak in the southwest. **p126**

**32** **Nancy Peak & Devils Slide**
Short but scenic circuit through karri forests and granite outcrops. **p128**

**33** **Bald Head**
Trek along a narrow peninsula surrounded by incredible seascapes to a lonely headland. **p130**

**34** **Nuyts Wilderness**
From karri and tingle forests to the wild Southern Ocean. **p132**

**35** **Hamelin Bay to Elephant Rock**
Beaches, coastal heath, islands and blowholes make for an epic day out. **p134**

# Explore

# Southwest Forests to the Sea

The southwest corner of Western Australia (WA) with its mild climate, high rainfall and rich, varied landscapes, is a naturalist's nirvana. Bushwalkers will relish the tall native forests, fragile alpine ecosystems, brilliant white beaches and deep turquoise oceans free of tropical nasties. Walking here is easy as tracks, national parks and camp sites are plentiful.

## Albany

Sitting on picturesque King George Sound, this former whaling station is now the largest town in the southwest and makes a good base for exploring the nearby Stirling Ranges, Porongurup and Torndirrup National Parks. There's plenty of markets, cafes, museums, pubs and accommodation options to suit most walkers as well as several outdoor stores. It's a 4½-hour drive (410km) from Perth and 1½ hours (120km) to Walpole.

For a rollicking evening or just a quiet tipple, the grand old **White Star Hotel** (whitestarhotel.com.au) serves up a wide selection of local and imported beers and wines, not to mention music. No visit to Albany is complete without a trip to the sobering yet excellent **National Anzac Centre** (nationalanzaccentre.com.au) sitting on the hill above the town.

## Walpole

This small farm-service town is surrounded by magnificent forests, national parks, walking tracks and pristine beaches. With the Bibbulmun long-distance walking track passing right through the town there's a range of accommodation and several food options including a supermarket. The **visitor centre** (walpole.com.au) stocks walking maps and can arrange trail transport.

Locals will tell you the best coffee in town is at **Four Sisters Cafe**, strangely inside the BP service station. It also does a mean toastie.

## Margaret River

Perth's favourite weekend gourmet getaway (280km, 3¼ hours) is surrounded by vineyards, cheese factories, breweries and some wicked surfing breaks. Expect plenty of fine dining, luxurious cottages and five-star prices. However, things are much more relaxed over on the nearby coast where fishing villages like Gracetown, Prevalley and Hamelin Bay all have affordable camping grounds.

With too much wine to choose from, why not try some craft beer instead. **Brewhouse** (brewhousemargaretriver.com.au), in karri forest at the entrance to town, has some of the craftiest. **Down South Camping** (downsouthcamping.com.au) has a reasonable selection of outdoor gear.

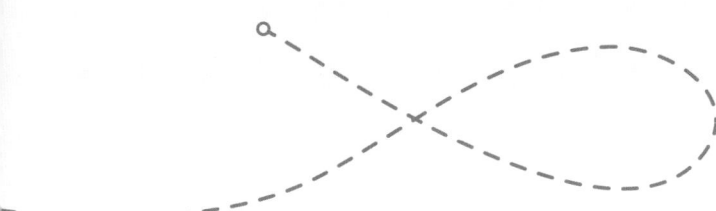

## Resources

**Cape to Cape Track** (capetocapetrack.com.au) Lists transport operators and 'walker-friendly' accommodation for the Margaret River coast.

**Parks & Wildlife** (parks.dpaw.wa.gov.au) Parks & Wildlife Service website.

**TransWA** (transwa.wa.gov.au) Southwest bus schedules and tickets.

**Bibbulmun Track** (bibbulmuntrack.org.au) Information on walks around Walpole.

**Porongurup Promotions** (porongurup.com) Tourism site for Porongurup.

**Margaret River Region** (margaretriver.com) Slick official booking engine.

**Rainbow Coast** (rainbowcoast.com.au) Eclectic, informative site covering Albany, Walpole and Denmark.

## When to Go

The lush southwest is walkable all year. Wildflowers are at their best in early spring, while winters can be cold and wet. Avoid the heat of late spring and summer days by starting early. Summer bushfires are an increasing reality.

## Where to Stay

The southwest is inundated with great accommodation options; this is the place to splash out on something cosy. **Nornalup Riverside Chalets** (nornalupriversidechalets.com.au) are nice and secluded but still within easy distance to Walpole. Albany has some good heritage options, none quirkier than **Albany Foreshore Guest House** (albanyforeshoreguesthouse.com.au). Gracetown and Hamelin Bay have wonderful laid-back camping grounds, and bush campers shouldn't miss a night in the **Big Brook Arboretum** near Pemberton. And for walkers who'd like a decent shower and comfy bed all within staggering distance of some seriously frothy stuff, the **Edge of the Forest** (edgeoftheforest.com.au), a mere 80m from Margaret River's Brewhouse, should do you just nicely.

## What's On

**Killer Whales** (Jan–Mar) Active in the waters of Bremer Bay, some 180km from Albany.

**Albany Folk 'n' Shanty Festival** (shantyfest.com; Easter) Folk music and sea shanties. Bring your own parrot.

**Taste Great Southern** (tastegreatsouthern.com.au; Mar/Apr) An 11-day Albany noshfest showcasing local produce.

**Margaret River Pro** (margaretriver.com; May–Jun) An international surfing competition that has plenty of spinoff gigs.

**Denmark Festival of Voice** (denmarkfestivalofvoice.com.au; May/Jun) A three-day festival featuring everything your vocal chords are capable of.

**Gourmet Escape** (gourmetescape.com.au; Nov) This Margaret River food frenzy peaks with tastings, workshops and celebrity chefs.

## Transport

Busselton and Albany both have domestic airports, car rental and local taxis. TransWA runs buses linking all hub towns to Perth and each other. Naturally Walpole (facebook.com/Naturallywalpole) can arrange trailhead transport around Walpole while a transport operator in Augusta can arrange Cape to Cape transfers. You will need your own vehicle to access most of the other trailheads.

125

# 31

# Bluff Knoll

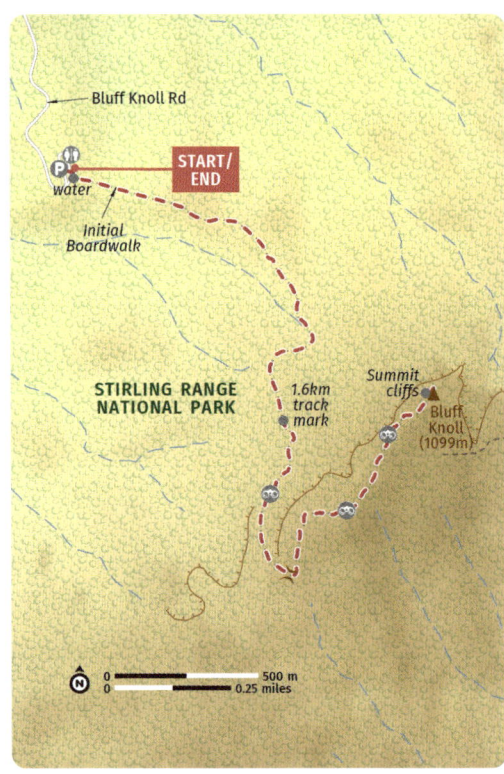

| DURATION | DIFFICULTY | DISTANCE | START/END |
|---|---|---|---|
| 2½-3½hrs | Moderate | 6.4km | Bluff Knoll car park |

| TERRAIN | | Well-formed track & steep steps |
|---|---|---|

Wilderness views and wildflowers compete for attention on this classic walk to the highest peak in the Stirling Ranges. A biodiversity hotspot, Bluff Knoll (1099m; pictured) is also one of the few places in WA to ever see snow. Bring a jacket.

From the car park a brief section of flat boardwalk leads straight towards the imposing bulk of Bluff Knoll, before the first of many broad steps are encountered. The trail winds up through a magnificent collection of endemic **wildflowers** – banksias, verticordias, eucalypts, and higher up, darwinias.

The path rapidly gains height as it climbs south and soon other Stirling peaks are revealed, including the sharp point of **Toolbrunup** to the west.

On reaching a low **alpine saddle** between imposing crags the path swings 180 degrees back to the north. It's not uncommon for **low cloud** to sit in this saddle as cool coastal air meets the warmer inland mass.

Keep an eye on the track markers as the now rocky trail traverses the exposed **montane plateau** where whiteouts can occur anytime. Even on a hot summer's day the wind chill on this plateau catches many people out.

The trail crosses several flat rock slabs providing **great views**, though the best are still to come.

Broad ledges just beyond the **summit** provide incredible views to the north and west, while also providing some shelter from the incessant wind – a perfect spot for a snack.

Retrace your route carefully back to the saddle and down to the car park.

# 32

# Nancy Peak & Devils Slide

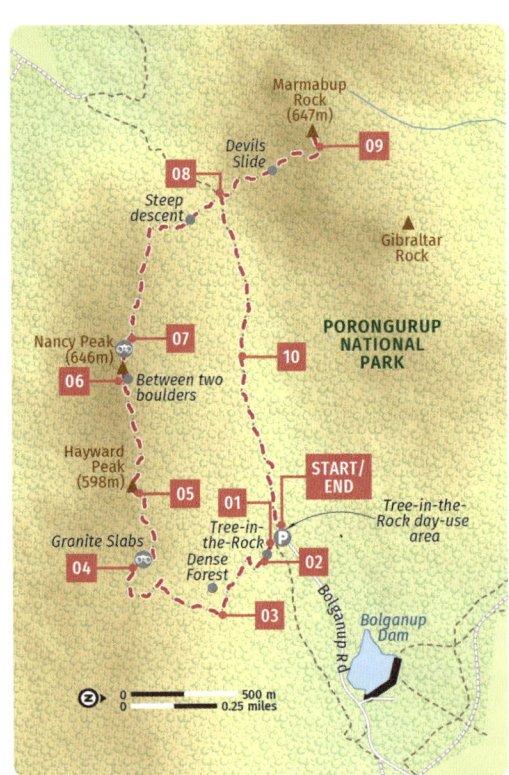

| DURATION | DIFFICULTY | DISTANCE | START/END |
|---|---|---|---|
| 3-4hrs return | Moderate | 7km | Tree-in-the-Rock day-use area |

| TERRAIN | Karri forest, granite slabs |
|---|---|

This is an absolute gem of a walk that is full of surprises. Starting in verdant karri forest you'll climb onto the huge granite blobs of Porongurup, ticking off peaks on a ridgeline traverse with amazing views, before dropping back to a saddle, climbing to the top of an even higher granite lump, then strolling leisurely back to the car park immensely satisfied. It makes an excellent afternoon's outing to complement an energetic morning spent in the nearby Stirling Ranges.

## Getting Here
Porongurup National Park is 50km from Albany and a similar distance from the Stirling Ranges. You'll need your own vehicle.

## Starting Point
From Porongurup drive 3km along Bolganup Rd to the Tree-in-the-Rock day-use area, where there's toilets and picnic tables.

**01** Enter **dense karri forest** immediately from the car park and keep a watch for striking **red-eared firetail finches**.

**02** Within 100m pass the aptly named **Tree-in-the-Rock**, a large karri tree seemingly growing out of a large granite boulder.

**03** Enjoy the **lush ferns** and **shady forest** as the trail gently climbs onto the flank of Haywards Peak (598m).

**04** Exit the trees onto the first of many granite slabs offering good views of the surrounding farm land and stark granite peaks of **Porongurup National Park**.

## Granite Skywalk

Most visitors to Porongurup will want to tick off this raised walkway that is described as either a 'feat of engineering' or an 'ugly steel caterpillar' that encircles the lofty granite tor of Castle Rock in the park's east. At only one hour (4km) return from the Castle Rock picnic area, it's an easier option if you're not up for the exertions of Nancy Peak.

The walk (pictured) gently ascends through jarrah forest to the first of two lookouts. From here the going gets a little more strenuous and some rock scrambling and ladder climbing is involved to reach the second summit. The views are fine, but nowhere near as good as from Nancy Peak and the Devils Slide.

**05** The track now alternates between slabs and thick scrub as it climbs over **Haywards Peak**.

**06** Follow the granite crest of the range to the high point of **Nancy Peak** (646m), with the track narrowing as it passes tightly between boulders.

**07** Just 50m past the summit, a particularly rounded boulder provides an **impressive view** northwest to the Devils Slide.

**08** Descend 600m to a saddle and four-way track junction back in the forest.

**09** Follow the marked path steeply straight up the other side to the top of the **Devils Slide** (647m), a huge sloping granite boulder with a superfluous 'trail end' marker on the top.

**10** Return to the four-way junction, turn left and enjoy an easy amble on a wide fire trail down through **karri forest** alive with birdsong to the car park.

 **Take a Break**

Notice those vineyards on the drive in? Need a nice vino and cheese plate, or perhaps just coffee and cake? While there's plenty of wineries nearby for a tasting, not many offer food. So head directly to the friendly, family-run **Ironwood Estate** (ironwoodestatewines.com.au), where the wines win awards, the food is elegantly simple and the view of the Porongurups just sublime.

# 33
# Bald Head

| DURATION | DIFFICULTY | DISTANCE | START/END |
|---|---|---|---|
| 4-6hrs return | Moderate | 12.5km | Bald Head car park |

| TERRAIN | Sandy coastal heath, granite slabs |
|---|---|

Get ready for a big day out on one of the most exciting yet relatively unknown day walks in the southwest. For some reason this magnificent walk along the sandy spine of a narrow isthmus to a bare rocky headland suspended above the rampant Southern Ocean is off everybody's radar, including Parks & Wildlife's.

## Getting Here
Torndirrup National Park is only 20km from Albany at the southern entrance to King George Sound. There is no public transport, though a taxi is possible.

## Starting Point
The walk starts at the car park just off Misery Beach Rd. From Frenchmans Bay Rd follow signs for Salmon Holes then turn left onto Murray Rd and right onto Misery Beach Rd. The turnoff is on the right.

**01** The route initially heads due east on a flat boardwalk for several hundred metres before climbing onto the big granite slab of **Isthmus Hill**, with good views of Salmon Holes to the south.

**02** For a marginally better view, follow an unmarked side track for five minutes.

**03** Traverse the main slab north and pick up the track again in the top left corner.

**04** The track curls around Isthmus Hill on its northern side, providing great views of **Misery Beach** and **King George Sound** before the whole **Flinders Peninsula** is revealed to the east, with Bald Head away in the distance at the very end.

## More Torndirrup

**Natural Bridge & The Gap** The Gap path ends on a viewing platform suspended over a nasty slash in the granite cliffs; still a work in progress for the Southern Ocean. Likewise, Natural Bridge has been undermined by waves for millennia. Both features are linked by high-accessibility walkways. Sunsets are dramatic and the rock climbing excellent.

**Blowholes** (1.6km/40 minutes return) Venture down in wild weather to see the waves funnelled up through gaps in the granite cliffs.

**Stony Hill & Peak Head** (4.3km/90 minutes return) An enjoyable walk to the peak on the comma-shaped headland at the bottom of the park. Stony Hill is near the car park.

SAM JEFRS/SHUTTERSTOCK ©

**Best for**

**AMAZING VIEWS**

**05** On the narrowest point of the isthmus it's possible to look down at **beaches on both sides**. An access track and stairs lead to the southern beach.

**06** The sandy trail continues heading east, winding around or climbing over knolls, cutting through coastal heath and **magnificent wildflowers** on the way to Limestone Head.

**07** After cresting the head and descending into a shallow saddle, you'll encounter a short cement section as the track climbs out the other side.

**08** Emerging onto slabs, follow the large **cairns**.

**09** Descend into a **sand blow**.

**10** Reach another set of cairned slabs. Follow the route carefully, along the spine of the ridge.

**11** A steep sandy descent leads to the last saddle before Bald Head.

**12** Climb steeply onto **Bald Head** (pictured).

**13** Reach the **terminal cairn**, where the sides slope away in three directions to the restless Southern Ocean. Retrace your route back to the car park.

 **Take a Break**

You'd be forgiven for thinking you'd stumbled into a Parisian backstreet on visiting **Gourmandise & Co** (gourmandiseandco.com.au), a French-style patisserie on Albany's stylish Stirling Tce. Excellent coffee, homemade quiches, pies and of course delicious pastries complement the artisanal ambience. Don't miss its plat du jour lunch specials

# 34

# Nuyts Wilderness

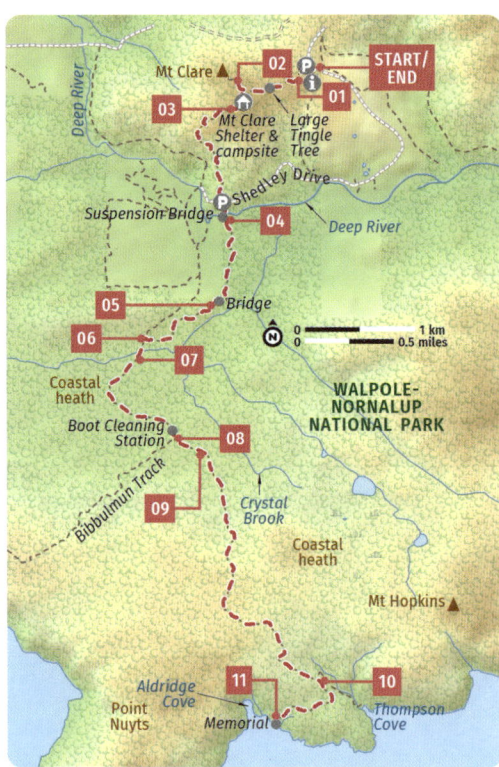

| DURATION | DIFFICULTY | DISTANCE | START/END |
|---|---|---|---|
| 5-6hrs return | Moderate | 19km | Mt Clare car park |

| TERRAIN | Karri forest, sandy coastal heath |
|---|---|

An interesting and seldom-walked route leads from lush tingle and karri forest across flowering coastal heath to lonely cliffs on the continent's southern edge. While not quite 'wilderness' – the old 4WD fishing track to Aldridge Cove, though unsigned, is quite obvious – there is still a sense of isolation and remoteness after turning off the busy Bibbulmun Track that provides access to Nuyts. Bring plenty of water and sunscreen.

## Getting Here

Walpole is 120km (90 minutes) from Albany and 416km (five hours) from Perth. TransWA buses connect Walpole to Perth, Albany and Margaret River.

## Starting Point

From the South Coast Hwy 7km west of Walpole, take Tinglewood Rd to Mt Clare car park. The walk leaves by an info panel incorrectly listing the return distance as 16.2km; it's actually 19km.

**01** Head west towards **Mt Clare** on the well-marked Bibbulmun ('Bib'). Within 100m join a vehicle track, then pass a massive buttressed **tingle tree**.

**02** Ignore the side track to Mt Clare unless you've a lust for granite slabs; the view from the scrubby peak is uninspiring.

**03** Fill out the intentions book at **Mt Clare Shelter**, a designated Bib camp site with picnic tables, water and nearby toilet.

**04** Head steeply downhill through tingle and karri forest for 1.3km, cross unsealed Shedley Dr and within 100m you'll reach

## Dutch Connection

Pieter Nuyts, of the Dutch East India company, helped chart the southern Australian coastline with Captain François Thijssen aboard the *Gulden Zeepaert* (Golden Seahorse) in 1627, the first recorded European visitors. Blown off course on their way to Batavia (Jakarta), they mapped most of the Great Australian Bight and Nuyts' name graces landmarks across the southern coast. After the voyage, the increasingly arrogant and downright dodgy Nuyts dabbled in politics in North Asia, but made a terrible diplomat and controversy dogged him everywhere. Eventually sacked by the Dutch and imprisoned by the Japanese, he somehow made it home to Holland, becoming a mayor.

a **suspension bridge** over the Styx-like **Deep River**.

**05** The shrinking forest becomes sandier underfoot as **kangaroo paws plants** (pictured) appear and within 1km you'll see another **smaller creek**.

**06** Scrub takes over and another 1km brings a wide track junction. Turn left onto sandy 4WD ruts.

**07** **Xanthorrhoea grass trees**, with their distinctive black, spear-like flower spike, line the flat track as it crosses coastal heath.

**08** Around 1.5km from the track junction is a **boot-cleaning station**, which is a good rest stop.

**09** Ignore the Bib turnoff and continue straight ahead, following the wheel ruts towards the coast. **Wildflowers** bloom along the track, including dryandra, kangaroo paws, banksias and chorizema. Boulder-capped Mt Hopkins appears off to the left.

**10** Around 3.2km from the Bib, a side track points to **Thompson Cove**. Keep on the main track as it swings right for 800m to **Aldridge Cove**.

**11** The track ends above rock slabs with **excellent views** of the cove, the crashing waves and a **memorial** to a missing walker.

### Take a Break

The Sri Lankan chefs at **Nornabar** (nornabar.com) in tiny Nornalup cook up Asian-inspired taste sensations using fresh produce and showcasing local vino, making this place worth the 10km drive from Walpole. Add some jazz and a comfy beer garden and you won't be walking anywhere.

# 35

# Hamelin Bay to Elephant Rock

**Best for**

☑

**WILDLIFE**

| DURATION | DIFFICULTY | DISTANCE | START/END |
|---|---|---|---|
| 5-6hrs return | Moderate | 16km | Hamelin Bay Beach car park |

| TERRAIN | Beach, coastal heath, blowholes |
|---|---|

Spend a wonderful day exploring the incredibly scenic and many-featured Margaret River coastline. This long, rewarding walk follows a lovely section of the multiday Cape to Cape Track as it traverses pristine beaches, sandy headlands, fragile heath and enigmatic limestone blowholes to arrive at a flat rock surrounded by the Indian Ocean. Islands, shipwrecks, wildflowers and plentiful birdlife, not to mention the odd reptile, dot the route. Bring plenty of sunscreen, food and water for the day.

## Getting Here
Hamelin Bay is 36km south of Margaret River, or 39km by the more interesting Caves Rd. The closest TransWA bus stop is Karridale, 8.5km away. South West Driving Services in Augusta (19km) and Margaret River Passenger Transport can arrange drop-offs/pickups.

## Starting Point
Start from Hamelin Bay Beach car park (not the boat ramp but the car park to the east), where there's toilets and water. You can halve this walk by arranging a pickup at Cosy Corner car park.

**01** Follow the sandy access track from the car park directly to the **beach** (pictured) and turn left, walking along the sand towards **Hamelin Island**. Both bay and island bear the name of Jacques Félix Emmanuel Hamelin, the French captain of the *Naturaliste*, who along with Nicolas Baudin aboard the *Géographe*, explored and mapped the Australian coastline in 1801.

**02** Head along the beach for 300m then turn left up the **boat ramp**. The waters along the entire Leeuwin-Naturaliste National Park coastline fall under the protection of **Ngari Capes Marine Park**. 'Ngari' is a Noongar word meaning 'salmon' and Noongar *boodja* (Country) occupies the whole southwest corner of WA, from Jurien Bay to Esperance. The Noongar comprise 14 different language groups united by one common lore, distinct from any other Aboriginal and Torres Strait Islander peoples. This walk lies on Wardandi *boodja*.

**03** Look for stairs nearby on the right for the **Cape to Cape Track** (CtC). These lead to a small benched **lookout** with a view over several rotting piles, all that remain of the original 1882 jetty built to service the rapacious local timber industry.

**04** Continue to more lookouts on the nearby limestone **White Cliff Point**, where there are good views of both Hamelin and Foul Bays, and offshore to Hamelin Island. A panel explains how Hamelin Bay made a poor choice of harbour, lying exposed to the prevailing northwesterly winds, which accounted for 11 shipwrecks in the bay's not-so-calm, reef-laden waters.

**05** Take a short steep sand track down the side of the cliff, next to a fence, to land on the beach of **Foul Bay**. It may well be foul if the wind is blowing so head for the rocks in the distance.

**06** Just before the rocks, the track climbs steeply up the dunes to a 4WD track.

**07** Walk along the 4WD track 600m as it heads inland away from the beach to a signposted junction for the CtC on the right.

**08** The CtC Track initially heads southwest through **lush, thick forest**. Beware of snakes in this damper section during the warmer months.

## Cape to Cape Track

This 124km walk links the lighthouses of **Cape Leeuwin** and **Cape Naturaliste** on the Indian Ocean coast, predominantly within **Leeuwin-Naturaliste National Park**. Utilising old 4WD access tracks, the walk crosses coastal heath, deserted beaches, windswept headlands and the odd rocky clifftop as well as passing through several fishing hamlets where commercial camping grounds complement the few national park camp sites. The well-marked route is not particularly onerous, though some sections are long and mostly unshaded. Water stops and wind direction (seasonally changing) are other factors to plan for carefully. Most people take between five and seven days. See capetocapetrack.com.au.

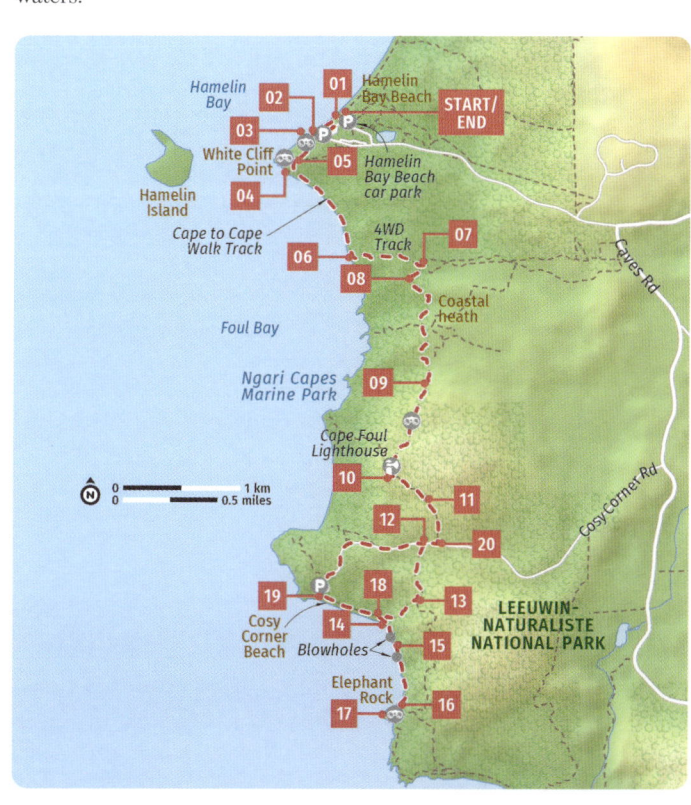

**09** Follow the CtC Track as it meanders south, climbing onto a dry plateau of stunted coastal heath offering **excellent views** to the northeast and giving some idea of the power and direction of the wind.

**10** Dinky **Foul Bay Lighthouse** is reached next, on top of a low hill. The strong winds, currents and rocky islets along this coastline were particularly dangerous to shipping. The original Hamelin Island lighthouse was decommissioned in 1967 and replaced by this automatic one, which is still in use.

**11** Keep heading south on the now wide track as it winds around the hill, past **Xanthorrhoea grass trees**, to drop down onto Cosy Corner Rd.

**12** Turn right and follow the road briefly before picking up the track again on the left.

**13** Watch out for a track junction on the right, which will bring you down steeply to the eastern end of Cosy Corner Beach.

**14** From the **beach** you should be able to see Elephant Rock, the flat, bare lump at the end of the point to your left (south). It might look close but it's still at least 1km away and you first need to traverse the miniature limestone blowholes – the grey area of rocks between you and the point.

STEVE WATERS ©

**15** The track winds in and out of the hollow **blowholes**. Take care, as many are bottomless and exit directly onto the crashing waves below.

**16** Just before the point, the track turns inland and climbs a dune to a **viewpoint** over Elephant Rock.

**17** **Elephant Rock** (pictured) is accessible at low tide in calm weather from its southern tip. Be aware that **rogue waves** can occur at any time. Do not linger here; if you're looking for a lunch spot then either the small beach just south of Elephant Rock, or Cosy Corner Beach, are safer choices.

## Limestone Caves

The blowholes at Cosy Corner are just one example of the limestone foundations underlying much of Leeuwin-Naturaliste National Park. Over 100 caves can be found in the region including the following:

**Calgardup** A self-explore cave 300m long, accessible by boardwalk. Helmets and torches are provided at the entrance.

**Mammoth** A large and spectacular cave; thylacine fossils have been found here.

**Lake** The only cave in the region with a permanent lake, it's also one of the deepest.

**Giant** The longest, deepest and most adventurous self-guided cave. Expect ladders, scrambles and squeezes.

**Jewel** Close to Augusta, this remarkable, large, four-chambered guided cave is known for its straw stalactites.

**Moondyne** Small guided groups are led by torchlight in this cave, which has been restored to 'pre-tourist' condition. Helmets, overalls and gloves supplied.

**18** Return past the blowholes and walk down the length of **Cosy Corner Beach** to the obvious path at its western (ie furthest) end.

**19** Climb up steeply to the car park. If you've arranged a pickup then end the walk here, otherwise return along Cosy Corner Rd until you reach the CtC Track leading to Foul Bay Lighthouse.

**20** Retrace your outward route back to Hamelin Bay, where you can skip the beach plod by taking the footpath on the far side of the boat ramp through the first car park to the beach car park.

# Also Try...

## Toolbrunup

| DURATION | DIFFICULTY | DISTANCE |
| --- | --- | --- |
| 3-4hrs return | Hard | 4km |

This Stirling Ranges peak (pictured) is rated by many bushwalkers as a more interesting and challenging undertaking than popular Bluff Knoll.

Climb steeply from Toolbrunup car park, 4km off Chester Pass Rd, up through forest to an opening across a boulder field. The path then alternates between forest and boulder fields before giving up on the forest altogether. Look for markers as the route heads straight up a boulder-strewn slope. At the top of the boulders the route enters thick scrub before yet more boulder action, more scrub and finally a rock scramble onto the summit pyramid. From the small saddle choose either summit – the western one is flatter, and better for a picnic; the eastern marginally higher. Both offer superb 360-degree views.

## Giant Tingle – Frankland Camp

| DURATION | DIFFICULTY | DISTANCE |
| --- | --- | --- |
| 4-5hrs return | Moderate | 18km |

A pleasant loop in giant tingle and karri forest leads to a secluded riverside lunch spot.

Start at the Giant Tingle Tree car park in the tall forests above Walpole. After looping around the Giant Tingle, head east on the Bibbulmun Track through magnificent forest, cresting a low hill to a track junction. Turn right following the wide management track gradually downhill, where you can glimpse the Frankland River through the trees. Leave the fire trail by a narrow marked side track on a corner just before a creek crossing. Cross another dirt road and within 1km arrive at Frankland River Shelter, an excellent place for lunch and possibly a swim. Follow the Bib along the river until Sappers Bridge, then keep following the river, now on a fire trail that joins your outwards route. You can avoid the long hill trek by keeping straight and meeting the road back to the car park.

ANDREW ATKINSON/SHUTTERSTOCK ©

## Coast Walk

| DURATION | DIFF | DISTANCE |
|---|---|---|
| 8hrs one-way | Hard | 17km |

Deep blue ocean, brilliant white beaches, huge granite outcrops and seaside kangaroos make for a spectacular walk in Cape Le Grande National Park (pictured).

Begin at Rossiter Bay, 50km east of Esperance. The walk follows pristine coastline as it curves around beaches and hidden coves to Le Grand Beach. On the way you'll have incredible views of the the granite islands of the Archipelago of the Recherche. The walk can be broken into smaller stages, with camping grounds at Lucky Bay and Le Grand Beach.

## Numbat Trail

| DURATION | DIFF | DISTANCE |
|---|---|---|
| 4-5hrs return | Moderate | 12km |

Naturalists won't want to miss the incredible fauna and flora on this surprisingly challenging day walk close to Perth.

AWC's Paruna Sanctuary in Perth's Avon Hills is the scene for an interesting day's wandering among wandoo and jarrah forest, granite outcrops, wildflowers, orchids and native birds. There's plenty of picnic spots, lookouts and benches to enjoy the views, creeks, waterfalls and even a gorge. If the going proves tough, a shorter circuit is available. Arrange with AWC (australianwildlife.org) in advance.

## Gracetown Coast

| DURATION | DIFF | DISTANCE |
|---|---|---|
| 5hrs return | Moderate | 15km |

Enjoy stunning views along the wild coastline near Margaret River on this section of the Cape to Cape Track.

Begin at Gracetown, a small fishing village 20km from Margaret River. Head north from the boat ramp following the Cape to Cape markers as the track scales rocky headlands and traverses wildflower-laden heath and random sandy beaches before arriving at the remarkable cliffs of Wilyabrup, a rock-climbers' paradise. Bring plenty of water and sunscreen. Return the same way.

Finders Ranges (p144)

# Flinders to Fleurieu

**36  Mt Remarkable Summit**
Make a dramatic ascent in the southern Flinders Ranges. **p144**

**37  The Riesling Trail**
Take a wine-region wander along a reinvented railway route. **p146**

**38  Morialta Gorge Three Falls**
Tackle this gorgeous gorge hike, hidden in the Adelaide foothills. **p148**

**39  Mylor to Mt Lofty**
Follow the Heysen Trail through the super-scenic Adelaide Hills. **p150**

**40  Belair National Park Waterfall**
Detour from Adelaide's suburbs into South Australia's oldest national park. **p154**

**41  Marion Coastal Trail**
Take in sweeping clifftop views, fascinating geology and pods of passing dolphins. **p156**

**42  Blowhole Beach to Cape Jervis**
Walk the Heysen Trail's last (or first) hurrah – a spectacular coastal trek. **p158**

# Explore
# Flinders to Fleurieu

Many of South Australia's best day walks cling to the state's southern coastlines – there's a whole lot of hot desert further north! But the hilly spine running between the rugged desert-edge Flinders Ranges, the Clare Valley, the Adelaide Hills and the fertile Fleurieu Peninsula also delivers some dazzling day walks, easily accessible from big-smoke Adelaide.

## Adelaide

Facing west onto the shimmering Gulf St Vincent (superior sunsets!), Australia's fifth-largest city (population 1.34 million) is also its most underrated. A leafy metropolis below the crescent-shaped Adelaide Hills, 'ADL' has ditched its 'City of Churches' tag and now embraces life's finer things: fine festivals, fine food, fine music and (OK, forget the other three) fine wine. Home to SA's main airport, Adelaide makes a logical base, fanning out north to the Flinders Ranges, south to the Fleurieu Peninsula and into the wine regions in between.

## McLaren Vale

A tick under an hour's drive south of Adelaide, the vine village of McLaren Vale (population 4040) and its encircling wine region offer myriad accommodation options and plenty of places for a pre- or post-hike feed. Access to the fab coastal trails around the southern Fleurieu Peninsula is straightforward. See mclarenvale.info for more information.

## Clare

Functional Clare (population 4050) is the hub of the Clare Valley viticultural scene, with plenty of decent places to stay and eat, plus easy access to the Barossa Valley (an hour south) and southern Flinders Ranges (an hour north). It's not the most scenic of towns, strung along an endless main street, but the coffee is hot and the beer is cold. Check out clarevalley.com.au for local info. If you're planning some walks in the northern Flinders Ranges, consider basing yourself further north in Quorn or Wilpena Pound.

##  When to Go

South Australia is the hottest and driest state on the planet's hottest and driest landmass. Obviously, if you're walking here during summer (December to February), aim for a day that's not forecast to be 42°C with a howling northerly wind! Conversely, winter (June to August) is a lovely time to explore the hills and coastline from the Flinders to the Fleurieu, with mild days and plenty of sunshine (and no snakes!). The grapevine colours in autumn (March to May) are atmospheric around the McLaren Vale, Adelaide Hills, Barossa Valley and Clare Valley wine regions, which

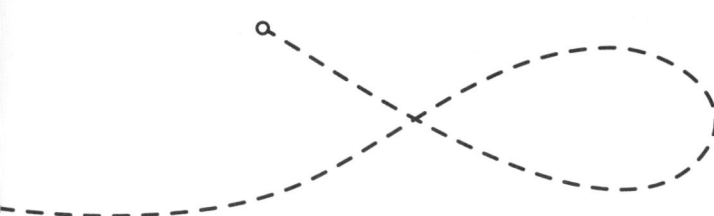

feature some terrific hiking trails. Further north, Flinders Ranges' wildflowers are spectacular in spring (September to November).

## Where to Stay

From the southern tip of the Fleurieu Peninsula to the northern Flinders Ranges, you'll find all kinds of accommodation, from budget hostels and caravan parks to highway-side motels, historic B&B cottages and luxe big-city hotels. Check the contents of your wallet then book something near your bushwalk: see southaustralia.com/plan-your-trip/places-to-stay for comprehensive listings.

## What's On

Until quite recently, South Australian vehicle licence plates proudly proclaimed 'SA - The Festival State'. Adelaideans, in particular, love a good party: during 'Mad March', the high-brow, the weird and the petrol-powered collide in a crazy confluence of festivals that lasts the whole month (book your beds way in advance):

**Adelaide Fringe** (adelaidefringe.com.au)

**Adelaide 500** (adelaide500.com.au)

Seasonal SA wine festivals also see accommodation book up quickly. You might want to sidestep (or fully embrace) the following as you're travelling around:

**Crush** (crushfestival.com.au; Jan) In the Adelaide Hills.

**Clare Valley Gourmet Weekend** (clarevalley.com.au/whats-on; May)

**Sea & Vines Festival** (seaandvines.com.au; Jun) In McLaren Vale.

**Winter Reds** (winterreds.com.au; Jul) In the Adelaide Hills.

**Barossa Gourmet Weekend** (barossagourmet.com; Sep)

 **Transport**

Many walks around the fringes of Adelaide and the Adelaide Hills are accessible via public transport (buses and trains; see adelaidemetro.com.au), but services can be scandalously infrequent, particularly on weekends. Having your own vehicle will afford you much more flexibility plus allow you to access remote trailheads, and you can crank up the loud motivational tunes! Bike hire is readily available, but hey, you're here to walk, not ride, right?

### Resources

**National Parks & Wildlife Service South Australia** (parks.sa.gov.au) Click on 'Know before you go' then 'Bushwalking' for links and walk classification info. Also the place for online parks pass bookings (required for vehicles).

**Walking SA** (walkingsa.org.au) A fabulous resource with comprehensive walk descriptions, maps and regional search capability.

**Trails SA** (southaustraliantrails.com) State-wide walk listings and maps, plus local eating, accommodation and transport suggestions.

**Heysen Trail** (heysentrail.asn.au) Detailed info and maps on the amazing 1200km Heysen Trail, rambling north–south between the Flinders Ranges and the Fleurieu Peninsula.

**Bureau of Meteorology** (bom.gov.au/sa) Forecasts, live updates and a rain radar.

# 36

# Mt Remarkable Summit

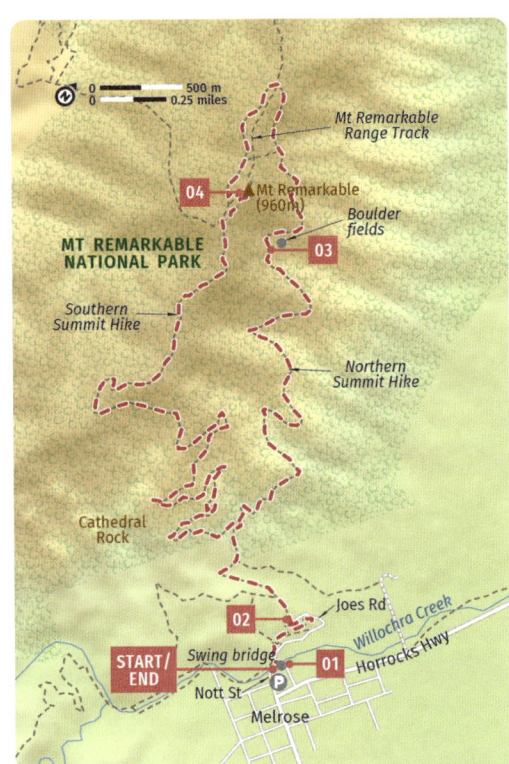

| DURATION | DIFFICULTY | DISTANCE | START/END |
|---|---|---|---|
| 4hrs return | Moderate | 14km | End of Joes Rd, Melrose |

| TERRAIN | Narrow dirt tracks & rocky scree slopes |
|---|---|

The remarkable Mt Remarkable rises 960m above the rural plains of the southern Flinders Ranges...or is it 995m, as per the plaque on the summit? Gauge for yourself as you tackle the spectacular ascent up the flanks of this lonesome peak. Along the way you'll traverse river-like slopes of fractured boulders, pass the site of a tragic accident and soak up breathtaking views across the picturesque little town of Melrose below.

## Getting Here

Melrose is a 275km, 3¼-hour drive north of Adelaide via Port Wakefield Hwy (A1) then Crystal Brook and Laura.

## Starting Point

Park near the historic Willochra Creek swing bridge on Joes Rd in Melrose. Public toilets are on nearby Nott St.

 Founded in 1853, super-charming **Melrose** is the oldest town in the Flinders Ranges. It's tempting to hit the cafe or one of the town's two pubs along with the local mountain bikers (Melrose is a MTB centre these days) – but hey, you've got a mountain to climb! Cross the winter-flowing Willochra Creek via the **old swing bridge** (parts of which have been here since the 1890s) and head for the stark white **WWI monument** on the hillside above. You can follow Joes Rd, but the scrabbly dirt 'Kiss The Sky' bike track is a more direct route.

**02** The **summit trail** (pictured) begins at the gate behind the obelisk, dedicated to nine local men who died during the Great War (a

## Melrose Nature Hike

If you're not quite up for a barnstorming attempt at the summit, take a more leisurely wander around Mt Remarkable's foothills on the Melrose Nature Hike. It's an undulating 2.6km, 1½-hour bush circuit, following the same route as the summit hike as far as the WWI memorial, before branching off on its own trajectory. **Cathedral Rock viewpoint** is a good spot for a snack break, before you circle back to Melrose with an optional detour to see an old copper mine that was worked until the early 1900s. You'll be sharing the track with mountain bikers for some of the way. See walkingsa.org.au for trail notes and maps.

**Best for**

A POST-WALK DRINK

more tactful name could probably have been chosen for the 'Dodging Bullets' sculpture nearby…). Signed as the 'Northern Summit Hike', the steep-sided orange-dirt track (watch your step) crosses dry creek beds as it rises. Pass the Southern Summit Hike junction (you'll return via this route later on) and zigzag ever-upwards, views opening up of silos and wheat fields bisected by gun-barrel-straight country roads. Fast lizards dart for cover as you pass by.

**03** A series of impressively barren **boulder fields** feature as you climb, broken rocks cascading down the mountain in super-slow motion. The largest of these scree slopes, about 4.5km into the walk, was the site of a tragic plane crash in July 1980. A light plane flying from Leigh Creek to Adelaide crashed into the mountainside in bad weather, killing all three people on board. Amazingly, the crumpled fuselage is still there, a bleak white husk clinging to the rocky terrain.

**04** After crossing a fire trail, **Mt Remarkable summit** is actually a bit underwhelming: there's a rusty trig point, a few picnic benches and a plaque with its contentious statement of altitude…but trees blocking all the views! Backtrack 50m to the start of the Southern Summit Hike and head downhill: **sensational views over Melrose** appear with pleasing frequency as you follow the waymarkers for 7.5km back into town.

 **Take a Break**

As welcome as summer rain, the appealing 1854 **North Star Hotel** (northstarhotel.com.au) in Melrose is a real beauty. It's a noble stone pub renovated in city-meets-woolshed style. Stay the night, sit under spinning ceiling fans in the bistro, or sip a cold post-hike beer.

145

# 37

# The Riesling Trail

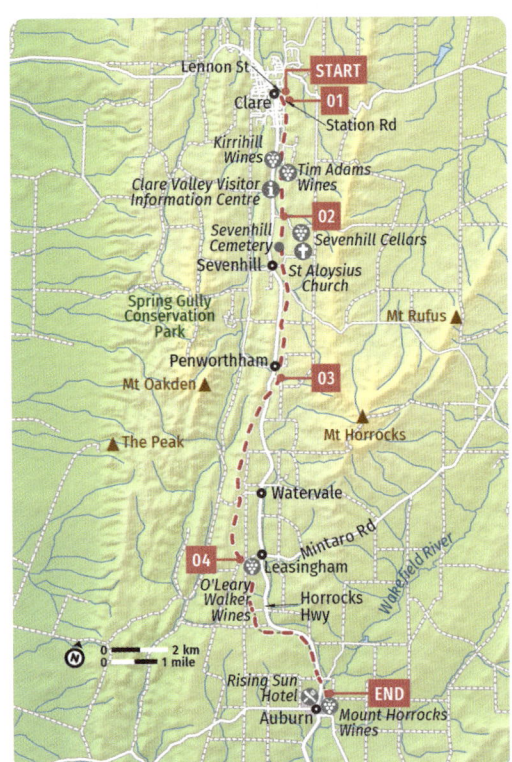

| DURATION | DIFFICULTY | DISTANCE | START/END |
|---|---|---|---|
| 5-6hrs one-way | Moderate | 25km | Lennon St, Clare/Curling St, Auburn |

| TERRAIN | Well-maintained undulating gravel track |
|---|---|

The beautiful Riesling Trail (pictured) is a lengthy but easygoing walk through the Clare Valley, following the route of a former railway, an unprofitable line that closed in 1983. One of SA's essential wine regions, this slender valley is known for its sweet-scented rieslings and mineral-rich reds. Feel like sampling some? There are more than enough cellar-door diversions along the trail to delay your progress. Complementing the vines are golden wheat fields, endearing country towns and big open skies.

## Getting Here

Drive two hours (145km) north of Adelaide to Clare, following Main North Rd then the Horrocks Hwy.

## Starting Point

The trail access point on Lennon St in Clare is a handy place to start, with plenty of car parking.

**01** The sturdy timber Clare train station is long gone, but rusty hints of its presence remain on the corner of Lennon St and Station Rd. The Riesling Trail officially begins 8km north of here at Barina, but this extra distance might make your trek to Auburn too much legwork for one day. From the car park here, the firm grey-gravel trail steadily rises, leaving Clare behind, passing **copses of elms** and crossing a few country roads. **Mr. Mick Cellar Door and Kitchen** is the first winery you pass, which is in Clare's suburbs. **Tim Adams** (timadams wines.com.au) is right on the trail.

## The Rattler Trail

Can't get enough of those rolling hills and wide mid-northern skies? Extend your Clare Valley experience with a jaunt along the 19km **Rattler Trail**, heading south from Auburn to Riverton along the same former rail corridor as the Riesling Trail. It's a newer trail than its winery-dotted brother to the north (opened in 2010), and shorter and less hilly, making it an easier outing for both hikers and bikers. There aren't many winery cellar doors along the Rattler – it's more of an agricultural landscape – but it's super-scenic nonetheless. A cold ale at the endearing old Riverton Hotel awaits...

**Best for**

**A POST-WALK DRINK**

**02** The 1917 **Quarry Rd Bridge** is a curious relic of the old rail line: rebuilt in 1995, it's a broad steel arch spanning between hefty concrete buttresses. The trail rolls across it, continuing below eucalypt boughs to the outskirts of **Sevenhill**, a town founded by Jesuits in 1851. **Sevenhill Cellars** (sevenhill.com.au), the valley's oldest winery, is here, alongside **St Aloysius Church** (1866) and **Sevenhill Cemetery**, just off the trail. The Riesling Trail's apex is a few kilometres further on – the peak of your slow 90m ascent over 10km from Clare. It's a steady 178m descent from here into Auburn, 15km away.

**03** Just south of **Pentwortham**, the trail passes beneath the Horrocks Hwy. In 1839 the highway's namesake explorer John Horrocks camped by a red-gum tree here, now a **400-year-old specimen** still growing alongside the trail. About 9km shy of Auburn, the most scenic section of the trail unfolds, offering **glorious views extending to distant hills** across a patchwork of grapevine and baked-wheat colours.

**04** Beyond the concrete remnants of a railway crossing at Leasingham, **O'Leary Walker Wines** (olearywalkerwines.com) is next to the trail. The route then follows the highway through shady stands of whispering pines, crossing the Wakefield River into pretty **Auburn**. The old Auburn train station now hosts **Mount Horrocks Wines** (mounthorrocks.com): toast your big day out with a tasting and a bottle to go.

### Take a Break

After a long day on the trail, dust off your boots and stroll into the **Rising Sun Hotel** in Auburn – one of country SA's best-known pubs. It's a classic 1850 boozer serving inventive, seasonal pub grub with plenty of local wines. There's accommodation out the back, too, but mostly, it's a top spot for a beer.

# 38

# Morialta Gorge Three Falls

| DURATION | DIFFICULTY | DISTANCE | START/END |
|---|---|---|---|
| 3hrs return | Moderate | 7.5km | Morialta Conservation Park car park |

| TERRAIN | Clifftop tracks, bush paths; steep sections |
|---|---|

In Adelaide's northeastern suburbs, rugged Morialta Gorge is a hidden gem. This grand circuit takes you past waterfalls, clifftop lookouts and tracts of native scrub. Immersed in the bush, it's hard to believe there's a city of 1.34 million Adelaideans just over the ridge.

From the main car park (hot tip: arrive early to get a space), head up the **steep stone steps** signed towards 'Kookaburra Lookout'. Winding up through **stands of olives and casuarinas**, this could be the Sierra Nevadas or Crete…but the bush scents are undeniably Australian. **Views back towards Adelaide** open up, but watch your step – the trail is rocky and steep-sided.

From **Kookaburra Lookout** there's a brilliant view down into the gorge, with the colourful specks of other hikers far below.

Following the 'Three Falls Grand Hike' signs, the trail continues its steady climb, passing a detour to **Morialta Falls** (pictured) and crossing Fourth Creek where **Second Falls** tumbles into the gorge. Continuing upstream, two sturdy boardwalks skirt below cliffs where abseilers defy gravity. Beyond a steep concreted section is **Third Falls**, with its deep pool and viewing platform – snack time?

Heading home, the trail skirts the northern fringe of Morialta Gorge, the ochre-coloured walkway descending to a stand of white gums then rising to **Deep View Lookout** (vertigo sufferers beware – yes, the gorge is deep!). From here, parrots and poached egg daisies keep you company on the zigzag descent to the car park.

**Best for**

**WILDLIFE**

# 39
# Mylor to Mt Lofty

| DURATION | DIFFICULTY | DISTANCE | START/END |
|---|---|---|---|
| 4-5hrs one-way | Moderate | 18km | Mylor Oval/ Mt Lofty Summit |

| TERRAIN | Dirt tracks & roadside walking; some steep sections |
|---|---|

In traditional Peramangk Country, this lengthy amble is a snapshot of the good life in the Adelaide Hills. It's a diverse day out along part of SA's epic 1200km Heysen Trail, from wheat-coloured fields through stringybark forests; past cafes, cool-climate wineries, an old stone mill and a creekside pub and along picturesque rural roads with a steep uphill surge to Mt Lofty Summit. Show-stopping views over the Adelaide Plains are your ultimate reward.

## Getting Here
You can access Mylor on public buses, but driving is a more flexible option (you'll just need to organise a ride back to your car from Mt Lofty). Note many sections of the trail are closed during fire-danger season.

## Starting Point
Kick things off on Mylor's leafy main street (Strathalbyn Rd). You can park your car for free alongside Mylor Oval, across from Harvest Mylor Cafe.

**01** **Mylor**, settled in 1891, sure is a pretty little village, with a charming cafe, overhanging boughs an old-school primary school and stone cottages. From the immaculately mowed town oval, head north along Strathalbyn Rd and cross the **honeysuckle-hung bridge over Leslie Creek**. Beyond Aldgate Creek, just a few metres further along, turn right onto Whitehead Rd and head uphill: ignore the signs to the rather unexpected Wat Sri Rattana Wanaram Thai Buddhist monastery and follow the little red Heysen Trail route markers instead. There's a definite whiff of agriculture in the air as you pass the horsey fields here, before you reach the 45-hectare **Mylor Conservation Park** at the end of the road. Follow the well-trodden dirt track into this remnant pocket of tall stringy-bark forest, sharing the path with watchful magpies and kookaburras, sidestepping bull ants and the odd horse poo as you go.

**02** After 1km of 'forest bathing' (soaking up the verdant forest vibes, aka *shinrin-yoku*...it's big in Japan), exit the park onto dusty Hooper Rd, turn left and truck downhill to meet Strathalbyn Rd again. Cross over and turn right onto the skinny pathway, just a few metres from the road but happily concealed within dense scrub. Lined with **native flowers**, the trail traces the road for 2km, skirting past **Nation Ridge Road Bushland Reserve** before crossing Strathalbyn Rd again and heading downhill along Aldgate Tce. At the end of the road, the trail dips down into an overgrown valley where a tributary of Cox Creek slowly trickles by. Eastern brown snakes are common in the Adelaide Hills, but some heavy stomping, whistling and hand-clapping should clear your path of any resident reptiles. Emerging from the valley, turn left onto Ayr St then right onto Beadnell Cres – both suburban streets – continuing for a few hundred metres before a steep pathway ducks down towards the lush expanses of Bridgewater Oval.

**03** **Bridgewater** these days is quiet suburban Adelaide Hills enclave, but back in 1857 it was a thriving hub, centred around its impressive stone flour mill and adjacent pub, both of which front onto the **duck-filled Cox Creek**. The creek, named after early explorer Robert Cock, has yielded its fair share of gold over the years – prospectors still sieve through the mud here after a good downpour. From **Bridgewater Oval** (any cricket happening today?), follow the creek along the concrete path below Mt Barker Rd and across the bridge into the **kids'**

## Waterfall Gully Hike

If you've got anything left in the tank after 18km and the thigh-busting final Mt Lofty ascent, extend your walk with the 3km downhill run to **Waterfall Gully** (pictured). This is every Adelaidean's favourite hill climb: you'll pass plenty of sweaty joggers and cardio crusaders making the steep uphill hike. The feathery 30m waterfall at the bottom – aka 'First Falls', one of seven along the route – is particularly camera-worthy after rains in the hills (an event that happens more often up here than down in the city). Other highlights include remote stone cottages (one a YHA, one a ruin), twittering wrens and snoozy koalas. There's a cafe at the bottom for a self-congratulatory ice cream.

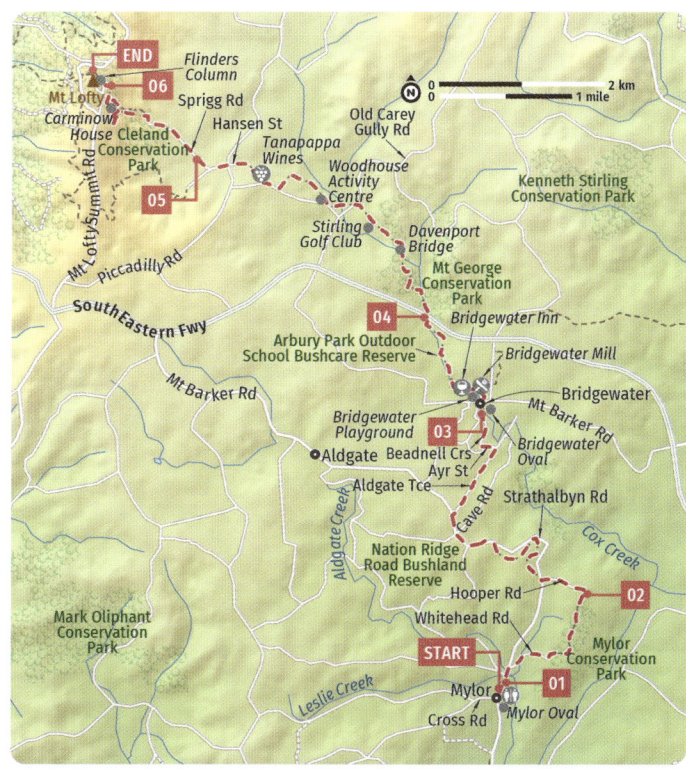

playground. **Bridgewater Mill** is beyond the stepping stones crossing the creek: have a stickybeak at the slick restaurant inside, or refuel at the attendant cafe. You're about two-fifths of the way to Mt Lofty Summit here...and you're going to need your strength! On a warm day, the siren's call of the **Bridgewater Inn's shady beer garden** is a loud one: suck on your water bottle instead and veer right up the stone steps just beyond the mill. The trail follows the creek for a while, ducks through a graffiti-spangled tunnel below the Adelaide–Melbourne rail line, then enters **Arbury Park Outdoor School Bushcare Reserve**. Creek remediations here have seen the return of the threatened **rakali** – a native rat, one of Australia's two freshwater amphibious mammals (the other one being the much more famous platypus).

**04** After you've been immersed in bushland for a few hours, the traffic on the South Eastern Fwy comes as a rude shock. Duck through the 50m concrete tunnel underneath (admiring the further efforts of the local spray-can crew) and enter the 85-hectare **Mt George Conservation Park**. Beyond a large dam on the right, towering stands of stringybark shroud the trail as you rise then drop back down to cross Cox Creek once again at the **timber Davenport Bridge**. You might want to generate some more anti-snake commotion through this section of the trail: on a hot summer's day, this cool creek bed is irresistible to the local wildlife. Look for **superb blue wrens** and the crimson flash of **red-browed finches** zipping through the undergrowth, and **Pacific black ducks** and **grey teals** paddling in the creek. The golfers at the estimable **Stirling Golf Club** are a different kind of native wildlife: beware their wayward tee shots as you navigate your way across the fairways, cross Old Carey Gully Rd and leapfrog the stile into the grassy fields beyond.

**05** The **super-scenic Piccadilly Valley** (pictured) spreads its orchards and vineyards across the hillsides between Summertown and Stirling. The trail enters the valley via the **Woodhouse Activity Centre**, a sprawling complex of playing fields, high-ropes courses and downhill tube-slide runs. Follow the Heysen Trail markers past the weary-looking corporate bonding groups, up a steep roadway then right alongside Spring Gully Rd to another stile. On the far side, follow the trail downhill (somewhat disconcertingly...aren't we supposed to be climbing a summit!?) past the vine rows of **Tanapappa Wines**. The Adelaide Hills are a long-established cool-climate wine region, with abundant rainfall and temperatures around 5°C cooler than down on the Adelaide Plains. Tanapappa is just one of 50-plus cellar doors here: make a mental note to return to sip some fine sauvignon blanc. From Tanapappa, wander onto the end of Hansen St, cross Piccadilly Rd

### Heysen Trail Online

If you're walking with your device in hand/pocket, check out heysentrail.asn.au/heysen-trail/interactive-map for a zoomable map of the Heysen Trail as it doglegs its way through this part of the Adelaide Hills – a handy resource if you've overlooked one of the little red Heysen Trail route markers along the way. It's a little inaccurate in places due to ongoing re-routing, most notably where the trail makes its final ascent to Mt Lofty Summit: ditch the digital realm and follow the route markers here instead.

then head downhill (again!) along Sprigg Rd for a few hundred metres. Follow Sprigg Rd where it forks off to the right: a **glorious view of Mt Lofty Summit** opens up to the northwest, capped by the three Mt Lofty broadcast towers and the castellated stone turrets of Carminow House, built in 1885 and still someone's eccentric private palace.

**06** Between the Piccadilly Valley and Mt Lofty Summit is **Cleland Conservation Park**...and a very steep trail! Enter the park at Gate 27 on the bend in Sprigg Rd and head directly uphill. After a few hundred metres make a right-hand turn, following the Heysen Trail markers up a steep fire trail, zigzagging ever higher. After a final zig, **Carminow House** appears in all its anomalous architectural glory: from here it's a short and relatively level jaunt north to the **summit**. There's a cafe, a gift shop and an info desk here, but forget all these for the moment – how about that view? At 710m above sea level, this is the highest point in the Mt Lofty Ranges (aka the Adelaide Hills), with the **shimmering Gulf St Vincent** and the **big city** spreading out for endless miles below. The dinky white obelisk here is **Flinders Column**, erected in 1902 to mark the centenary of the naming of Mt Lofty by English explorer Matthew Flinders. Of course, the Peramangk people had been looking down over these plains for millennia before Flinders showed up. This wonderful walk has been a guided tour of their Country – a truly beautiful part of South Australia.

### Take a Break

About 7km into the walk you'll wander into Bridgewater, a historic Adelaide Hills suburb with a cute pub and the towering **Bridgewater Mill** (thebridgewatermill.com.au) alongside Cox Creek, dating back to the 1850s. There's a high-end restaurant inside, but divert to the little Coffee Grounds cafe in the adjacent stone cottage for a caffeine hit and a slice of cake.

# 40

# Belair National Park Waterfall

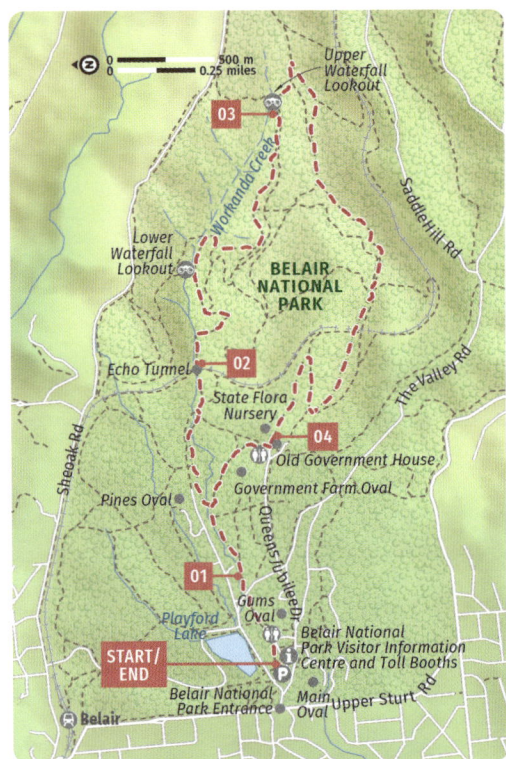

| DURATION | DIFFICULTY | DISTANCE | START/END |
|---|---|---|---|
| 3hrs return | Moderate | 8.5km | Gooch Dr car park |

| TERRAIN | Well-trodden dirt tracks & roadside walking; some steep sections |
|---|---|

Established in 1891, Belair (pictured) is the state's oldest national park. SA's early governors retreated to their stately summer home here: they're long gone, but you can still enjoy this terrific walking trail, taking you past the Old Government House and winter waterfalls, along ridges and through craggy, bush-clad wilderness, just 13km from downtown Adelaide.

## Getting Here

Belair is one of Adelaide's southeastern suburbs; Belair train station is on the park boundary. It's just as easy to drive and park off Upper Sturt Rd.

## Starting Point

Save yourself the national park entry fee by parking in the free car park just off Gooch Dr, before the park toll booths.

**01** Pick up a trail map at the visitor centre and hit the **Lorikeet Loop Walk** nearby, winding past cricket ovals, tennis courts and barbecue areas emitting appetising summery smells. You'll hit the **Waterfall Hike** after 1km: branch off to the left over the little bridge, making your way steadily uphill past a plaque commemorating a 1936 boy scout 'corroboree' here, attended by 4000 young knot-tying tent dwellers.

**02** You'll soon come to **Echo Tunnel**, a narrow, 50m-long concrete culvert (duck your head!) beneath the Adelaide–Melbourne rail line. **Workanda Creek** dribbles through here: the tunnel offers a cool, momentary respite from the sun. On the far side the trail ascends some steep timber steps, delivering you (and your racing pulse) to a breezy ridge. Monarch butterflies and humming bees are your companions as you divert left to **Lower Waterfall Lookout**. After winter rains, Workanda

## Aldgate Valley

Belair is on the doorstep of the Adelaide Hills (technically the Mt Lofty Ranges – Peramangk Country). With crisp air, woodland shade and labyrinthine valleys, it's usually a few degrees cooler up here than down in Adelaide. The pretty hills villages of Stirling and Aldgate are famed for their dazzling deciduous colours. Oddly, Aldgate has also been home to both late AC/DC singer Bon Scott and Mel Gibson over the years. On a less rock 'n' roll tack, the 6km **Aldgate Valley Nature Walk** runs from Aldgate to nearby Mylor; follow the bandicoot signs from the little park across the road from the Aldgate shops (map from ahc.sa.gov.au).

CAROLINE BRUNDLE BUGGE/GETTY IMAGES ©

Creek tumbles over the sheer cliff here, with clear-day **views extending to shimmering Gulf St Vincent**.

**03** Back on the trail – which momentarily follows a broad vehicular fire track – continue uphill onto a bushy plateau. The charred trunks here are the remnants of a 2014 bush fire, ignited by a goods train on a 40°C day. **Spectacular Upper Waterfall Lookout** is next – a craggy sandstone cliff where Workanda Creek once again takes a vertical shortcut. Check out the little cave at the cliff base – a good spot to refuel with a sluice of juice and a muesli bar.

**04** The return route largely adheres to gravelly fire trails, passing several human-made objects that hint at a return to civilisation – a graffiti-spangled concrete reservoir and a rusty water tank below high-voltage power lines – then winding back downhill with distant coastal views through the eucalypts, beyond shimmering rooftops. Return to the fringes of suburbia at **Old Government House**, a photogenic stone homestead built in 1860, with SA's first indoor pool! Check out the **State Flora Nursery** nearby, then rejoin the Lorikeet Loop Walk back to where you started.

 **Take a Break**

You could truck back into Adelaide, but why not take a quick 10km detour up Sheoak Rd to the lovely Adelaide Hills town of Stirling, where the **Stirling Hotel** (stirlinghotel.com.au) awaits? The bistro here is a free-flowing, all-day affair (classy pub grub and pizzas), with boundless cold beer on tap.

# 41

# Marion Coastal Trail

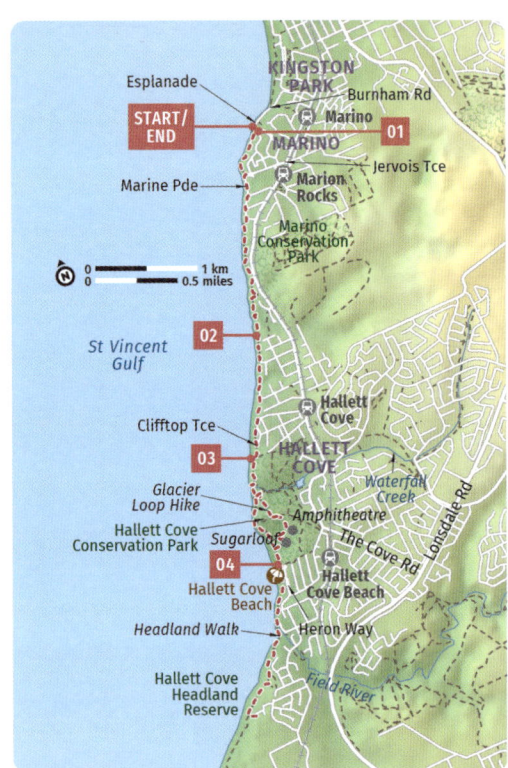

| DURATION | DIFFICULTY | DISTANCE | START/END |
|---|---|---|---|
| 3½hrs return | Moderate | 10.5km | Esplanade, Marino |

| TERRAIN | Clifftop dirt trails, extensive boardwalks & steep timber steps |
|---|---|

On the Fleurieu Peninsula, this meandering clifftop trail delivers mesmerising coastal views, alongside glorious Gulf St Vincent. Also known as the Hallett Cove Boardwalk, much of the trail follows spectacular elevated boardwalks, with lengthy flights of timber steps to test your quads. Watch for passing dolphins, sweaty joggers and circling seabirds, before exploring the crumbling ice-age geology of Hallett Cove Conservation Park and Hallett Cove Beach.

## Getting Here

It's an easy half-hour drive from Adelaide south to the trailhead. Or, catch a Seaford Line train to Marino Station then walk 10 minutes west to the coast.

## Starting Point

Hit the trail on the Esplanade (the continuation of Burnham Rd) at Marino, where there's plenty of free on-street parking.

**01** At the **Esplanade trailhead**, local artist Marijana Tadic's sculpture *Contemplation* (2006) resembles an upturned hull. But fear not – Gulf St Vincent is protected from Southern Ocean swells by Kangaroo Island, and upended boats here are a rarity. From the end of the Esplanade, track around the headland on a level dirt trail, then take the Marine Pde footpath to its conclusion, where the dirt trail resumes.

**02** The trail proper kicks off from here, weaving along the cliff edge, with **fishing boats bobbing offshore**. Windswept coastal heath, wild daisies and squat succulents cling to the verges, conjuring visions of the Cyclades.

## Headland Walk

Extend your Fleurieu adventures with an hour spent exploring Hallett Cove Headland, just over 1.5km from Hallett Cove Beach. Walk south along the shore, ducking around the mouth of the diminutive Field River before scaling the steep headland within Hallett Cove Headland Reserve. The view north back along the gulf coast from here is a real showstopper (try not to visualise Adelaide's infamous white-elephant desalination plant, just over the rise to the south). Avid botanists should keep an eye out for rare native species along the track, including dwarf hakea (*hakea rugosa*) and mallee box (*eucalyptus porosa*).

Huge **mansions** flank some sections of the trail – crumbling '60s haciendas and new-century architectural marvels – all of which have bedazzling views, extending to the Yorke Peninsula on a clear day. The trail dips into a series of scrub-filled ravines, steep sections traversed by zigzagging flights of timber steps: 110 down, 85 up, 75 down…with regular detours to the craggy shore. Water fountains crop up along the way, but they're sporadically operational – bring a bottle in your backpack.

**03** **Hallett Cove Conservation Park** caps the end of Clifftop Cres – a precious reserve of internationally significant geologic and glacial formations, dating back to an ice age 280 million years ago. The Coastal Trail gives you a taste of the park's features, or detour inland beyond the sometimes-flowing **Waterfall Creek** onto the wheelchair-accessible **Glacier Loop Hike**. This trail offers a closer look at the much-photographed **Sugar Loaf** (pictured) and **Amphitheatre** formations, before rejoining the Coastal Trail 1km further south.

**04** **Hallett Cove Beach** is a stone-strewn affair, touted as the possible site for a Sydney-style ocean-bath development. Until this happens you can cool off in the gulf, or duck into the cafe for a bite before you turn around and retrace your steps.

 **Take a Break**

Poised above stony Hallett Cove Beach, the **Boatshed Cafe** (boatshedhc.com.au) is a classy eatery with views to rival the Coastal Trail itself. It's the perfect halfway house in which to refuel before you backtrack north along the coast. There's a takeaway kiosk here, too, if you've worked up an aroma on the trail that you'd rather keep to yourself.

# 42

# Blowhole Beach to Cape Jervis

| DURATION | DIFFICULTY | DISTANCE | START/END |
|---|---|---|---|
| 4hrs one-way | Moderate | 11km | Blowhole Beach/ Cape Jervis |

| TERRAIN | Dirt & sandy tracks along rocky coastline |
|---|---|

The Heysen Trail is 1200km long – epic! If you don't have a few spare months to hike it, walking its final (or first) 11km along the Fleurieu Peninsula's south coast is a superb snapshot. From rugged Blowhole Beach in Deep Creek Conservation Park, the trail hugs the dramatic, windswept coastline all the way to Cape Jervis. Jagged cliffs, sandy coves and a few human-made surprises feature en route.

## Getting Here
From Adelaide, plug Blowhole Beach into your phone/GPS and drive 109km south (1¾ hours).

## Starting Point
Access Blowhole Beach via a steep 4WD track in Deep Creek Conservation Park (national parks pass required). No 4WD? Park at Cobbler Hill car park on Blowhole Beach Rd and walk 2km downhill.

**01** The sheltered arc of **Blowhole Beach** is a stunner. It's tempting to wade into the gentle waves here, but there's 11km of trail ahead – better get walking! Follow the little red Heysen Trail markers beyond the creek at the bay's western end, rising up to straw-coloured hillsides. Bounding kangaroos (and plenty of flies, in summer) keep you company as the trail traverses several ravines, winds along lichen-covered shoreline and through windswept saltbush. Look for **pods of dolphins** and **migrating southern right whales** (June to September) in Backstairs Passage offshore.

**02** Some of SA's most unusual accommodation is tucked into a gully at **Sprigg Inlet**, on the end of Rarkang Rd about 3.5km into the walk. Designed in 1968 by Finnish architect Matti Suuronen as a modular concept house, the

## Deep Creek Circuit

Like the look of this part of the Fleurieu Peninsula? For further in-depth analysis, tackle the **Deep Creek Circuit** within Deep Creek Conservation Park. It's a steep and challenging loop (12km over five to six hours) dipping down to photogenic Deep Creek Cove (good for a swim) before returning via bush-filled ravines and open grassland. Look forward to brilliant views along the coast and across Backstairs Passage to Kangaroo Island (just 'KI' to its friends and associates). See parks.sa.gov.au for info. You'll need a national parks pass for vehicle access (it's probably too far to walk in to the trailhead from the park entrance).

UFO-shaped **Futuro House** (thefuturohouse.com) is one of 60 or so surviving examples around the world. It's currently part of the marvellous **Naiko Retreat** (naikoretreat.com.au), a luxury surf-shaped villa across the valley. File under 'Special Occasions' and keep walking...

**03** Beyond a couple of stiles and some **old fishing shacks** near the end of Talisker Rd, a sheer cliff plummets down to a photogenic little beach, only accessible by boat. The trail continues through stands of casuarinas to the grey-shale **Fishery Beach**.

A chunky power cable exits the well-barricaded concrete power plant here, running under Backstairs Passage to electrify Kangaroo Island.

**04** The jumping-off point for Kangaroo Island ferries, **Cape Jervis** (pictured) comes into view as your walk nears its conclusion. For the last few kilometres the sandy trail passes through low coastal scrub, past the crumbling redbrick chimney of a ruined cottage at **Land's End** and into the dunes south of the trailhead. Orange monarch butterflies flit between corn daisies, guiding you towards the drinks fridge inside the ferry terminal. Mission completed, pick up your pre-organised ride back to your car at Blowhole Beach.

## Take a Break

This is a remote part of the Fleurieu, with limited foodie offerings. You can get a biscuit and a drink at the Kangaroo Island ferry terminal at Cape Jervis, but for something more substantial travel to Normanville, 32km north. On the main street, **1 Little Sister** (onelittlesister.com.au) is a city-style cafe doing a roaring trade in coffees, big breakfasts and pizzas.

# Also Try...

## Wangarra Lookout

| DURATION | DIFFICULTY | DISTANCE |
| --- | --- | --- |
| 3hrs return | Moderate | 7.5km |

The undisputed highlight of the northern Flinders Ranges is Ikara (Wilpena Pound), an 80-sq-km sunken valley ringed by jagged ridges (naturally formed – don't let anyone tell you it's a meteorite crater!). The hike to Wangarra Lookout (pictured) delivers knockout views across the whole basin.

Wilpena Pound Resort, run by the local Adnyamathanha people, hosts the Wilpena Pound Visitor Information Centre. Pick up a trail map here, pay your Ikara-Flinders Ranges National Park entry fees and head south. Lined with red gums, acacias and native pines, the trail follows the rarely flowing Wilpena Creek to Pound Gap, a narrow cavity in Ikara's otherwise unbroken ring of colossal crags. Just inside the Pound, the Hills Homestead ruins tell a tale of failed farming in the early 1900s. From here, scale Ikara's steep slopes to the upper Wangarra Lookout – a sweaty but utterly rewarding climb.

## The Shiraz Trail

| DURATION | DIFFICULTY | DISTANCE |
| --- | --- | --- |
| 2-3hrs one-way | Easy | 9km |

Similar to the Riesling Trail in the Clare Valley, the Shiraz Trail follows a disused rail route (closed in 1972) through the lush vine-lands of the McLaren Vale wine region on the Fleurieu Peninsula.

From the appealing old Willunga train station, a time-warped Victorian architectural vision, the trail scoots past Willunga High School before entering wine country proper. It's an easygoing, level stroll for the most part, along a sealed path shared by cyclists and dog walkers. To sample the local product, detour along McMurtrie Rd and sip some shiraz at classy Mitolo Wines (mitolowines.com. au) or estimable Wirra Wirra (wirrawirra.com). The trail finishes at the McLaren Vale Visitor Information Centre: there's a cafe here, or winery maps and brochures if you're in need of more wine time. Alternatively, walk in the opposite direction and finish up in Willunga's main-street pubs and cafes.

CHAMELEONSEYE/SHUTTERSTOCK ©

## Alligator Gorge Ring Route

| DURATION | DIFF | DISTANCE |
|---|---|---|
| 4hrs return | Moderate | 9km |

Hidden in the northern section of Mt Remarkable National Park in the Flinders Ranges, Alligator Gorge (pictured) is sensationally remote.

This adventurous trail starts at the car park on Alligator Gorge Rd, accessed via Wilmington, a 3½-hour drive north of Adelaide. Descend into The Narrows, a sheer ochre-coloured ravine just 2m wide in places, with Alligator Creek trickling through. The track also crosses The Terraces, a curiously rippled natural geologic feature, and traverses open bushland. National park fees apply. No sign of any gators…

## Wallowa

| DURATION | DIFF | DISTANCE |
|---|---|---|
| 3hrs return | Moderate | 10.5km |

Just an hour north of Adelaide, SA's most famous wine region is the Barossa Valley, producing robust reds. But it's not just vineyards here: encounter the valley's wild side in rugged Kaiserstuhl Conservation Park.

From Gate 1 on Tanunda Creek Rd, the Wallowa Hike cuts a U-shape through the park, passing through open stringybark forest, across creeks to a rocky lookout, before following a section of the Heysen Trail to Gate 2 on Rifle Range Rd. This is the turn-around point: backtrack to Gate 1, accompanied by kangaroos and raucous native birds.

## Dutchmans Stern

| DURATION | DIFF | DISTANCE |
|---|---|---|
| 5hrs return | Moderate | 10.5km |

Hinting at the loftier northern Flinders Ranges further north, Dutchmans Stern rises a dramatic 820m above the dusty plains 10km northwest of Quorn (four hours north of Adelaide).

This circuit walk around the mount, partly following the Heysen Trail, starts at the car park off Dutchmans Stern Rd. Look forward to sweeping views across the plains to Spencer Gulf, beyond stands of sheoak, native pine and sugar gum. It's not a particularly arduous hike (and it's good for families with older kids), but bring plenty of $H_2O$.

Mt Buffalo National Park (p170)

# Grampians to the High Country

**43  Wonderland Loop**
The best introductory walk to the spectacular Grampians. **p166**

**44  Mt Stapylton**
Watch sunset light up cliffs near this wonderful craggy peak. **p168**

**45  Mt Buffalo Plateau**
A delightful ramble past cliffs and boulders on a striking plateau. **p170**

**46  The Razorback & Mt Feathertop**
Amazing views on Victoria's most iconic mountain and ridge walk. **p172**

**47  Mt Cope**
Climb this easy peak for a captivating high-country panorama. **p176**

# Explore

# Grampians to the High Country

Victoria's finest regions for mountain walks are Grampians National Park (Gariwerd) and the High Country. Though separated by a solid day's drive, they are indelibly linked by the Great Dividing Range, the chain of mountains and valleys stretching from western Victoria up to northern Queensland. In the west of the state, the Grampians are a series of rugged sandstone ranges with a rich Aboriginal heritage. In Victoria's northeast, Mt Buffalo National Park is a geological marvel of granite formations, frost plains and cascades. Nearby, the High Country's tallest peaks rise to over 1800m and are incorporated into the vast Alpine National Park. This is fantastic walking country.

## Halls Gap

The only central town in the Grampians, Halls Gap is spread out along Grampians Rd in a stunning setting at the foot of the Wonderland Range, about 250km from Melbourne. It's a quiet place for much of the time, but come weekends and holiday times it can be packed out with visitors all trying to get their piece of the Grampians. Though small, the town has a supermarket, cafes, a few pubs, a wide selection of accommodation options and other amenities for tourists and outdoorsy types. It's an ideal place to base yourself for walks in the hills, especially if you have your own vehicle.

## Bright

Best appreciated in autumn, when its multitude of deciduous trees are in full colour, Bright is an all-year tourist destination sitting prettily beside the Ovens River. There are frequent running and cycling events here too, and in winter it's a central base for snow sports at nearby Falls Creek, Mt Hotham and Mt Buffalo. The proportion of cafes relative to its size is surprising, but in holiday times you'll appreciate why – Bright's population explodes during the summer and Easter peak. It has the full gamut of services for tourists and outdoor enthusiasts, and there is an extensive range of accommodation on offer. While there are other smaller towns nearby that are also worth considering as a base – including Porepunkah, Harrietville, Mt Beauty and even Omeo – Bright is the preferred option logistically because it's got the best facilities in the region to help you prepare for your foray into the bush.

 When to Go

The peaks of the Grampians are not overly high, so snow is rare and walks can be undertaken at any time of year. Spring and autumn are ideal, and summer is popular but can be scorching.

Walks in the High Country, including Mt Buffalo, are generally at higher elevations that are snow-covered between June and September, so are best avoided at this time, particularly so for the ice-prone higher peaks. Additionally, some roads close in the mountains during winter, restricting access to many walking areas. Late spring to mid-autumn is peak walking season here.

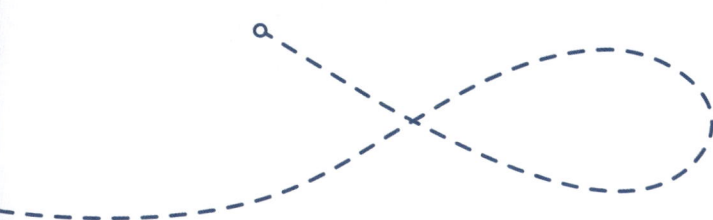

## Where to Stay

Both the Grampians and High Country regions offer a huge variety of accommodation – from camping areas and caravan parks to homestays and resorts – and Halls Gap and Bright are both blessed with decent selections to suit all budgets. Bushwalkers heading to Mt Buffalo National Park might be interested in overnighting at **Lake Catani Campground** (parks.vic.gov.au/where-to-stay), the delightful camping area high on the plateau. Facilities are basic but it's an unbeatable location beside the lake and near the Mt Buffalo Chalet.

## What's On

**Grampians Music Festival** (grampiansmusicfestival.com; Feb) Features a lineup of local talent staged in a superb setting.

**Bright Autumn Festival** (brightautumnfestival.org.au; Apr/May) This long-running event highlights the changing seasons and local produce and art, and culminates with the Gala Day street parade.

**Grampians Grape Escape** (grampiansgrapeescape.com.au; May) This annual event showcases local wines, foods and music.

**Bright Alpine Climb – 4 Peaks** (4peaks.com.au; early Nov) Walking and running evening where competitors climb four local mountains over four days; Mt Buffalo, Mt Feathertop, Mt Hotham and Mystic Mountain.

## Transport

The main towns near the Grampians and High Country have good **V/Line** (vline.com.au) train/bus combination services from Melbourne (Southern Cross Station), but to access most trailheads you'll need your own wheels. Halls Gap can be reached by train from Melbourne to Ballarat, where passengers alight for a bus to Ararat or Stawell, and then make a further bus change for Halls Gap. For Bright, trains run from Melbourne to Wangaratta, where a connecting bus takes you the rest of the way. Train and bus tickets are available from **Public Transport Victoria** (ptv.vic.gov.au). There are no car-rental outlets in Halls Gap or Bright.

## Resources

**Parks Victoria** (parks.vic.gov.au) Official website for Victoria's national parks.

**The Grampians** (visitgrampians.com.au) The Grampians' best online resource.

**Mt Buffalo National Park** (visitmountbuffalo.com.au) The best site for up-to-date information on Mt Buffalo.

**Alpine Visitor Information Centre** (visitbright.com.au) Has just about all you need to know about Bright and the surrounding district.

**Bright Escapes** (brightescapes.com.au) Handy reference for accommodation bookings in and around Bright.

**Victoria's High Country** (victoriashighcountry.com.au) Information on all areas of the High Country and northeast Victoria.

# 43

# Wonderland Loop

| DURATION | DIFFICULTY | DISTANCE | START/END |
|---|---|---|---|
| 3hrs return | Moderate | 9km | Halls Gap |

| TERRAIN | Steps & steep ascents along a good track |
|---|---|

Crags, canyons, waterfalls and grand vistas are all jam-packed into this half-day walk through the enchanting Wonderland Range. It's possibly the most iconic day walk in Grampians National Park: if you can only do one walk in the park, make it this one. Start early if it's hot.

## Getting Here
Conveniently, Halls Gap can be reached by public transport.

## Starting Point
Begin at the tourist shelter and car park, directly opposite the supermarket in Halls Gap.

**01** Head west from the shelter, just south of **Stony Creek**, cutting through the caravan park and following signs to the Pinnacle. The described clockwise loop walk goes against the advice of most other publications and park information boards, but doing the walk in this direction gets the steepest leg of the walk done first and rewards walkers with a possible dip at Venus Baths near walk's end.

**02** The route ascends steadily below **Mackeys Peak**. Head up the first of many steps and continue climbing, with occasional **viewpoints** and **bench seats** along the way to break up the journey; one particularly long set of steel steps is a real thigh-burner. The grade levels considerably on the crest of the **Wonderland Range**, but be careful to follow the yellow markers over rock slabs to the **Pinnacle** (pictured), 3.8km from Halls Gap. This dramatic 720m crag overlooks Halls Gap and Fyans Creek valley; behind you, rock outcrops provide a nice foreground to views of more distant ranges.

## Grampians Peaks Trail

The 160km **Grampians Peak Trail** (GPT) is a 13-day epic trek through Grampians National Park, from Mt Zero in the north to Mt Abrupt near Dunkeld. The route takes a challenging yet scenic course over peaks, through valleys, and along the ridges of the Mt Difficult, Wonderland, Serra and Mt William Ranges, and includes a crossing of the Grampians' tallest peak, Mt William (1167m). Glean more information at parks.vic.gov.au.

**Best for**

**A POST-WALK DRINK**

**03** Signposts and yellow track markers indicate the route to follow towards Wonderland car park. The trail passes through **Silent Street**, a narrow slot canyon, before descending past the tiny **Bridal Veil Falls** and a little further to the **Cool Chamber**, a cavern-like undercut in the rock.

**04** The descent continues, soon reaching the upper end of the Grand Canyon. Ignore the less-interesting bypass track and enter the **Grand Canyon** down a set of short but steep steps (protected by guardrails), where the grade quickly eases. Bridges criss-cross the small creek and within just 10 minutes you exit the canyon to reach **Wonderland car park**. (It's possible to drive to this point if you have your own vehicle, which is handy for a shorter return walk to the Pinnacle.)

**05** Signs direct you towards Halls Gap, 3.2km distant, following a course close to **Stony Creek**. Pass the side track to **Splitters Falls** and continue along the path. The going is now much easier as the worst of those tedious steps is finally over. Further down, the track passes a few enticing creek pools and climbs over a low spur where the picturesque slabs and crags of **Elephants Hide** can be seen across the valley. **Venus Baths**, a set of refreshing shallow creek pools, are 10 minutes further, accessed along a short side trail. The main path broadens and is often busy for the final 15 minutes back to Halls Gap.

 **Take a Break**

If the term 'micro-brewery' has you watering at the mouth, **Paper Scissors Rock Brew Co** (paperscissorsrock.beer), next to the tourist office in Halls Gap, sells a variety of tasty brews and has a street-food-inspired menu. Sit at the tables outside and enjoy views to the Wonderland Range.

# 44

# Mt Stapylton

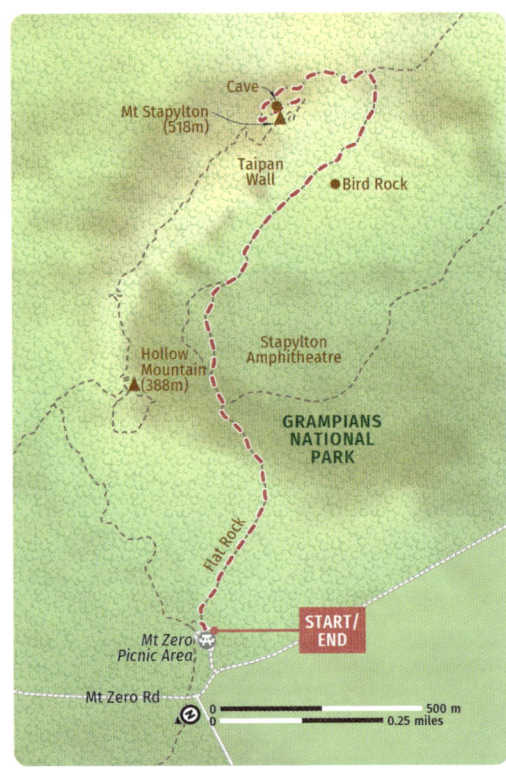

| DURATION | DIFFICULTY | DISTANCE | START/END |
|---|---|---|---|
| 1½hrs return | Moderate | 4.8km | Mt Zero Picnic Area |

| TERRAIN | Rocky track with some scrambling |
|---|---|

This short but superb northern Grampians outing, with exceptional views from sandstone outcrops along the way, is ideally suited to walkers who love an easy scramble. One particularly attractive feature is that little planning is required; a fine day, sturdy shoes and a little effort is all that's needed. Aim for a late-afternoon departure and watch the cliffs of Mt Stapylton simmer as sunset approaches.

The route heads south from Mt Zero Picnic Area (40km north of Halls Gap) and heads up the long sloping slab of **Flat Rock** along a route marked by yellow dabs of paint. After 15 minutes a panorama of Stapylton Amphitheatre, Mt Stapylton and the **ochre-hued cliffs** of Taipan Wall unfolds from the top of Flat Rock.

The path is easy to follow as it passes beneath the slopes of **Hollow Mountain** and leads through **Stapylton Amphitheatre** onto a rocky ramp below **Taipan Wall** (pictured). Ascending past the picturesque **Bird Rock** formation the route reaches a ridge crest, then loops north below crags of Mt Stapylton's eastern wall. The route gets a little more challenging as it climbs higher through a gully and then swings south, ascending past a couple of **wind-scoured caves** on a sideways sloping ramp. Though it's a bit exposed most walkers won't find any difficulty here.

The trail ends at a marker just short of the actual summit of **Mt Stapylton** (498m), where the peaks and ranges of the Grampians dominate the scene to the south. While it might look possible to scramble further, any route is seriously exposed and it would be foolhardy to attempt to climb to the top from here. After you've had your fill of the view, make your way back along the outward route.

# 45

# Mt Buffalo Plateau

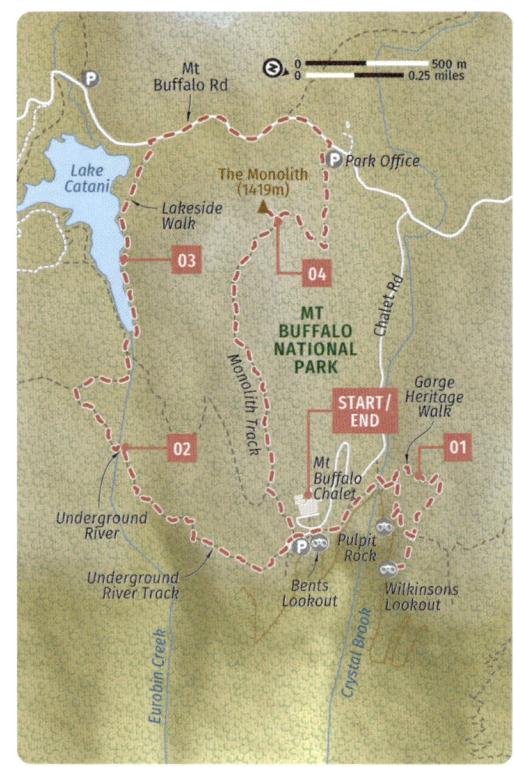

| DURATION | DIFFICULTY | DISTANCE | START/END |
|---|---|---|---|
| 2½hrs return | Moderate | 9km | Mt Buffalo Chalet |

| TERRAIN | Well-used tracks with some short climbs |
|---|---|

This delightful route takes in the Gorge and the Monolith, two of Mt Buffalo National Park's most popular geographical features, and makes for an excellent foray into the joys of this sub-alpine plateau. It's not a hard walk by any means, but this jaunt could conceivably be split into two, as the described route consists of two loop walks radiating from the Mt Buffalo Chalet. If you're after a short stroll you could complete just the Gorge Heritage Walk, the first part of the main walk, as it is the shorter (2.5km) and easier of the two loops.

## Getting Here

It's 31km from Bright to the chalet in Mt Buffalo National Park. There is no public transport to the park so you'll need your own vehicle.

## Starting Point

Begin at the car park, directly opposite the historic chalet, at the path signed 'Gorge Heritage Walk'.

**01** Start by peering over the edge of nearby **Bents Lookout**, which teeters on a cliff edge forming the gorge. Then head along **Gorge Heritage Walk**. This interpretive trail leads walkers on a historical and environmental journey around the gorge as if led by Alice Manfield, or Guide Alice as she was better known, whose family ran one of the early establishments on the plateau. As you proceed, admire the views over the Ovens Valley from **Pulpit Rock** and **Wilkinsons Lookout**, which are awe-inspiring, a term not used lightly.

**02** On returning to the **chalet**, wander down to the eastern end of the car park, where you should follow the **Underground River Track**. This will lead you downhill to a gully where

## The Horn

Don't leave the park without having made the trip to the **Horn** (pictured), the plateau's highest point. Beyond the Mt Buffalo Chalet the road heads further into the park, climbing past Lake Catani and Cathedral Saddle before arriving at Cresta Valley, the site of a small five-lift ski area until it was destroyed by a bushfire in 2006. A gravel road continues further and ends at a picnic area on the edge of an escarpment, 13km from the chalet. A walking track climbs from here to a large boulder crowning the Horn (1723m), safely protected by guardrails. The view is jaw-dropping.

boulders have clogged the valley and created the **Underground River**, which supports a rare species of glow-worm. Entering the cave-like formation is dangerous, but **Adventure Guides Australia** (adventureguidesaustralia.com) can take you through.

**03** Climbing out of the gully the track snakes its way to a prominent management track. Turn towards Lake Catani, but within just a few metres veer right onto the **Lakeside Walk**, which steers you around the northern shore of **Lake Catani** to reach Mt Buffalo Rd.

**04** The route follows the roadside north for 600m (beware of traffic) to reach the **Monolith Track** junction bearing east. This track meanders through forest to the foot of the Monolith, where a couple of side tracks and a short climb up a ladder leaves you puffing atop a rocky outcrop allowing **expansive views over the plateau** to the distant peaks of the Great Dividing Range. For many years, the adjacent tor – the **Monolith** itself – was adorned with an ageing and increasingly rickety ladder. Due to safety concerns the ladder has been removed but the views from the boulders nearby are nonetheless grand. Return to the Monolith Track and continue east. An easy finish to the walk leads through forest back to the chalet.

 **Take a Break**

At the time of research, the **Mt Buffalo Chalet** (which has been closed since 2007) was undergoing extensive renovation works. It's hoped that an eventual reopening will include a cafe for day-use visitors. If this happens, the chalet will make an unmissable spot to have lunch. Until such time, food and drinks are available from **Dingo Dell Café**, 6.4km southwest of the chalet, open on long weekends and holidays, or at the **Gorge Coffee Van**, which opens sporadically during peak times.

# 46

# The Razorback & Mt Feathertop

**Best for**
AMAZING VIEWS

| DURATION | DIFFICULTY | DISTANCE | START/END |
|---|---|---|---|
| 7-8hrs return | Hard | 21.6km | Great Alpine Rd |

| TERRAIN | Windswept track along exposed ridge with some steep climbs |
|---|---|

Mt Feathertop is one of Australia's most beautiful peaks and a bushwalking icon. Formidable slopes guard the mountain and precipitous spurs descend from the summit to the valleys below, giving the mountain a true 'alpine' feel. The most popular and scenic route to Mt Feathertop is along the narrow and often windswept Razorback ridge (pictured p175), which is mainly above the tree line and offers walkers splendid views. This is a long walk and you will need to be fully self-sufficient. Carry at least 3L of water (per person) in warm weather and food for the day. Avoid the snow- and ice-covered Razorback in winter.

## Getting Here

There is a 52km drive from Bright to the head of the Razorback on the Great Alpine Rd, 3km before the village and ski lifts at Hotham Heights. While there is no official car park, there is generally plenty of space to park beside the road. **Alps Link** (dysongroup.com.au/alps-link) runs buses three times per week between Bright and Mt Hotham, but it's impossible to get the schedule to work for a day walk. There are no other summer (ie non-winter) transport options between Bright and Mt Hotham.

## Starting Point

Begin opposite the A-framed Diamantina Hut. The Razorback walk is clearly signed. Before setting off, appreciate the scene in front of you. The view of Mt Feathertop and the Razorback is one of the most inspiring alpine panoramas in Victoria and photos taken from the road near here regularly feature in advertising material. While the mountain is beautiful year-round, the view from the road in winter is the best time to really appreciate Mt Feathertop's attractive form, when westerly winds create large cornices along the summit ridge. (Avoid the walk itself in winter.)

**01** Log your name into the 'Intentions Book' at the small information shelter, then set foot on the track heading north along the ridge. Immediately, the ridge narrows and soon a side track can be seen edging around the east of the **Razorback**, above the infant Diamantina River. Stay on the main ridge route as it climbs to a wonderful viewpoint on the hilltop at the head of Bon Accord Spur. Rest a moment at this high spot and consider the plight of early skiers travelling to Mt Hotham; the **Bon Accord Spur** and the small section of the Razorback you've just walked were once used as the main winter access route for visitors to Mt Hotham at a time before the road was cleared for winter traffic (see the Eric Johnson box, p174).

**02** Continuing, the trail dips steeply into the prominent Big Dipper saddle, then contours around the east side of the next hill to rejoin the crest of the Razorback. The route now follows the ridgetop most of the way to Mt Feathertop, and it's a delightful walk. A forest of regenerating post-bushfire snow gums hampers views for a while but the route soon climbs out of the trees at the head of **Champion Spur**. Mt Feathertop looms closer now, but it's still around 1½ hours to the summit.

**03** The path continues along the narrow ridge past the two pint-size hills of **Twin Knobs**, often dappled in **wildflowers**, and slips to the west-side **High Knob** (1801m) to reach a junction with a track climbing up Diamantina Spur. A relatively easy ascent of High Knob can be made from here; simply climb steeply straight up

## Snow Carnival

In the early 1920s skiing in Victoria had a surge in popularity. On Mt Feathertop, a trail was cut from Little Mt Feathertop down the upper Bungalow Spur to make a ski run where races could be held, and in 1923 the mountain hosted the Snow Carnival & Skiing Championships. Further events were run right up to the late 1930s, but when the Feathertop Bungalow (the main accommodation establishment on the mountain) was destroyed by bushfire in 1939, and with the advent of more accessible resorts at Mt Hotham and Mt Buller, ski events were held elsewhere and Mt Feathertop was left largely to hardy adventurers.

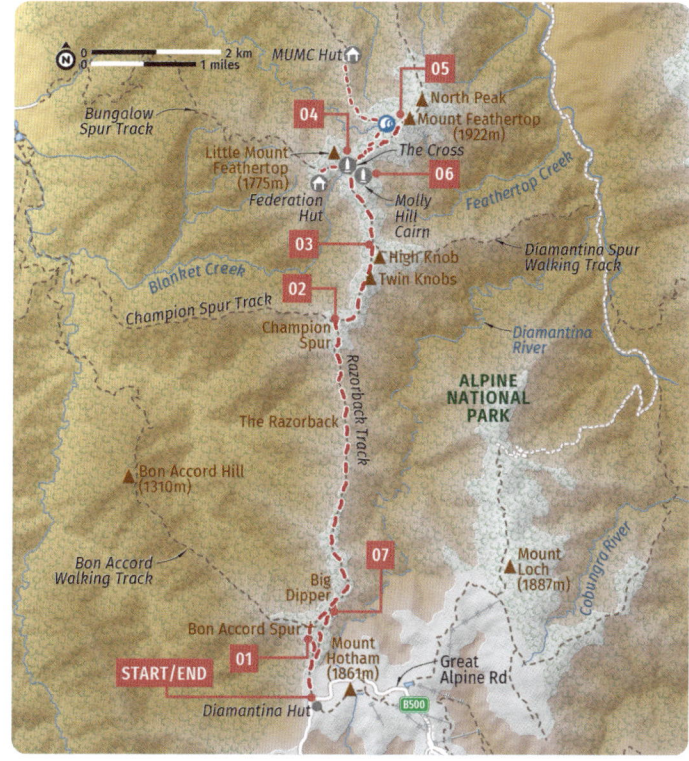

(there is no track) for commanding **views** of Mt Feathertop and the surrounding High Country. If you don't have the time to walk the entire way to Mt Feathertop, or the weather is closing in, High Knob makes a great destination in its own right.

**04** The main path guides you north, then leaves the ridgetop on the west side to cut across to a saddle adorned with a **cross** near **Little Mt Feathertop** (1775m). **Federation Hut** (and its associated camp site and toilet) is 500m off the main track but is worth a visit should weather not permit going further. There is a lovely **grassy grove** outside the hut, ideal for a picnic, but a detour here will add another 1km to the trip.

**05** The climb to Mt Feathertop beckons walkers; it feels close to enough to touch now. Leave the saddle at the cross and follow the track heading northeast, then in five minutes keep right on the track that leads back to the spine of the Razorback. (The track heading left leads to a **spring** – a reliable source of water – on the west face of Mt Feathertop, and continues further to the Northwest Spur and the dome-shaped **Melbourne University Mountaineering Club Hut**.) Back on the Razorback the route to the summit climbs obviously before you. The ascent through stunted alpine grasses and scree is steep but increasingly striking views unfold as you gain elevation. The highest point of **Mt Feathertop** (1922m) is the easternmost bump of the narrow summit ridge; here, you can almost stand astride the peak with steep slopes falling away on two sides, though there is no danger to bushwalkers. There are few places in the Victorian Alps that present a more impressive outlook.

**06** Shoulder your pack once more and descend back to the saddle at the foot of the summit climb. In good weather, ignore the outward trail that contours to the west toward Little Mt Feathertop and instead follow a faint footpad along the crest of the Razorback, rising to the large **Molly Hill Memorial Cairn** (pictured p172). This memorial is dedicated to an adventurer from the Ski Club of Victoria, who died in 1932 from injuries sustained after falling down an icy slope nearby. This is yet another grand viewpoint.

**07** Continue south along the ridgetop. Within about 10 minutes the main Razorback foot track will be joined, then simply retrace your steps to the Great Alpine Rd. This time, however, on reaching the **Big Dipper** saddle avoid the ridge climb and instead follow the side track to the east. This alternative route avoids the final short but excruciating climb at the end of a long day on the trail.

### Eric Johnson

When Mt Hotham was in its infancy as a ski centre in the 1940s, there was only one way for winter visitors to get up the mountain relatively quickly from Harrietville; the long, demanding and often hazardous Bon Accord Spur. From 1943 Eric Johnson, a Norwegian immigrant, operated a packhorse and sled service up the spur to deliver tourists, their luggage and other provisions to the Hotham Heights Chalet on Mt Hotham. Horses were often fitted with improvised snow shoes and he offered his service no matter how brutal the weather, often in the face of fierce blizzards. He eventually quit the route after a number of years and moved his service to Mt Buller. Sadly, he succumbed to illness in 1956, at the age of just 46.

### Take a Break

Liquid treats are served until late at the inviting **Snowline Hotel** (snowlinehotel.com.au), where you can grab a drink, sit on the deck and soak up valley views after a long day in the mountains. The food is highly recommended too, with decent grub on offer. If you have a little too much, there are basic motel-style rooms where you can sleep it all off.

# 47

# Mt Cope

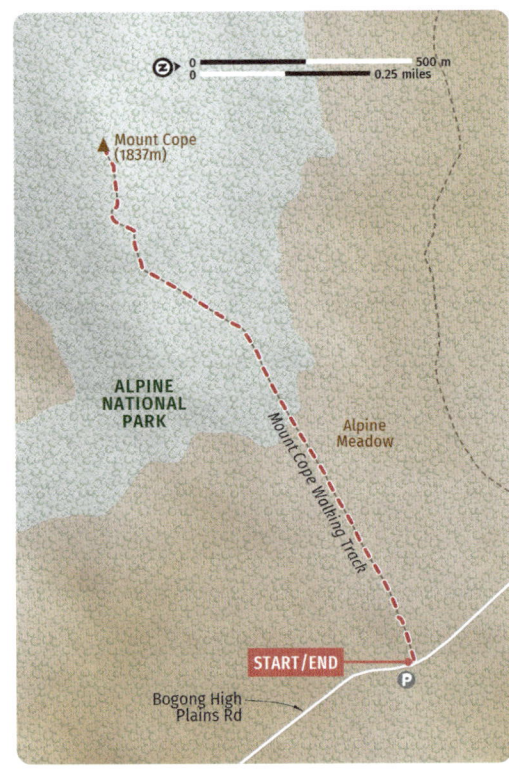

| DURATION | DIFFICULTY | DISTANCE | START/END |
|---|---|---|---|
| 1¼hrs return | Easy | 3.5km | Bogong High Plains Rd |

| TERRAIN | Gently undulating trail across plains with a minor ascent |
|---|---|

For a minor peak Mt Cope packs a punch. Easily accessible off Bogong High Plains Rd, 13.5km southeast of Falls Creek, Mt Cope's low stature belies the panorama that extends over the surrounding plains and valleys. If you're driving the Alpine Discovery Loop between Falls Creek and Omeo, and your time is tight, this delightful short stroll is a good introduction to the Victorian High Country.

A sign indicates the start of the walk. Don't expect a broad path or loads of other walkers here; you're likely to have the mountain to yourself. The **narrow trail** heads southwest from the road but walking is easy and, in summer, wildflowers provide a delightful distraction as you wander across the **alpine meadow**.

The route over the plateau pitches upward just a little on approaching the summit. Calling this a 'mountain' might seem over the top, but **Mt Cope** (pictured) actually tops out at 1837m, making it one of the state's highest peaks. The **boulders** crowning the peak provide views of Victoria's two tallest mountains, Mt Bogong (1986m) and Mt Feathertop (1922m). It's also impossible not to notice the **dead timber** scattered across the region, a stark reminder of bushfires that swept through the High Country in 2003 and 2006–07. Fire licked at the slopes of Mt Cope again in 2020.

Backtrack to the trailhead to end the walk. Moving on, if driving east you're in for a real treat. The **Blue Duck Inn** ((03) 5159 7220) at Anglers Rest, 39km from Mt Cope, is a quaint country pub beside the Cobungra River dating from 1900. It's a mandatory stop for lunch or a post-walk beer, and there are cabins out back if you decide to stay the night.

# Also Try...

GLENN VAN DER KNIJFF ©

## Mt Bogong

| DURATION | DIFFICULTY | DISTANCE |
|---|---|---|
| 7-8hrs return | Hard | 19km |

As befits the highest peak in Victoria, the ascent of Mt Bogong (1986m) is not easy, though the rewards are great.

Thankfully the challenging 1400m ascent is compensated for by the grandstand-like views from the treeless summit. If the weather is cloudy or inclement, leave Mt Bogong for another time; attempt the walk only in the summer months and only if the forecast is for clear and calm weather.

    Mountain Creek Camping Area is the starting point, 14.5km from the town of Mt Beauty. The circuit ascends the mountain along the steep Staircase Spur, diverts along the summit ridge to the large cairn marking the top, then descends Eskdale Spur and Mountain Creek valley. Mt Bogong looks its best under a sparkling mantle of snow and ice, but many lives have been lost on the mountain in winter so at this time it's best left for experienced and suitably equipped adventurers.

## Mt Loch

| DURATION | DIFFICULTY | DISTANCE |
|---|---|---|
| 3hrs return | Easy | 10km |

With views toward Mt Feathertop that perhaps eclipse those from the Razorback, Mt Loch is a worthwhile destination if you don't have the time for the long Razorback & Mt Feathertop walk.

Starting 1km west of Hotham Heights ski village at Mt Loch car park, follow a fire track along the Australian Alps Walking Track (AAWT). The route keeps close to the ridge until the AAWT veers southeast away from the fire track. But stay on the fire track as it swings north and passes just below the summit of Mt Loch, where a short signposted diversion climbs to the top. Capped in volcanic basalt, the 1887m summit offers a wonderful panorama toward Mt Feathertop and the Bogong High Plains.

    Heading back, a detour along the AAWT leads to Derrick Hut (pictured) – a pleasant picnic location amid elegant snow gums – before returning to the car park.

ALIZADA STUDIOS/SHUTTERSTOCK ©

## Mt Abrupt

| DURATION | DIFF | DISTANCE |
|---|---|---|
| 2½hrs return | Moderate | 6.6km |

The brooding mass of Mt Abrupt (pictured) towers above farmlands in the southern Grampians and offers grandstand views of the jagged Serra Range.

A trail begins beside Grampians Rd, 7km north of Dunkeld, and climbs steadily to reach the crest of the Serra Range. Higher up, it's worth noting the amazing work of the track builders who've meticulously sculpted the stone steps that lead rather steeply for the final 500m ascent. Enjoy the panorama from the top (828m) before backtracking to the car park.

## Sugarloaf Peak

| DURATION | DIFF | DISTANCE |
|---|---|---|
| 1.5hrs return | Hard | 1.8km |

In the Cathedral Range near Buxton, Sugarloaf Peak (923m) draws walkers who love to take on this little beast of a hill.

The difficult route involves steep scrambles over exposed slabs, so it's not for young children or the faint-hearted. But if you've got a head for heights and enjoy an exciting challenge, this walk is for you. Impressive views from the summit ridge add to its appeal. From Sugarloaf Saddle, ascend the demanding Wells Cave Track, returning along the easier Canyon Track. Avoid Wells Cave Track if it's wet.

## High Plains Huts

| DURATION | DIFF | DISTANCE |
|---|---|---|
| 2hrs return | Easy | 6km |

One for history buffs, this popular circuit visits two quaint huts without any major hills. A little gem of a walk for a family outing or half-day stroll.

A path departs Bogong High Plains Rd, 10km southeast of Falls Creek, and quickly brings you to Wallace Hut, an 1889 graziers hut with National Trust classification. Continue to Rover Chalet and on to Cope Hut, a 1929 skiers hut still used by outdoor enthusiasts today. The route loops onto Bogong High Plains Rd, then diverts along a foot track back to Wallace Hut before returning to the car park.

Wreck Beach (p194)

# The Prom to the Great Ocean Road

**48** **Lilly Pilly Gully & Mt Bishop**
A lovely forest walk and a fantastic viewpoint. **p184**

**49** **Oberon Bay**
Hit three splendid beaches on this out-and-back walk. **p186**

**50** **Squeaky Beach**
A kid-friendly walk to a stunning bay. **p188**

**51** **Lorne Forests & Waterfalls**
Pass diverse forests and quaint waterfalls on this long walk. **p190**

**52** **Wreck Beach**
See golden sands and shipwreck relics at this secluded beach. **p194**

# Explore

# The Prom to the Great Ocean Road

The vast coastline of Victoria is home to a diverse range of environments and a wealth of walking opportunities. The two best regions are Wilsons Promontory National Park (aka The Prom), a landscape of dramatic granite outcrops and wild coves, while to the west of Melbourne the world-famous Great Ocean Road meanders past waterfalls, rainforests and wave-lashed beaches. These areas are rambler heaven and are home to some of the best-loved walking destinations in the state.

## Foster

If you're looking to stock up on supplies, Foster is the nearest town to Wilsons Promontory. It's not a large place but it does have a selection of eateries, a pub and a couple of supermarkets. Foster also has affordable accommodation, making it an OK base for the Prom provided you have a vehicle; it's a 60km one-way drive to the Tidal River tourist hub at the Prom.

## Tidal River

Not a town but a tourist hub, Tidal River makes a good base for the Wilsons Promontory walks described in this book. There are a selection of accommodation options and a general store selling basic supplies and takeaway food. Staying here is all about convenience and ambience; if you're after a base town with cafes, shops and fuel, head to Foster or look elsewhere.

## Lorne

Lorne is a busy year-round resort town on the Great Ocean Road. The setting is simply beautiful, with forests tumbling down the hillside right onto the outskirts of town and a fine beach beside the main road. It's full of restaurants, cafes and bars, and there's also a large supermarket and a wide range of accommodation options for all budgets. A number of walks start either in town or just a short drive away.

## Apollo Bay

Sleepier than Lorne and surrounded by pastoral countryside, Apollo Bay attracts plenty of tourist traffic. A small town with loads of accommodation and services, it makes a good central base for walks and drives along the Great Ocean Road.

## Port Campbell

Diminutive Port Campbell is a town that's usually packed with tourists, especially during daylight hours when busloads of travellers pop through to visit nearby Loch Ard Gorge and the Twelve Apostles, the Great Ocean Road's most famous drawcard. Despite its size, Port Campbell is a pretty decent base town for the Shipwreck Coast, with accommodation, fuel and food available in abundant supply.

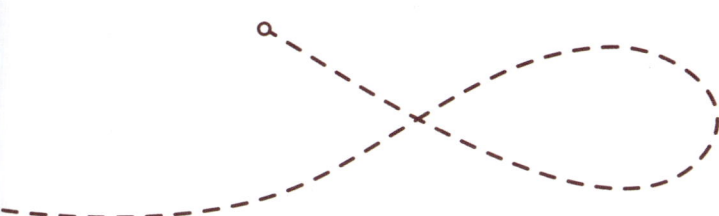

## Resources

**Parks Victoria** (parks.vic.gov.au) Official website for Victoria's national parks.

**Visit Prom Country** (visitpromcountry.com.au) Useful website for information on the Prom and surrounds.

**Great Ocean Road** (visitgreatoceanroad.org.au) Everything you need to know about the road and associated sights, walks and services.

**I Am Lorne** (iamlorne.com.au) Lorne's homepage, with links to accommodation, sights, walks and waterfalls.

**I Am Apollo Bay** (visitapollobay.com) Loads of information on sleeping, eating, sights and walks.

**I Am 12 Apostles** (visit12apostles.com.au) Main tourist website for the Twelve Apostles and Port Campbell.

**Walk 91** (walk91.com.au) Can help with equipment hire, transport, itineraries and shuttles for outings along the Great Ocean Walk.

 ## When to Go

Walking anywhere along Victoria's coast is best done in spring to autumn, with November to May being the peak, but for beach walking the warmer summer months are ideal. The coast can be wet any time of the year, but pick a nice day in winter or spring and you have the chance of viewing waterfalls at their best. For all popular seaside areas book accommodation well in advance, particularly for peak weekends, public holidays and school summer holidays.

 ## Where to Stay

Despite the lack of nearby towns to Wilsons Promontory, there is a large variety of sleeping options – from basic caravan parks to upmarket homestays – in the triangle between Fish Creek, Foster and Yanakie. At Wilsons Promontory itself, nothing beats staying at central **Tidal River** (parks.vic.gov.au/where-to-stay), where you'll find basic camp sites, rustic huts and 'wilderness retreats'.

Along the Great Ocean Road, the plethora of sleeping options is overwhelming. Suffice to say, everything and anything is available, and many options have picturesque locations beside beaches, rivers or forests. For convenience, the tranquil riverside and seaside **Lorne Foreshore Caravan Park** (lornecaravanpark.com.au) is hard to beat.

 ## What's On

**Great Ocean Road Running Festival** (greatoceanroadrunfest.com.au; ⏲ May) This festival includes a marathon between Lorne and Apollo Bay. Road closures affect travel along the Great Ocean Road.

**Falls Festival** (fallsfestival.com; ⏲ Dec) Annual multi-day music festival usually held on a local farm surrounded by rainforest.

 ## Transport

Foster and towns along the Great Ocean Road are well-linked to **V/Line** (vline.com.au) public transport. A few buses a day run from Melbourne (Southern Cross Station) to Foster. For Great Ocean Road destinations, trains run frequently from Melbourne to Geelong, where buses connect passengers to destinations including Lorne, Apollo Bay and Port Campbell. As with most walking areas in Victoria, having your own vehicle or rental car will give you flexibility to get from the hub towns to trailheads. Tickets for trains and buses are available from **Public Transport Victoria** (ptv.vic.gov.au). Car rental is best organised in Melbourne.

# 48

# Lilly Pilly Gully & Mt Bishop

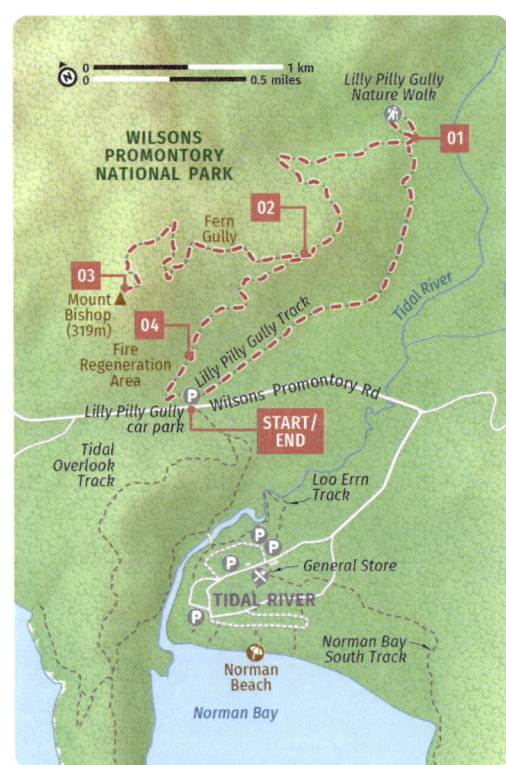

| DURATION | DIFFICULTY | DISTANCE | START/END |
|---|---|---|---|
| 3hrs return | Moderate | 10km | Lilly Pilly Gully car park |

| TERRAIN | Good tracks & steady climb, no steps |
|---|---|

Magnificent stands of eucalypt, an unexpected rainforest, fluorescent-green fern gullies and one of Wilsons Promontory National Park's best viewpoints are the attractions of this popular circuit, probably the top forest walk at the Prom. The park protects a huge variety of flora, and the slopes of Mt Bishop and Lilly Pilly Gully support some great stands and mixtures of woodland. At only 10km and with generally gradual ascents, this outing suits most moderately fit walkers.

## Getting Here

Wilsons Promontory is 200km southeast of Melbourne, while Tidal River – the park's tourist hub – is a further 29km south of the park entrance. There is no public transport to the Prom.

## Starting Point

Lilly Pilly Gully car park is 26.5km from the entrance station, just before Tidal River. The walk starts at the lower end of the car park.

**01** A broad path heads east, passing through stunted forest at the base of Mt Bishop at first, then through groves of **taller forest** as you approach Lilly Pilly Gully. Interpretive signs along the route highlight many interesting facets of the Prom. You'll reach **Lilly Pilly Gully Nature Walk** (pictured), a 600m boardwalk and interpretive loop through a pocket of rainforest, after 2.1km. The loop is particularly interesting and informative signs highlight the **warm temperate rainforest** that survives in this locale, the most southerly example of such forest in Australia.

## Tasmania Land Link

During the last ice age, the hills forming the backbone of the Prom were part of a greater range of peaks, known as the Bunurong Range, that stretched from Wilsons Promontory to the northeastern tip of Tasmania, providing a contiguous land link. When sea levels rose after the ice age, low-lying areas were engulfed, leaving the peaks of Wilson Promontory and the islands of the Furneaux Group, including Flinders Island and Cape Barren Island, protruding above the sea.

**02** The route climbs for the first time, wending its way up the eastern flank of the ridge connecting Mt Bishop to Mt Leonard. Thankfully, this is one of the rare walks where there are few, if any steps, to negotiate. The forest opens up a little as the route ascends, with fleeting glimpses through the trees of **Mt Oberon** and the taller **Mt Ramsey** across the valley. A signpost indicates the point where the out-and-back track to Mt Bishop heads off the main path.

**03** The track climbs gradually up the hillside, passing a **glorious fern gully**, and eventually tops out on the ridge just prior to reaching Mt Bishop. Not really a mountain at all, **Mt Bishop** (319m) is really just a prominent outcrop of boulders on a major ridge leading to Mt Leonard but it offers an excellent perch to take in views of the Prom's west coast. The breathtaking scene includes **Tidal River**, **Norman Bay** and the white sands of **Squeaky Beach**, and in many ways is better than the views from Mt Oberon.

**04** Head back down to the track junction and bear right for the final 1.5km to the car park through forest still rejuvenating following a bushfire in 2009. To highlight the capacity of Australian flora to recover after fire, one **information panel** near the end of the walk shows a photo taken from that location immediately after the 2009 bushfire razed the area. It's hard to fathom that the photo was taken in the same location, such is the regeneration that's taken place.

 **Take a Break**

At nearby Tidal River, the **General Store** stocks a basic range of supermarket-type goods as well as souvenirs and takeaway food. It also has a small coffee counter that does brewed coffee and other drinks, and outdoor tables are good for watching the comings and goings at the camping ground.

# 49

# Oberon Bay

| DURATION | DIFFICULTY | DISTANCE | START/END |
|---|---|---|---|
| 4-5hrs return | Moderate | 16.5km | Tidal River Visitor Centre |

| TERRAIN | Good tracks, beach strolling; few climbs |
|---|---|

In a region of myriad bays and beaches, this jaunt ticks off three magnificent yet very different beaches all as part of a longish – but not at all difficult – coastal walk. Though there is little shade anywhere along this walk, a nearly constant breeze blows along the shore here, helping to keep you cool on even the hottest days. If it is warm, bring a hat, loads of sunscreen and perhaps even a beach towel.

## Getting Here
Wilsons Promontory National Park is 200km southeast of Melbourne, while the Tidal River tourist hub is a further 29km south of the park entrance. There is no public transport to the park.

## Starting Point
The walk starts just west of the visitor centre near a toilet block. The track is signed 'Norman Bay South' and 'Oberon Bay'.

**01** The route heads immediately into a large belt of **tea trees** but the walking is easy as the path tunnels through the thickest sections. Cross a road and continue to the southern end of **Norman Beach**, where a path heads towards Oberon Bay. Views of Norman Beach soon appear before the track climbs over a ridge separating Norman Bay from **Little Oberon Bay**. Pass the Norman Point side track and swing east to reach the wild beach and rough waters of Little Oberon Bay. The beach is a stunner, a mix of glistening white sand bookended by rocky headlands, and if the sun is shining you'll need sunglasses. But note while the water may look inviting it's far too dangerous for swimming.

## Disaster Magnet

In recent decades Wilsons Promontory has had more than its fair share of natural disasters. A bushfire in 2005 led to the evacuation of over 600 people from the park. Then, in 2009, lightning started a bushfire that scorched 25,000 hectares of forest and heath – half of the entire park. To exacerbate the damage, in 2011 around 370mm of rain fell in a 24-hour period, washing away hillsides and flooding valleys. Evidence of these events is all around; dead tree skeletons are a stark reminder of fire, while eroded gullies and landslips are scars from the 2011 downpour.

**Best for**

**A COOLING SWIM**

**02** At the far end of the beach the path rises onto a shelf where a sign points the way to Oberon Bay. The sign reads 'Oberon Bay Camp 2km' but don't be fooled: it's close to 2km to Oberon Bay but actually 3km to the Oberon Bay camp site. Remove your shoes on arrival at **Oberon Bay** (pictured) – you'll need to anyway to cross Growler Creek – and meander south, dipping your toes into the gentle surf. The beach is broad and serene, and more secluded the further south you go. If the water is not too frigid, consider a dip in the generally shallow surf, but be aware that no beaches at the Prom are patrolled.

**03** On reaching **Frasers Creek** near a **prominent sand dune**, a track heads inland to the **Oberon Bay camp site**. There is a toilet here beside a large patch of grass, while the camp sites are a short walk inland. There is some shade beneath nearby tea trees, making this a **good picnic location**.

**04** Make your way back to the southern end of Norman Beach, but instead of returning to the visitor centre, walk first along the beach to **Tidal River**. This tea-stained stream is coloured with tannins from decomposing flora upstream. Though it looks dirty it's actually sparkling clean and OK for a dip.

**05** Wander upstream until you approach a **footbridge**. The river will block your progress, so head towards the **camping ground** along any of the tracks south of the river, and cut through the camp to return to the visitor centre.

## Take a Break

The nearest source of nourishment is at Tidal River's **General Store**, but this walk is ideally suited to a picnic lunch at the Oberon Bay camp site. If you can't provide your own lunch, buy goodies at Tidal River and bring them with you.

# 50
# Squeaky Beach

| DURATION | DIFFICULTY | DISTANCE | START/END |
|---|---|---|---|
| 2½hrs return | Easy | 10.1km | Tidal River Visitor Centre |

| TERRAIN | Well-formed trails & beach walking with only minor ascents |
|---|---|

For many visitors, their first incursion into Wilsons Promontory National Park is to Squeaky Beach, and it's easy to understand why. The beach is one of the park's most adored features and also one of its most beautiful. The white sands are blinding in the sun and riddled with quartz, rubbing under your toes to create the 'squeak' sound the beach is famous for. Easily completed in a half-day, this ramble is within the capabilities of most walkers and is ideal for children.

## Getting Here
Tidal River tourist complex is 230km from Melbourne, and 29km south of the park entrance. There is no public transport to the park.

## Starting Point
Locate the Loo Errn Boardwalk at the eastern end of the car park opposite the visitor centre.

**01** Wander along the **Loo Errn Boardwalk** to **Tidal River**, a tannin-stained creek that meanders toward the coast. One **tranquil pool** beside the boardwalk reflects riverside tea trees and Mt Bishop across the valley; if you can, visit early in the morning to appreciate this spot at its best.

**02** The boardwalk ends at a **footbridge** and on the far side a track is signed to Squeaky Beach. The path weaves along the hillside above Tidal River for 15 minutes, offering views of Tidal River and **Norman Bay**, to reach a **track junction** on the crest of the ridge extending to Pillar Point. Take note of this point: the return route heads along the signed Tidal Overlook Circuit.

## Staying at the Prom

Staying at the Prom is a highlight for many travellers. Thankfully there is a range of accommodation options at Tidal River, though getting a place for the night is another thing, particularly between January and March and the busy holiday periods such as Easter. A ballot system is used for making camp site bookings during the peak Christmas and January period, and the ballot opens in the preceding June. At other times, early bookings are essential and can be made up to 12 months prior to your planned arrival. Bookings and further information can be found through **Parks Victoria** (parks.vic.gov.au/where-to-stay) or **Tidal River Visitor Centre**.

**03** Veer left and you'll shortly pass another junction, where the direction to Squeaky Beach is clearly marked. The route passes a minor lookout then loops across the north side of the headland forming Pillar Point, where a **magnificent vista** over low coastal scrub toward Leonard Bay and Squeaky Beach presents itself. The track descends past **rock platforms** and one particularly **large boulder**, split in half by the forces of nature; kids will love scrambling around here. It's now just a few steps to the sands of **Squeaky Beach**. There is no shade but if the water is calm it's not a bad place for a swim, though you're unlikely to have the beach to yourself; children from all over Victoria visit Wilsons Promontory National Park as part of official school camps.

**04** Stroll to the far end of the beach to a **small creek and boulder outcrop**, which makes a pleasant place to have a break and another area for kids to play.

**05** Head back toward the car park along the outward route, but on reaching the ridge between Leonard and Norman Bays deviate onto **Tidal Overlook Circuit** (pictured). This alternative route climbs to a viewpoint – the **Tidal Overlook** – which was built in memory of park rangers and workers from all over the world who've lost their lives while on duty. Back on the trail the route weaves through dry forest then swings around the hillside back to the Tidal River footbridge and onto Loo Errn Boardwalk.

 **Take a Break**

The park has little choice when it comes to eateries, but a basic range of supermarket-type food can be obtained from the **General Store** at the Tidal River tourist complex. Sharing the same building is a takeaway store and cafe counter selling brewed coffee and limited other goodies.

# 51

# Lorne Forests & Waterfalls

**Best for**

**WILDLIFE**

| DURATION | DIFFICULTY | DISTANCE | START/END |
|---|---|---|---|
| 5-6hrs return | Moderate | 17.5km | Sheoak Picnic Area |

| TERRAIN | Undulating trails, some steep ascents |
|---|---|

In a region blessed with more than its fair share of natural attractions, this full-day outing takes walkers on a circuitous route to some of Lorne's best waterfalls and forests. Admittedly the walk is made harder by virtue of its length, but with such a variety of geological features on offer, and with the bonus of being readily accessible from the centre of Lorne, it's an excellent introduction to Great Otway National Park. Any time of year is suitable, but winter and spring provide the best opportunities to see the waterfalls flowing at their most magnificent.

## Getting Here

Sitting seaside on the Great Ocean Road, Lorne is 145km southwest of Melbourne. Sheoak Picnic Area is 4km west of Lorne, accessed from Allenvale Rd, and can be reached by vehicle, on foot or by local taxi.

## Starting Point

The path signed 'The Canyon' starts at the northern end of the delightful Sheoak Picnic Area, near the picnic tables.

**01** Departing **Sheoak Picnic Area** the path immediately passes through a **wonderful section of forest** and tree ferns, and crosses a timber footbridge. Cut across Allenvale Rd and Sharps Track in quick succession, then descend first to **Won Wondah Falls**, and shortly after **Henderson Falls** (along a short side track; pictured p193).

**02** The track continues towards the **Canyon** (pictured left), an unusual little gorge comprising small cliffs and boulders that looks out of place among the forest and quite different from other features seen locally. At the far end of the Canyon the route squeezes through boulders to emerge onto a good trail. The way ahead begins as a descent along a foot track, then an old vehicle track, towards Phantom Falls.

**03** Joining a more significant path, the route immediately comes to the short side track to the base of **Phantom Falls**. If the weather gods are on your side, recent rainfall will ensure that flows in St George River are high, creating a crashing waterfall. In drier times, the falls may be just a trickle. Phantom Falls is one of the taller waterfalls near Lorne.

**04** Return to the top of the falls and push on towards Allenvale. The main route is easy for five minutes but soon begins a descent, steeply at first, above **St George River**. The grade soon eases and the route eventually reaches the bucolic pastures and apple orchard at **Allenvale**. There is private property here, sometimes selling local produce, but the clearly marked trail guides walkers around the orchard before crossing the river to reach **Allenvale Mill car park**.

**05** There's no easy way to avoid the next section, an uninteresting but thankfully easy 2km walk along Allenvale Rd back to **Sheoak Picnic Area**. Having looped back to the starting point, covering 8.5km along the way, this makes an ideal place for a **picnic lunch**. The facilities here are excellent, including toilets and a large shelter. Another viable alternative for lunch is to visit **Qdos**, just a few minutes' drive back along Allenvale Rd. If you started the walk late and time has got the better of you, or if you've simply had enough, you also have the option to finish the walk here. We'd recommend pushing on, though, given the sights in store ahead.

## Iconic Coastal Drive

The beaches and waterfalls of the Otway region were already tourist attractions by the 1890s, but in the early 1900s much of the coast west of Lorne was difficult to reach. Construction began on a coastal road in 1919, to be built in memory of soldiers who fought in WWI. By the time the **Great Ocean Road** opened in 1932 around 3000 men had worked on the project, many themselves returned servicemen, and the road became recognised as the world's largest war memorial. Included on the Australian National Heritage List, the road is now renowned as one of the world's great coastal drives.

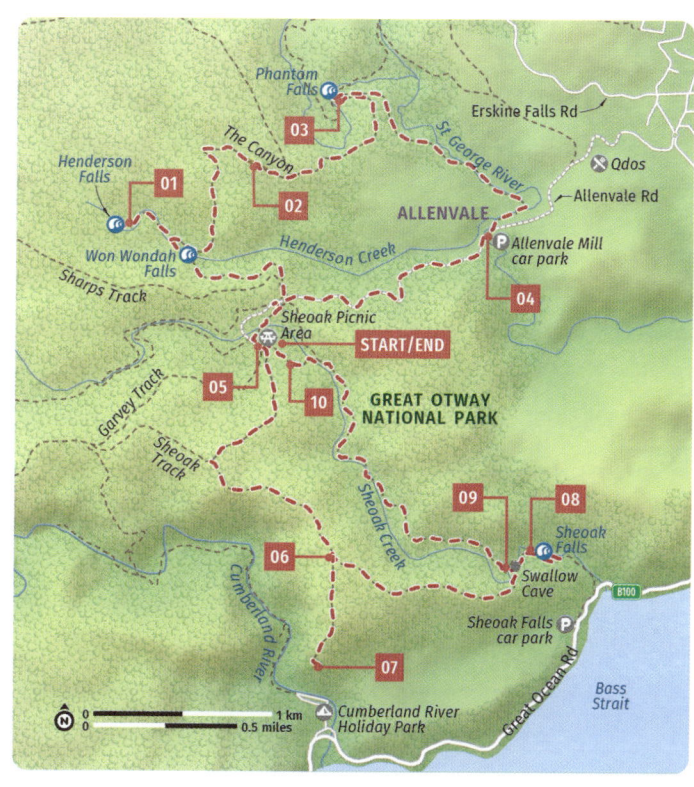

**06** At the southern end of the picnic area continue on an old management track, leaving lush forest behind as the track climbs steeply through **dry forest** in the direction of Castle Rock, eventually levelling out as you approach **Sheoak Track**. Turn left onto Sheoak Track 1km from the picnic area and within 15 minutes of easy strolling you'll arrive at the Castle Rock track junction.

**07** There is a steep descent to the viewpoint at **Castle Rock**, hovering on the edge of a cliff face, but don't miss it; the outlook here over the **Cumberland River** towards the ocean is impressive. The camping ground you see below you, **Cumberland River Holiday Park** (cumberlandriver.com.au), is set in an idyllic location and is one of the more spectacularly sited camping grounds along the entire Great Ocean Road. Backtrack to the junction on Sheoak Track and bear east, where the route descends steadily, soon joining a foot track.

**08** The path drops towards **Sheoak Creek**, joining a more heavily used track above a set of cascades. Before heading back to Sheoak Picnic Area, pop down the track to the base of **Sheoak Falls** first, 10 minutes away, where the creek spills over a ledge into a pool below. The Great Ocean Road is a mere 500m away, so you're likely to see other walkers here. Head back up the track and continue towards Swallow Cave and Sheoak Picnic Area.

**09** Sheoak Creek is soon crossed in a pretty little valley and there are large **stepping stones** to help keep your feet dry. If water levels are high, you may need to grab a stick for support, or avoid the crossing altogether if the creek is in spate. Immediately after the crossing a quick detour to **Swallow Cave**, a little down-valley beside the river, is recommended; with luck, you may see swallows making the cave their home, particularly during the spring nesting season.

**10** The day's jaunt finishes with a 2.5km walk through a lovely valley, amid increasingly **verdant forest** as you walk upstream. Nearing Sheoak Picnic Area the route veers onto **Sheoak Nature Walk**, the path at times passing beautiful tree ferns under a canopy of towering eucalypts.

## A Bygone Industry

You may have noticed information boards along the walk highlighting relics from a 19th-century timber operation. Realising the potential of the forests of the Otways region, loggers arrived in the 1850s and set to work felling the valuable tall trees and building a network of tramways and other infrastructure to help transport the logs from the forests to the mills. Logging quickly became the area's main industry, but tourism and farming gradually took over as sources of income, and thankfully logging of these wonderful forests has now ceased. This period of history is not forgotten entirely, and many of the old tramway easements are put to good use today as walking trails.

## Take a Break

On the way to Sheoak Picnic Area you'll drive right past **Qdos** (qdosarts.com) on Allenvale Rd, an excellent venue in a lovely forest setting to kick-start your day and set you in the right mood for a walk. Qdos serves a variety of breakfast offerings, a selection of sweet goodies and decent coffee. It's a great place to relax, load up on calories and take in the sights and smells of the forest before heading into the Great Otway National Park. Its centrepiece gallery isn't half bad, either.

# 52
# Wreck Beach

| DURATION | DIFFICULTY | DISTANCE | START/END |
|---|---|---|---|
| 1½hrs | Easy | 6.1km | The Gables car park |

| TERRAIN | Easy path, beach walking; some steps |
|---|---|

While ticking off a small section of the long-distance Great Ocean Walk (GOW), this outstanding walk's real highlights are the golden sands and shipwreck artefacts of Wreck Beach (pictured). The walk is within the capabilities of most walkers but be prepared to battle the unrelenting beach-access steps, nearly 400 of them. Given its beauty and historical interest, it's quite remarkable that Wreck Beach isn't one of the Great Ocean Road's iconic sights…yet.

A 10-minute amble from the car park leads to the **Gables Lookout**, for fine views over coastal bluffs toward **Moonlight Head**. Backtracking a little, the route heads west onto the GOW to reach a signposted junction, where the steps to **Wreck Beach** descend to the west. The **sublime seashore** here, part of the Shipwreck Coast, is perfect for wandering, so if the tide is out mosey northwest to the **rusting relics** of the *Marie Gabrielle*, visible in the distance, then continue a little further to the anchor of the *Fiji*. Don't be tempted to walk through to Moonlight Beach and beyond at low tide, as Parks Victoria warns against it.

Return to the top of the steps, gather your breath and consider your options. The outward route back to the Gables car park is worth considering in hot weather as there may be a little shade. For a more circuitous route turn left onto the GOW to quickly reach **Wreck Beach car park**, from where you can follow the gravel Wreck Beach Rd. The coastal scenery is pleasant rather than epic, but the road offers easy walking and soon joins Moonlight Head Rd. Turn right, pay your respects as you pass by pint-sized **Moonlight Head Cemetery**, and within a few minutes you'll return to Gables car park.

Best for

SOLITUDE

# Also Try...

GLENN VAN DER KNIJFF ©

## Southern Prom Circuit

| DURATION | DIFFICULTY | DISTANCE |
|---|---|---|
| 4-5 days return | Moderate | 64.5km |

Wilsons Promontory National Park's classic multiday walk, this journey takes in some of the area's finest beaches and coves, and there is a real wilderness feel along much of the route.

As most of the sights are not within reach of day walkers, you're likely to encounter only other overnight hikers along the majority of this walk, and the feeling of seclusion is palpable. Beginning at Telegraph Saddle the walk passes Sealers Cove, Waterloo Bay, historic Wilsons Promontory Lightstation, South Point and Oberon Bay before ending at the Tidal River visitor hub. In peak summer months the trail (pictured) is busy, and the section from Telegraph Saddle to Sealers Cove and Waterloo Bay is particularly popular. Book camp sites well in advance at parks.vic.gov.au/stay or by phone. Walkers need a permit, obtainable from Tidal River Visitor Centre.

## Great Ocean Walk

| DURATION | DIFFICULTY | DISTANCE |
|---|---|---|
| 8 days one-way | Moderate | 100km |

The most popular multiday walk along the Great Ocean Road and one of Victoria's 'Icon' walks, the Great Ocean Walk (GOW) is an exciting trek from Apollo Bay to the Twelve Apostles, the region's most famous geological feature.

If you have time to spare, the right gear and suitable experience, the GOW offers an unforgettable adventure through towering rainforest, coastal hinterland, windswept clifftops, rocky headlands and deserted beaches. The only restrictions on walkers are that they must travel east to west and there are limits on the size of walking parties due to availability of tent sites at some of the bushwalker camps. Detailed information on the GOW can be found at greatoceanwalk.com.au, and camp site bookings – mandatory for walkers using overnight camping areas – can be made at parkstay.vic.gov.au/great-ocean-walk-bookings or by phone.

GLENN VAN DER KNIJFF ©

## Mt Oberon

| DURATION | DIFF | DISTANCE |
|---|---|---|
| 2hrs return | Moderate | 6.4km |

Of all the peaks at Wilsons Promontory, Mt Oberon (558m) is the one that's on most people's hit list.

It stands like a beacon above Tidal River and is capped in granite boulders providing a bird's-eye view over Norman Bay, Pillar Point and the peaks of the southern Prom. The ascent itself isn't too hard, with a steady but not excessive gradient along a management track for most of the way. The walk starts at Telegraph Saddle but the car park fills up quickly so in peak times the park runs a free shuttle from Tidal River.

## Lower Kalimna Falls

| DURATION | DIFF | DISTANCE |
|---|---|---|
| 2hrs return | Easy | 5.8km |

In an area known for its plethora of waterfalls, Lower Kalimna Falls stands out as perhaps the most appealing of them all.

Though only small (6m), Kalimna Creek leaps over a chamber eroded into the rock and dives into a pool below. Beginning at Sheoak Picnic Area, the walk follows the remnants of an 1860s-era tramway easement, a vestige of a once-thriving timber industry. The route continues up a shallow valley, passing through verdant forest generally close to bubbling Sheoak Creek. There are some side tracks but the route is clearly signposted.

## Gibson Beach

| DURATION | DIFF | DISTANCE |
|---|---|---|
| 1hr return | Easy | 3km |

While the beach facing the Twelve Apostles is out of reach to walkers, at nearby Gibson Beach (pictured) you can get close to two equally picturesque sea stacks, Gog and Magog.

Steps descend the coastal cliffs from Gibson Steps car park to the shore from where – assuming the tide is not in – you can walk from one end of the beach to the other. Even when the tide is ebbing, you may need to remove your shoes to duck around the boulders that litter the sands. Don't contemplate swimming here; this beach is for selfies and strolling only.

**Wineglass Bay (p208)**

# Tasmania's Highlands & Coastlines

**53** **Dove Lake Circuit**
Loop around this photogenic lake at the foot of Cradle Mountain. **p202**

**54** **leeawuleena/Lake St Clair**
Hike the final day of the Overland Track – a forest ramble around Australia's deepest lake. **p204**

**55** **Cataract Gorge Adventure**
Explore Launceston's gorgeous gorge, with surprises both artificial and natural. **p206**

**56** **Wineglass Bay & Hazards Beach**
Visit the famous golden goblet, returning via sheltered sands and craggy coastline. **p208**

**57** **Organ Pipes Circuit**
Lose an afternoon exploring the flanks of Hobart's marvellous kunanyi/Mt Wellington. **p210**

**58** **Cape Hauy**
Join the Three Capes Track hikers on a jaunt to this spectacular cliff-edge cape. **p214**

**59** **Crescent Bay**
Discover this hidden white-sand gem not far from the Port Arthur Historic Site. **p216**

**60** **South Cape Bay**
Forget your deadlines and responsibilities on this trek to a primal stretch of coastline. **p218**

# Explore
# Tasmania's Highlands & Coastlines

Tasmania and bushwalking go together like socks and hiking boots, Hobart and history, oysters and chilled sauvignon blanc... The island's pristine wilderness and sublime hiking trails have been well and truly discovered by the rest of the world, but you can still find solitude here amid ancient landscapes in remote edge-of-the-planet locations.

## Hobart

Backed by impressive kunanyi/Mt Wellington on the shores of the slate-grey Derwent River, Tasmania's historic capital (population 224,000) is booming, riding a tourism-charged wave of affluence and opportunity. Fabulous food is everywhere, the festival calendar is full and the harbourside pubs and bars are kickin' after dark. Hobart is the perfect base for walks across the southern half of the state. The west coast and Lake St Clair are also more accessible from the south than the north of the island.

## Launceston

In the state's north on the kanamaluka/Tamar River banks, Tasmania's second city (population 87,330) is a quietly endearing place. Well-preserved architecture, an effervescent student population and plenty of good places to eat and drink make it a fun place to hang out as you explore the walks around the island's north. Cradle Mountain is a two-hour drive from 'Lonnie', while the northern half of the east coast is more accessible from here than from Hobart.

## Bicheno

If you're planning a walk on the east coast (who doesn't want to see Wineglass Bay?), Bicheno (population 950) is an unpretentious fishing town that manages to sidestep the glitzier tourist trappings of nearby Swansea and Coles Bay. The beaches and seafood here are superb, and there are plenty of low-key places to stay.

## When to Go

Summer in Tasmania (December to February) means warm days and long evenings – perfect walking weather. The shoulder months (October, November, March and April) can also be mild, but rain is much more likely. Only the hardiest, most experienced of souls contemplate walking anywhere here in winter (June to August), but if you do you'll have the trails all to yourself!

## Where to Stay

Tasmanian accommodation covers all the bases, from rudimentary caravan parks and city backpacker joints to midrange motels, international chain hotels and high-end

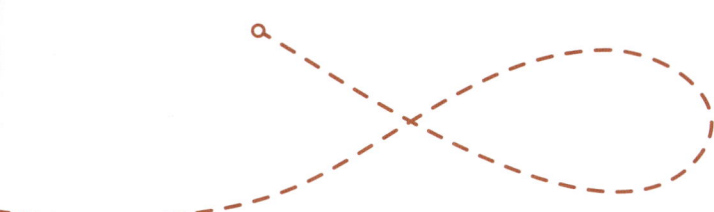

boutique resorts in glorious natural settings. Airbnbs are also plentiful. Location is key: pick a town near your walk and see what's on offer. Book early and expect a serious price spike over summer, especially in Hobart and Launceston, even for the most modest of caravan-park cabins. See discovertasmania.com.au/where-to-stay for listings.

## 👍 What's On

Tasmanian winters are chilly: it's no surprise that most of the key festivals here happen over summer. As summer is also prime walking season, book your beds well in advance. That said, there's a new breed of Tasmanian festivals that celebrate, rather than spurn, the island's Gothic winter darkness.

**MONA FOMA** (mofo.net.au; 🕒 Jan) Hobart's Museum of Old & New Art (MONA) extends the love to Launceston with this edgy festival of music and art (FOMA).

**Cygnet Folk Festival** (cygnetfolkfestival.org; 🕒 Jan) Three-day hippie fiesta in the southeast: good vibes, low-key performances and workshops.

**Festivale** (festivale.com.au; 🕒 Feb) Launceston's City Park hosts three days of eating, drinking and entertainment.

**Ten Days on the Island** (tendays.org.au; 🕒 Mar) The island's premier arts event, running biennially (odd-numbered years).

**A Taste of the Huon** (atasteofthehuon.com.au; 🕒 Mar) A celebration of fine food and wine in the Huon Valley, in the fertile southeast.

**Dark MOFO** (darkmofo.net.au; 🕒 Jun) In the cold depths of winter, MONA's Dark MOFO delivers a noir package of unhinged, seductive and joyful happenings.

**Sydney to Hobart Yacht Race** (rolexsydneyhobart.com; 🕒 Dec) The world's most arduous open-ocean yacht race heads for Hobart. The arrival celebrations are totally OTT.

**Taste of Tasmania** (tasmania.com/events/taste-of-tasmania; 🕒 Dec/Jan) Tasmania's big-ticket culinary event, Hobart's week-long 'Taste' is a frenzied food fest around New Year's Eve.

## ✈️ Transport

Daily direct domestic flights from Sydney and Melbourne (and sometimes Adelaide and Brisbane) jet into Hobart and Launceston. Alternatively, the twin *Spirit of Tasmania* ferries cross paths (literally ships in the night!) as they chug between Melbourne and Devonport. Bring your own car on the ferry, or hire one at the airport and head for the wilds.

## Resources

**Tasmania Parks & Wildlife Service** (parks.tas.gov.au) Extensive info on Tasmanian parks, reserves and activities, plus online parks pass bookings. Check out the '60 Great Short Walks' listings.

**Tourism Tasmania** (discovertasmania.com) Extensive activity and operator listings; click on 'What to Do' then 'Outdoors and Adventure'.

**Great Walks of Tasmania** (greatwalkstasmania.com) A collective of eight operators running private guided bushwalks.

**TasTrails** (tastrails.com) More than 100 walk listings around Tasmania, with notes and maps.

**Bureau of Meteorology** (bom.gov.au/tas) Tasmanian weather is notoriously fickle: check the forecast before you wander into the wilds.

**Greater Hobart Trails** (greaterhobarttrails.com.au) Walks in and around Hobart.

**LISTmap** (maps.thelist.tas.gov.au) Online topographic maps.

# 53

# Dove Lake Circuit

| DURATION | DIFFICULTY | DISTANCE | START/END |
|---|---|---|---|
| 2-3hrs return | Easy | 6km | Dove Lake car park, Cradle Mt |

| TERRAIN | Lakeside boardwalks, good dirt trails |
|---|---|

One of Australia's top-rated day walks, this lake loop in the wilds of Cradle Mountain-Lake St Clair National Park is an essential Tasmanian experience. Immerse yourself in a landscape of ancient alpine plants, white-quartz beaches, tannin-stained waters and heaven-sent mountain views. It's the walk that everybody clamours to do here, so be prepared for some company along the trail (get here early if you can).

## Getting Here

Cradle Mountain is 150km west of Launceston (a two-hour drive), or 78km from Devonport (one hour).

## Starting Point

Free shuttle buses run from the Cradle Mountain visitor info centre (pay your park fees here) to Dove Lake car park (which has toilets) every 15 minutes. Or you can drive here outside peak times.

**01** At the **Dove Lake car park** (did you spy any wombats around Ronny Creek on the way here?), scribble your name in the walkers' log, then head off around the western side of the lake. You can walk in a clockwise direction, too – either way, look forward to a **picture-postcard view of Cradle Mountain** across the rippling lake. It's a well-made, level gravel trail for the most part with plenty of boardwalks, moving through alpine heath, buttongrass and pink mountain berry bushes.

**02** About 10 minutes into the walk, the trail ducks down to a ramshackle old **boatshed** on the shore. Built from rough-cut King Billy

## Cradle Mountain

Aside from the mandatory loop around Dove Lake (pictured), Cradle Mountain offers many other excellent walks. Grab a map from the visitor centre and shuffle along the 45-minute return stroll to **Knyvet Falls**, the three-hour return hike along the **Cradle Valley Boardwalk** to the Overland Track trailhead, or the six- to eight-hour-return **Cradle Mountain Summit** hike – a tough but spectacular climb with incredible views in fine weather. As always in the Tasmanian high country, be prepared for snow and 100km/h winds in midsummer, or warm sunshine and twittering birds in the depths of winter.

LIZ MILLER/SHUTTERSTOCK ©

pine by the national park's first ranger in 1940, it's an impossibly photogenic structure: pause to snap the mandatory **boatshed-and-mountain photo**. Back on the trail, views extend to the craggy slopes and little beaches across the water.

**03** Beyond a gentle rise near the far end of the lake (the **picnic bench** here is perfect for, well, a picnic), the trail enters the **Ballroom Forest**. This moss-covered thicket of myrtle beech is hushed and magical – a dense pocket of rainforest interwoven with an elevated boardwalk. Beyond the trees at the base of Cradle Mountain (which seems somehow smaller here), the boardwalk takes a dramatic turn, suspended out over a cliff edge as it wraps itself around the lake.

**04** Heading back around Dove Lake's eastern shore, the vegetation becomes thicker and the atmosphere more dank: look for crimson waratah blooms and spiky pandani trees. Not far offshore, the small, shrub-cloaked **Honeymoon Islands** add to the sense that humans are an incongruous presence here...and that the wilderness will always prevail. As the car park comes back into view, detour to the lookout platform atop **Glacier Rock**. This huge quartz boulder is scarred with grooves from the glacier that formed Dove Lake – a reminder of the primal forces that shaped this exquisite part of the planet.

 **Take a Break**

Most of the hotels, lodges and wilderness resorts along Cradle Mountain Rd have in-house cafes and/or restaurants. The pick of the bunch is probably **Hellyers Restaurant** (cradlevillage.com.au), at Cradle Mountain Wilderness Village, where small plates come with big views over Cradle Valley and the treetops.

# 54

# leeawuleena/ Lake St Clair

| DURATION | DIFFICULTY | DISTANCE | START/END |
|---|---|---|---|
| 5-6hrs one-way | Moderate | 17.5km | Lake St Clair Visitor Info Centre |

| TERRAIN | Rough lakeside trail through dense, damp forest |
|---|---|

Don't have the time to hike the entire Overland Track? More sightseer than mountaineer? Tackle the final day of the 'OT' as a day walk, skirting around the western edge of shimmering leeawuleena/Lake St Clair, Australia's deepest lake. The boat ride to the lake's northern end is a fun way to get your bearings, before you strike out back around the thickly forested shore, heading south.

## Getting Here

It's a 178km drive to Lake St Clair from Hobart (2½ hours) – an easier drive than from the north of the state.

## Starting Point

Lake St Clair Visitor Information Centre has parking, a national parks desk (buy your parks pass here), toilets and a cafe. Park fees apply.

**01** **Lake St Clair Visitor Information Centre** is at the southern end of the lake at tranquil Cynthia Bay. Check in for your pre-booked ferry ride (lakestclairlodge.com.au) at the reception desk in the cafe; the jetty is a short walk beyond the big Overland Track sign. Chugging across the misty lake, the 25-minute ride to **Narcissus Bay** is super-scenic. Weary Overland Track walkers tend to bypass the final day's walk around the lake and catch the ferry back from Narcissus instead – but they miss an intimate encounter with leeawuleena, the Tommeginne name for Lake St Clair, meaning 'sleeping water'. It's 170m deep (some estimates suggest 200m); the trout here certainly do sleep deeply.

## Overland Track

Tasmania's Overland Track, arguably the most famous multiday walk in Australia, is a 65km, five- to seven-day odyssey (with backpack, containing all your worldly goods) through incredible World Heritage–listed alpine mountainscapes. The track runs from Ronny Creek near Cradle Mountain to leeawuleena/Lake St Clair – the final hike around the lake shore we've detailed as this day walk. If you have solid fitness and are well prepared for Tasmania's erratic weather, it's a very achievable independent adventure. If you're not naturally disposed towards alpine wilderness, consider signing up for a guided walk. See overlandtrack.com.au for info.

**02** The trail begins behind **Narcissus Hut**, one of the Overland Track cabins, heading across a marshy plain below towering **Mt Olympus** (1472m; pictured). The trail follows an elevated boardwalk, where snakes like to bask in the morning sun. The mountain is beautiful, but keep your eyes at ground level and stomp loudly: the locals will slither out of your way when they hear you coming. Beyond the marsh, the trail enters an **ancient rainforest** – a damp realm of gnarled roots, colossal trunks and burbling creeks. The pathway is never far from the lake, but the dense forest only permits an occasional glimpse of the water.

**03** Around two hours into the walk, the track descends to the shore at **Echo Point**, where a rustic cabin and jetty are evidence of human habitation. Behind the cabin, the trail passes a series of **gargantuan swamp gums** standing in splendid solitude. More formally known as *Eucalyptus regnans*, these Tolkienesque trees can grow up to 100m tall. When one of these giants succumbs to gravity and falls towards the lake, it squashes the undergrowth and opens up a view across the water.

**04** At **Watersmeet**, where the fast-flowing Cuvier River meets the Hugel River, the forest dries itself out and becomes open woodland. Beyond the bridge, wide gravel fire trails suddenly fill with cheery couples and snack-munching families exploring the short trails around the visitor centre. The cafe's chilly drinks fridge beckons.

### Take a Break

There's a pricey cafe at the Lake St Clair Visitor Info Centre. A better bet is the bistro at the **Derwent Bridge Wilderness Hotel** (derwentbridgewildernesshotel.com.au) – a barn-shaped hotel with quite possibly the largest fireplace in Tasmania.

# 55
# Cataract Gorge Adventure

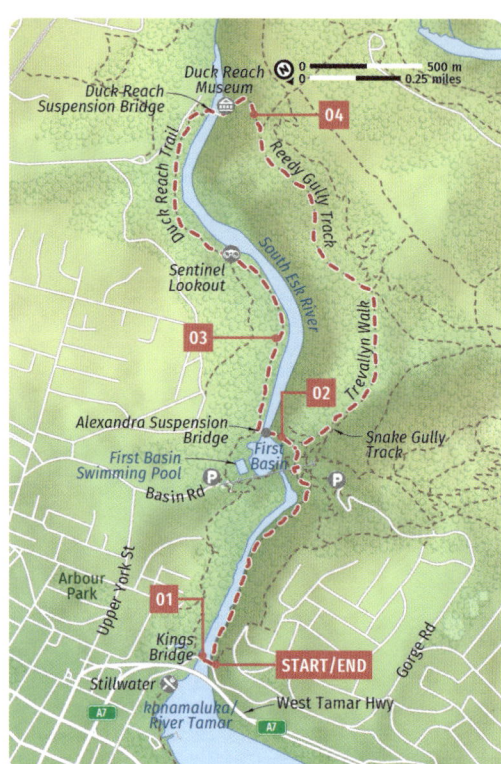

| DURATION | DIFFICULTY | DISTANCE | START/END |
|---|---|---|---|
| 2-3hrs return | Moderate | 7km | King's Bridge, Launceston |

| TERRAIN | Riverside & bush trails, some steep sections |
|---|---|

Cataract Gorge is a craggy canyon on the edge of downtown Launceston. For 'Lonnie' locals, it's a favourite spot to swim, hike, run and relax. Following the lower reaches of the South Esk River, this trail hugs sheer dolerite cliffs, crosses the broad Basin Reserve then heads upstream to the abandoned Duck Reach power station. There are two historic suspension bridges to wobble across, plus a return hike through serene bushland.

## Getting Here

From central Launceston it's a 10-minute walk (or quick drive) to the King's Bridge trailhead.

## Starting Point

The trail begins near the info panels at the northern end of King's Bridge. There's on-street parking nearby.

**01** Launceston's **ornate wrought-iron King's Bridge** was forged in Manchester, England, then shipped here in 1864. The grand span was assembled on a floating pontoon and lowered into place on the ebb tide. Impressive! Peer up the **South Esk River** (placid in summer, tumultuous in winter) then take the path along the gorge's sheer north face. Cliff-jumping teens plunge into the infamously cold river here in summer; more-sedate gorge fans enjoy the **beautifully floodlit cliffs** at night.

**02** A kilometre upstream, **First Basin** is a broad public reserve heralded by huge European and North American trees, including a monster sequoia planted in 1894. The **world's**

## Far from Cornwall

In 1798 George Bass and Matthew Flinders were the first Europeans to spy Launceston's kanamaluka/Tamar River estuary. Intent on beating the French in claiming Tasmania, the British then built a military post at the George Town rivermouth in 1804, on traditional Tyerrernotepanner lands. Soon after, an expedition upstream found the present-day site of Launceston, alongside Cataract Gorge and the tumbling South Esk River. The new colony took its name from the Cornish town – although the Tasmanian version came to be pronounced 'Lon-sess-ton' (or just 'Lonnie' to the locals) rather than the English 'Lawnston'.

longest single-span chairlift is here too (308m span, total length 457m), cranking along overhead. **Peacocks** wander aimlessly as you pass the shingle-roofed tea house and gaze across at the outdoor swimming pool, following the signs towards the **Alexandra Suspension Bridge** (pictured). Cross this swaying 67m beauty (built in 1904, rebuilt in 2004) to the far side of the gorge and head south.

**03** The trail continues 2km upstream to **Duck Reach** – a more rocky track with steep sections – passing **Sentinel Lookout** cantilevering out over the cliffs. Cross the river again via the **Duck Reach Suspension Bridge**, built in 1995 to replace the original, which was swept away by floods in 1969. The old power station – now an **atmospheric museum** – was one of the world's first publicly owned hydroelectric schemes, illuminating Launceston from 1895 to 1955. Duck inside for a look (pun intended).

**04** Take the steep **Reedy Gully Track** up the sweat-inducing 300m escarpment behind the station, past the lookout. The trail levels off as you rise from the gorge, moving onto a breezy ridge studded with sheoaks. Butterflies flit across the bracken (look for echidnas too!) as the trail slowly descends. After a couple of kilometres, turn right onto the slender **Snake Gully Track**, which follows a damp creek bed down to First Basin and the riverside path back to King's Bridge.

## Take a Break

Much-awarded **Stillwater** (stillwater.net.au), inside the historic 1832 flour mill near the entrance to Cataract Gorge, has long been Launceston's top dining dog. It serves laid-back lunches… then puts on the pizzaz for dinner. The seasonal menu and thoughtful wine list focus on local produce.

# 56

# Wineglass Bay & Hazards Beach

| DURATION | DIFFICULTY | DISTANCE | START/END |
|---|---|---|---|
| 4-5hrs return | Moderate | 11km | Trailhead car park |

| TERRAIN | Steep stone steps, dirt tracks, beaches |
|---|---|

You've seen the photos: now it's time to meet wondrous Wineglass Bay in person. Within Freycinet National Park, this steep trail climbs to the Wineglass Bay Lookout, then winds down to the sands (a swim is highly recommended). Cross a sandy isthmus to lesser-known Hazards Beach, then loop around through coastal casuarina groves back to your starting point. The lookout climb is ridiculously popular: be here early if you value your personal space!

## Getting Here
It's an easy 35-minute drive to the trailhead from Bicheno (47km), or 2½ hours from Hobart (198km).

## Starting Point
The trail begins at the car park (which has handy toilets) within Freycinet National Park; buy parks passes at the visitor centre.

**01** The little holiday town of **Coles Bay** (population 360) is quiet in winter but heaving with Freycinet visitors in summer: the local bakery, pub and pizza joint cope admirably with the influx. Interestingly, in 2003 Coles Bay became the first town in the world to ban plastic shopping bags! Around 1km from the town is the national park entrance; drive another 3.5km to the end-of-the-road trailhead at **Wineglass Bay car park**.

**02** Sign the bushwalkers' log, then take a long drink of water: the hike to the lookout is steep and sweaty work. From the **Coles Bay Lookout**, around 20 minutes in, look back at the rooftops of the township, shimmering in the

## Freycinet History

The first people to live on the Freycinet Peninsula were the Oyster Bay Aboriginal community. Their diet was rich in shellfish, evidenced by the many shell middens that still remain. In the 1830s Silas Cole (Coles Bay's namesake) burnt these shells to produce lime, which was mixed into mortar to build the nearby town of Swansea. Some 28 years earlier, Nicolas Baudin's French expedition had arrived and named Freycinet Peninsula after fellow explorer Louis de Freycinet. In 1916 Freycinet shared the honour with Mt Field in becoming Tasmania's first national park. Schouten Island was added to the park in 1977; the Friendly Beaches joined the park party in 1992.

**Best for**

**A COOLING SWIM**

NIGEL KILLEEN/GETTY IMAGES ©

east-coast sun. Pump your thighs ever-upwards, past the junction with the Boulderfield Track (big boulders!), until you reach the saddle between jagged Mt Amos and Mt Mayson, aka the Hazards. The sculptural timber bench here is tempting, but continue a few hundred metres more to the **Wineglass Bay Lookout**. Backed by a huge granite outcrop, the view down to the bay from here is a real winner.

**03** The path down to **Wineglass Bay** (pictured) isn't as steep as the ascent, levelling out through open woodland as you approach the sand. **Wallabies** often hop around on the beach, dragging their tails across hundreds of human footprints (it's worth reiterating – get here early to sidestep the crowds). Dunk yourself in the brine, munch a muesli bar then hit the trail to Hazards Beach.

**04** The sandy 1.5km path to **Hazards Beach** crosses a broad isthmus, passing a reedy lagoon to the south. The beach appears beyond a band of dunes, facing west across **Great Oyster Bay** towards Swansea. More sheltered than Wineglass, Hazards is a divine spot for a swim or some beachcombing among the kelp and scallop shells. From the beach's northern end, set off on the lengthy amble back to the car park, past sandy coves, bald granite outcrops and casuarina-clad slopes.

 **Take a Break**

Around 17km back from the Wineglass Bay trailhead, super-popular **Freycinet Marine Farm** (freycinetmarinefarm. com) grows huge, succulent oysters in the waters around Coles Bay. Its farm-gate cafe also dishes up fish and chips, mussels, scallops and abalone. Sit on the deck and sip some chardonnay with your hard-earned seafood picnic.

209

# 57

# Organ Pipes Circuit

**Best for**

**AMAZING VIEWS**

| DURATION | DIFFICULTY | DISTANCE | START/END |
|---|---|---|---|
| 4-5hrs return | Moderate | 9.5km | Springs car park |

| TERRAIN | Bushy paths; exposed, steep rocky sections |
|---|---|

This excellent hike delivers a smorgasbord of mountain highlights – it's just one of dozens of walks on Hobart's magical kunanyi/Mt Wellington. Look forward to sweet-smelling bushland and historic stone huts, spectacular rock formations, crumbling scree slopes and mesmerising views over the city and beyond. A few steep climbs over isolated rocky slopes will give your thighs a workout and accentuate your feeling of detachment from the city far below.

## Getting Here

Shuttle buses are an option (hobartshuttlebus.com), but driving provides more flexibility: it's 13km up Davey St to the Springs, via Pinnacle Rd.

## Starting Point

Lace up your boots at Trackhead 2 at the Springs. There's a cafe here, plus toilets, map panels and free car parking.

**01** Ribbed with its striking Organ Pipes cliffs (pictured p212), **kunanyi/Mt Wellington** towers 1271m over Hobart like a benevolent overlord. Around 700m above the city, there's not a whole lot to see at **the Springs** these days: a shipping-container cafe, some picnic tables, a car park and the start of the epic North-South mountain-bike track to Glenorchy... But if you'd visited between 1907 and 1967, you'd have been able to order tea and cake at the Hotel Mount Wellington, a much-loved (if never profitable) two-storey weatherboard beauty, with 16 bedrooms, a croquet lawn and sweeping verandah views. A tennis court was also planned, but the hotel burned down in Hobart's devastating 1967 bushfires in which

62 people died. Check out the **old hotel site** on the little detour road above the main car park, then hit the trail beyond the Trackhead 2 sign, heading for Sphinx Rock. The trail is self-evident, but a map from wellingtonpark.org.au/downloads isn't a bad idea.

**02** The well-trodden dirt trail heads into dense myrtle forest, running parallel to Pinnacle Rd but far enough below it to feel like you're in the wilds. It's a steady climb, passing lichen-covered rocks with the occasional city glimpse though the boughs. **Sphinx Rock** is about 30 minutes along the trail: a short detour through a safety gate delivers you to the top of this sandstone outcrop (which, it's fair to say, bears little or no resemblance to the Great Sphinx of Giza). **Brilliant views** extend from here across the city and south towards Kingston, South Arm and Bruny Island, named after French explorer Bruni d'Entrecasteaux who, in 1792, became the first person to chart this area. Dutch navigator Abel Tasman had also eyeballed these waters in 1642, but neglected to name anything after himself: he'd have to wait until 1856 for the 'Tasmania' concept to catch on.

**03** Back on the main track, it's a short hop over a couple of small creeks to the first of four historic stone huts along this walk. The doorless **Rock Cabin** (built from rocks) is right on the trail and has sheltered many a hiker from the mountain's capricious weather over the decades. A little further along, a steep, zigzagging detour downhill leads to compact **Lone Cabin**, another photogenic stone hut. It's not hard to imagine early mountain explorers huddling around the hearth here, as the storm raged outside. Return to the main trail, which becomes more rugged underfoot from this point. Track steadily downhill, passing through a metal stile to a bush clearing, in the centre of which stands the chunky stone **Junction Cabin**. Several mountain

## Journey to a Lost World

A real local secret (not so secret now, eh?), **Lost World** is an amazing boulder field near the summit of kunanyi/Mt Wellington, backed by a miniature version of the more famous Organ Pipes. Rock climbers, boulder-hoppers and bushwalkers venture here to lose a few hours in surreal solitude, to check out the views, or to play hide-and-seek among the massive fractured hunks of stone. To get here, take the little track heading north from the car park at 'Big Bend', 9km up Pinnacle Rd from Fern Tree – the last major hairpin bend before the summit. It's a 45-minute walk one way.

trails converge here (it's a junction) – scoff a snack at the table inside the hut then head uphill on **Hunters Track**.

**04** Like Sphinx Rock, **Crocodile Rock** is a chunky sandstone outcrop, formed from sediments laid down during the Triassic period 180 to 230 million years ago. Above this altitude igneous rock takes over: a thick sheet of grey dolerite barged its way in here during the Jurassic period, 170 million years ago (the mountain's famous Organ Pipes are fluted dolerite columns). Looming out of the bush above the trail, lofty Crocodile Rock packs a surprise punch: explore the small caves around its base then continue uphill. The trail soon opens onto a **vast scree slope** (pictured p210)– a slow cascade of fractured boulders tumbling inexorably down the mountainside. Iridescent orange trail markers on tall white posts mark the way across the sea of stones – a nod to the snows that cloak kunanyi over much of the winter (check hobartcity.com.au for snow updates). Continue up a steep zigzag section of the trail, across a small creek (the headwaters of the larger New Town Rivulet far below) then into another impressive boulder field. Pause to appreciate the **view** from here, reaching up the Derwent River valley to Hobart's famous MONA (Museum of Old & New Art) in the city's northern suburbs, jutting into the river on a small peninsula. Continue ever-upwards, turning left where the Hunter Track bumps into the **Old Hobartians Track**. You may be feeling a bit like an elderly Hobartian after all this

DEVAKA SENEVIRATNE/SHUTTERSTOCK ©

uphill hiking…but wait, there's more! There's a short but steep ascent from here to Pinnacle Rd, traversing another boulder field on the way.

**05** If you haven't had lunch yet, the **Chalet** is the place for you, an even kilometre above the surface of the Derwent River below. Alongside Pinnacle Rd, it's a much less rustic shelter than the Rock, Lone and Junction Cabins further down the slopes. If you need to refill your water bottle, there's a natural spring gushing out of the roadside embankment just below here. Pinnacle Rd itself is a sealed route running 12km from Fern Tree to the top of the mountain. Its construction was the brainchild of Albert Ogilvie, premier of Tasmania in the 1930s. When the Great Depression hit Hobart hard, Ogilvie deemed that all those unemployed hands would be best engaged in doing something helpful for the community. After several years of backbreaking labour, Pinnacle Rd opened in 1937. Initially very visible from the city and not entirely popular, the road became know as 'Ogilvie's Scar'. These days the route has mostly been obscured by trees – the two huge transmission towers on the mountaintop are much more of an aesthetic poke in the eye – and a drive up Pinnacle

### Famous Visitors

In February 1836 the esteemed English naturalist Charles Darwin sailed into Hobart and set out to scale kunanyi/Mt Wellington. Darwin was intrigued by the mountain's geology and flora, vividly describing the sunny day he spent here in his book *The Voyage of the Beagle*.

A less savoury mountaineer was bushranger Rocky Whelan, who lived in the aptly named 'Rocky Whelan's Cave' in 1854, a short walk from the Springs (650m downhill via the Fingerpost Track then Woods Track). Whelan was an escaped convict who'd done hard time in Sydney, on Norfolk Island, and finally in Van Diemen's Land where, upon his eventual recapture, he admitted to murdering a dozen men.

Rd to assess the city below has become a mandatory Hobart experience. Leave it all behind for now and head south towards the Organ Pipes.

**06** Pick up the trail behind the Chalet. The pathway veers momentarily uphill before levelling out and beginning its slow downhill run back to the Springs. Yet another broad, open boulder field soon appears, offering a **show-stopping view across the whole of Hobart**. The well-maintained trail soon rounds a bend and tracks across the base of the **Organ Pipes**. Soaring up to 120m high and visible from the city below, this astonishing dolerite wall was formed when molten dolerite cooled, shaping itself into regular hexagonal columns. Native birdsong and scarlet waratah blooms are a surreal addition to this already otherworldly scene. Crane your neck skywards (any rock climbers today?) then point your boots back along the trail. As you pass the turnoffs to both the Sawmill Track and Zig Zag Track, hints of a return to civilisation appear: overhead power lines, concrete culverts, the occasional plumbing inspection hatch... Weirdest of all is the University of Tasmania's **Cosmic Ray Observatory** – a peculiar little A-frame building next to the trail, behind a tall cyclone-mesh fence topped with unwelcoming barbed wire. What would the Muwinina people, kunanyi's Traditional Owners, make of this odd cosmic portal? Ponder this and the mountain's many other secrets as you pass the old Hotel Mount Wellington site and return to the Springs.

### Take a Break

After the old Springs Hotel burned down in 1967, there wasn't anywhere for a cup of coffee on kunanyi...until **Lost Freight** (lostfreightcafe.com) opened up a few years ago. It's a funky converted shipping container with excellent snacks to fuel your mountainside adventures.

# 58

# Cape Hauy

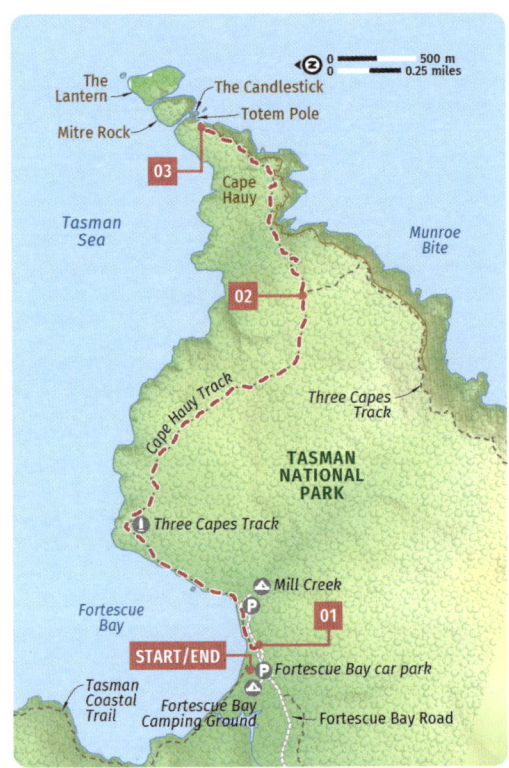

| DURATION | DIFFICULTY | DISTANCE | START/END |
|---|---|---|---|
| 4hrs return | Moderate | 9km | Fortescue Bay car park |

| TERRAIN | Steep stone steps, well-maintained trails |
|---|---|

On the fractured fringes of Tasman National Park, Cape Hauy (pronounced 'hoy') is a stunner – the third cape on Tasmania's famous Three Capes Track. Walking against the flow of Three Capes traffic, venture up and down (and up and down again) over rocky terrain to the end of the cape, where monumental dolerite cliffs plunge into the rolling ocean far below. The trail isn't super-long, but it will certainly put your cardiovascular condition to the test.

## Getting Here

From Hobart, drive 85km (1¼ hours) southeast to the Fortescue Bay turnoff on the Tasman Peninsula. The bay is a 12km dirt-road drive from here.

## Starting Point

The trail begins at the southern end of Fortescue Bay near Mill Creek: there are toilets, a car park, barbecues and a rangers' hut for parks passes here.

**01** A sweeping white-sand arc backed by thickly forested slopes, **Fortescue Bay** (pictured) has a chequered history. During the convict era the bay hosted one of the semaphore stations used to relay messages between Port Arthur and Eaglehawk Neck. Later, a timber mill operated here until 1952. Boilers and jetty ruins are still visible at Mill Creek near the trailhead (the magnificent tall forest along the drive into the bay seems to have recovered). These days Fortescue Bay is a primo camp site: book a long way ahead if you're planning on staying the night.

## Three Capes Track

The super-popular 46km **Three Capes Track** traverses Tasman National Park's lofty clifftops, taking in Cape Raoul, the sharp Blade rock formation at Cape Pillar and the eye-popping coastlines and cliffs around Cape Hauy (as detailed in this day walk). It's a four-day, three-night hike, with a boat trip from Port Arthur Historic Site to the trailhead, excellent hut accommodation and a bus back to Port Arthur from Fortescue Bay at the end. Walker numbers are capped at 48 per day, walking in one direction, so book well ahead (threecapestrack.com.au). It's also a good trail to tackle with the kids, or sign up for a guided hike with Three Capes Lodge Walk (taswalkingco.com.au).

JANETTE TEASCHE/GETTY IMAGES ©

**02** The well-made, level gravel trail traces the southern edge of Fortescue Bay, with **super views across the rolling swell** to the cliffs on the far side. A **sculpture** heralding the end of the Three Capes Track appears 1km along the pathway. Take a long gulp of water here before tackling the long flight of granite steps heading uphill, many of them beautifully crafted. The trail levels off near the top, moving through stands of conifers and yellow banksias. Take a break at the **summit**, 3km into your walk: the Three Capes hikers dump their packs here while they hoof it out to the end of the cape and back.

**03** The tip of **Cape Hauy** is just 1.5km from here – not far, but there are a whole lot of steep steps and switchbacks between you and the cliff edge. Distracting **coastal views** open up to the north and south as you make your charge. The wind picks up and the vegetation gets more wizened along the way, with **cliffs and chasms** dropping away to the ink-blue sea on all sides. The end of Cape Hauy isn't the place to linger if heights make your knees wobble. Or, if you and vertigo have never met, take a peek over the precipice: rock climbers toy with gravity on the **Totem Pole** and **Candlestick** dolomite sea stacks far below. For a less daredevil finale to your day's adventures, head back to Fortescue Bay for a cooling swim.

 **Take a Break**

Heading back to Hobart, turn right just before Dunalley's Denison Canal to discover the excellent **Bangor Vineyard Shed** (bangorshed.com.au). The cellar door doubles as a restaurant, serving local oysters (try the red wine vinegar, shallots and pepper dressing) and more substantial mains (sautéed abalone, calamari salad).

# 59 Crescent Bay

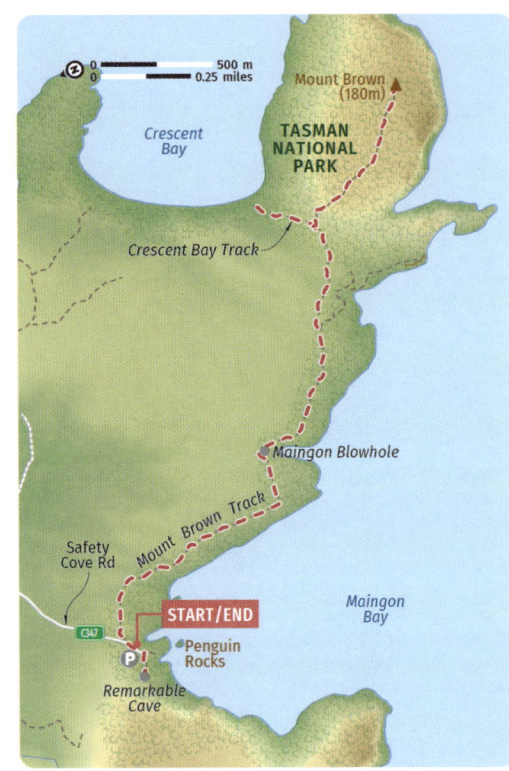

| DURATION | DIFFICULTY | DISTANCE | START/END |
|---|---|---|---|
| 3½hrs return | Moderate | 9km | Remarkable Cave car park |

| TERRAIN | Well-made, mostly level gravel trails |
|---|---|

A short hop from Port Arthur Historic Site, Tasmania's number-one tourist lure, this glorious white-sand beach remains relatively undiscovered – amazing! The pathway here and back is spectacular, winding along rugged, windswept coastline, with an impressive cave, blowhole and treeless peak to investigate en route.

Just 7km south of Port Arthur within Tasman National Park (98km southeast of Hobart; fees apply), **Remarkable Cave** extends under the cliffs and out to sea from the base of a collapsed gully. Waves surge through the tunnel and fill the gully with spray (and sometimes water – watch out!). From the car park, descend 115 steps (count 'em) to the **viewing platform**. Hardcore surfers sometimes brave the cave, paddling out through the opening to the wild reefs beyond.

The hike to Crescent Bay begins across from the car park. It's mostly a level gravel trail, cut through **low coastal heath and wind-bent bottlebrush**. Sloping granite terraces fall away to the ocean, with **views** extending south to the dolerite columns of Cape Raoul (which, according to local legend, the navy once used for target practice).

The slender chasm of **Maingon Blowhole** opens up in the heath a surprising distance inland. From the little bridge, peer down into the void at the white water surging below. A short, unsigned detour to the 174m summit of **Mt Brown** is next – a steepish, 30-minute return climb (rewarded by knockout views).

**Crescent Bay** (pictured) itself is a wonder. Head down onto the sand and marvel at the enormous dunes and rolling swell collapsing onto the beach. Rumour has it that a hotel development is planned for the bay: visit now before the rest of the world arrives!

# 60

# South Cape Bay

| DURATION | DIFFICULTY | DISTANCE | START/END |
|---|---|---|---|
| 4-5hrs return | Moderate | 16km | Cockle Creek |

| TERRAIN | Rugged bush trails, boardwalks & clifftop traverses |
|---|---|

Australia's most southerly day walk delivers you to one of the planet's last wild frontiers. Through rocky forest and along marshy boardwalks to a dramatic cliff edge, the South Cape Bay trail doubles as the final (or first) day of the epic South Coast Track – sit on the remote beach as the Southern Ocean thunders in and swap stories with the long-haul hikers as they shuffle by.

## Getting Here

Drive 122km (two hours) south of Hobart to Cockle Creek – the end of Australia's most southerly road. The last 19km are unsealed.

## Starting Point

The trail begins near the rangers' hut across the bridge over Cockle Creek (there is parking, but no toilets). Park fees apply.

**01** Within Southwest National Park, **Cockle Creek** is a divine pocket of **dunes and lagoons** on the southern end of Recherche Bay. In 1792 two French ships under the command of Bruni d'Entrecasteaux anchored here and granted the bay one of the many French names you'll find along Tasmania's east coast. Sign the walkers' logbook 50m along the trail, enjoying glimpses of Cockle Creek as you begin.

**02** The rocky, uneven trail rises steadily though dry sclerophyll forest (watch for **fantails** and squadrons of **glossy black cockatoos**) for 1.5km, before descending another 1.5km to a broad open plain. A **narrow boardwalk** extends

## South Coast Track

The challenging six- to eight-day, 85km **South Coast Track** starts (or ends) at Cockle Creek, linking this location with remote Melaleuca (mell-uh-loo-cuh), deep within Southwest National Park. Along the South Cape Bay section of the route (as described in this day walk) – the first or last leg of the South Coast Track – you'll pass bedraggled hikers gasping for the finish line, or be overtaken by chipper, clean-looking walkers striding out into the southern wilds. The Melaleuca trailhead is seriously remote: you have to fly in/out of here in a light plane – all part of the adventure! Check out southcoasttrack.com.au for more info.

**Best for**

**SOLITUDE**

from here across the 2.5km-wide **Heathers Creek marshland**, sweet with the scents of native heather and heath (hot tip: watch for snakes here, and wear long pants or gaiters to avoid scratches from the flora). Beyond the marsh the trail becomes sandy underfoot, hinting at the approaching coast. Skirt along the top of a deep gulch before descending into the lush gully alongside a burbling creek. Keep an eye out here for foraging **lyrebirds**, a species introduced from mainland Australia in the 1930s and '40s.

**03** The final push to **South Cape Bay** (pictured) climbs through bracken and bottlebrush, with the sound of breaking waves becoming ever louder. A **spectacular view** opens up from atop the final dune – a genuine 'Wow!' moment with either a sweeping clear-day view along the bay to Lion Rock, or, if the sea mist has rolled in, a chilly, horizon-less moonscape with giant waves booming invisibly nearby. Follow the cairns across the **crumbling grey-shale clifftops** (watch your step) to the steep steps down to the beach. **Redbill oyster catchers** and huge **oceanic gulls** patrol the sand as waves surge in and out, a jumble of battered logs and great knots of kelp strewn across the shore. Before you turn around and head back, pause for a moment to consider your position: between here and Antarctica is nothing but 2500km of freezing Southern Ocean. On an increasingly crowded planet, finding yourself alone on this frontier is a humbling and magical experience.

### Take a Break

This is BYO food territory…or backtrack 49km to Dover (via the Southport Hotel for a beer), where the excellent **Post>Office 6985** cafe offers cool decor, a sterling beer and wine list, and excellent wood-fired pizzas (try the scallop, caramelised onion and pancetta version).

# Also Try...

ASHLEY WHITWORTH/SHUTTERSTOCK ©

## wukalina/Mt William Summit

| DURATION | DIFFICULTY | DISTANCE |
| --- | --- | --- |
| 5hrs return | Moderate | 11km |

Rising a modest 216m above larapuna/Bay of Fires (pictured) in Tasmania's less-visited northeast corner, wukalina/Mt William is a haven for native wildflowers and wildlife.

Accessed via unsealed roads east of Gladstone, this relatively easygoing summit walk starts from Stumpys Bay Campground 4 at the northern end of Mt William National Park. Look for kangaroos, echidnas, wombats and wallabies as you cross the coastal heath, also home to 100 species of native birds including honeyeaters and flame robins. From the summit – which you'll most likely have all to yourself – views extend across the iconic white beaches of larapuna/Bay of Fires and out to the Furneaux Islands in Bass Strait. Bring plenty of water (most of Tasmania's rainfall happens on the west coast – by the time the clouds make it this far east they're usually empty!). National park fees apply.

## Hobart Rivulet Walk

| DURATION | DIFFICULTY | DISTANCE |
| --- | --- | --- |
| 2-3hrs return | Easy | 6km |

Following Hobart's original water source upstream from the city centre, this shady, scenic stroll makes a tranquil escape from the city streets, with history as your constant companion.

Hobart was initially sited across the Derwent River at Risdon Cove in 1803...before the reliable, cool-running Hobart Rivulet was discovered cascading down kunanyi/Mt Wellington. The settlement relocated and Hobart began to take shape. Today you can walk alongside the waterway from Molle St, heading west into South Hobart. Along the way you'll pass the site of the World Heritage–listed Female Factory, a notorious prison for convict women that operated from 1828–56 (one in four convicts transported to Tasmania was female). Cascade Brewery is next, with its haunting Gothic facade and lustrous liquids. It was established in 1824, and is Australia's oldest brewery. Take a beery tour, or head back down to the city.

REINDO/SHUTTERSTOCK ©

## Montezuma Falls

| DURATION | DIFF | DISTANCE |
|---|---|---|
| 3hrs return | Easy | 8km |

For a west-coast rainforest adventure, trek from the ghost town of Williamsford to one of Tasmania's loftiest waterfalls (104m), following an abandoned tramway route.

The North East Dundas Tramway opened in 1896, shunting ore from Williamsford to Zeehan until 1932. The rainforest then reclaimed the track...until the locals decided Montezuma Falls were worth looking at and beat back the bush. The Williamsford Rd trailhead is 9km south of Rosebery. It's an easygoing hike (pictured), offering a taste of the west-coast wilds.

## Apsley River Waterhole & Gorge

| DURATION | DIFF | DISTANCE |
|---|---|---|
| 4-5hrs return | Moderate | 7km |

Just north of Bicheno on the east coast is the turnoff to Douglas-Apsley National Park, an underrated realm of rocky peaks, dry forest, river gorges and swimming holes.

Apsley Waterhole is 15 minutes from the Rosedale Rd trailhead. Take a chilly dip (are there any endangered Australian grayling fish visible today?), then hike through the forest to Apsley Gorge for swim #2. Backtrack the way you came, or follow the Apsley River (in dry weather only) back downstream. National park fees apply.

## Hartz Peak Hike

| DURATION | DIFF | DISTANCE |
|---|---|---|
| 4-5hrs return | Moderate | 7.5km |

An accessible 1254m summit within Tasmania's World Heritage–listed Southwest Wilderness, Hartz Peak delivers astonishing 360-degree views.

Head 1½ hours south of Hobart through Geeveston to Arve Rd: from here it's an 11km unsealed drive into Hartz Mountains National Park. Begin your ascent across alpine moorland, passing mirror-flat Lake Esperance and Ladies Tarn. From the top, clear-day views take in Federation Peak and Precipitous Bluff. Bring all-season gear – snowstorms are common here, even in summer. National parks fees apply.

# TOOLKIT

The chapters in this section cover the most important topics you'll need to know about in Australia. They're full of nuts-and-bolts information and valuable insights to help you understand and navigate Australia and get the most out of your trip.

**Arriving**
p224

**Getting Around**
p225

**Accommodation**
p226

**Hiking**
p227

**Health & Safe Travel**
p228

**Responsible Travel**
p229

**Nuts & Bolts**
p230

**Wineglass Bay (p208)**
KLARA ZAMOURILOVA/SHUTTERSTOCK ©

# Arriving

Most visitors reach Australia by air, typically via the major international airports of Sydney (Warrane), Brisbane (Meeanjin) or Melbourne (Naarm). All state and territory capitals have an international airport, as do Cairns and the Gold Coast. Hobart's only direct international route is to/from Auckland.

## Travelling with Hiking Gear

Hiking gear can generally be packed around your regular travelwear. Just ensure that any used items are cleared of dirt, seeds, plant material and stowaway critters. If in doubt, declare it on your Incoming Passenger Card. In general, excess baggage is only required if you're bringing an extra backpack for overnight camping or specialty gear. Secure loose buckles and straps, or pack down into a durable duffle bag. Place items that might be considered potential weapons, such as tent pegs, trekking poles and Swiss Army knives, in your checked luggage, along with camping stoves, ensuring there is no detectable gas odour. Plan to buy lighters and fuel canisters when you arrive at your destination. EPIRBs and PLBs containing lithium-ion batteries below 100Wh, lithium metal content under 2g, and non-spillable varieties under 12V and 100Wh are permitted, providing they are safely stored to avoid accidental activation.

| | Melbourne | Sydney | Perth |
|---|---|---|---|
| **TRAIN** | No train | 15 mins $19-21 | 20 mins $5 |
| **BUS** | No direct bus | 60 mins $5 | 40 mins $5 |
| **TAXI** | From 30 mins From $50 | From 20 mins From $50 | 20 mins From $40 |
| **SHUTTLE** | 30 mins $24 | 20-30 mins $15-25 | 20-30 mins $24-50 |

### VISAS
Visas are compulsory for all visitors except New Zealanders. Popular options include the three-month Electronic Travel Authority (ETA) visitor visa and the extended Working Holiday visa. Check passport eligibility online. Apply in advance.

### CASH
Pre-loading travel credit cards can offer better value than an airport currency exchange. Be prepared for contactless payments; Australia has embraced tap-and-go, though keeping some cash is handy.

### CUSTOMS
The rules on what you can bring into the country are exceptionally strict, even down to muck on your boots. Scrub everything down and cross-check your packing list for unexpected contraband.

### AIRPORTS
Australia's seven major international airports provide ATMs, currency exchange, duty-free shopping, car rentals, pay phones, free wi-fi, foodie pit stops, and squeaky-clean bathrooms. Just don't expect affordability.

# Getting Around

**TRAIL ACCESSIBILITY**

Having reduced mobility shouldn't deter you from enjoying nature's beauty. Australia's network of firm, flat rail trails – repurposed from the country's abandoned train lines – are perfect for wheelchair users and vision-impaired hikers. Explore railtrails.org.au for more info. TrailRider all-terrain wheelchairs are an excellent option for rugged landscapes and often free to hire from national parks. These off-road enablers can be motorised or chaperoned by at least two 'sherpas', and in some state- and territory-managed parks, volunteer support can be arranged if booked in advance.

## DRIVING INFO

Australia drives on the left, with priority at roundabouts to your right

Many roads to hiking trails are unsealed; check your rental policy before driving

**.05%**
Legal blood alcohol limit is 0.05%

### Trains & Buses
Each state operates independent metro systems, offering efficient ways to navigate urban areas. Long-haul trains and bus routes link far-flung cities. Rural areas often lack public transport options, so brace for a potential warm-up trek to the trailhead.

### Car Rental
You will need a private vehicle to access many rural trailheads. Thankfully, Australia's rental market is competitive. In most cases, a standard car, allowing gravel road access in its rental agreement, should suffice. Consider an SUV with extra luggage space if you're carrying around gear.

### Electric Vehicles (EVs)
Australia is warming to EVs, with charging stations popping up nationwide, although with less frequency outside urban regions. Businesses, shopping centres and hotels may offer a free top-up for customers; otherwise, expect to pay $3.80 to $6.50 per 100km.

### Trail Navigation
Avoid relying on rural network coverage by pre-downloading base maps to your phone or satnav. Plan out and prepare hiking routes in advance with GPS-tracking apps like Google Maps and AllTrails; review hiker comments for updates, particularly in less popular locales.

## TRAVEL COSTS

**2WD/4WD rental**
from $80/180 per day

**Petrol**
fluctuates but around $2/litre; up to $3.60/litre in remote areas

**Melbourne metro**
$10/day

**Sydney metro**
$17.80/day Mon-Thu, $8.90/day Fri-Sun

LEFT: WS MUSHROOM/SHUTTERSTOCK ©, RIGHT: ANTON UKOLOV/SHUTTERSTOCK ©.

# Accommodation

**DARK SKY RESERVES**

With over 80% of the world's population living under light-polluted skies, Australia's wide-open spaces deliver a unique platform for unfiltered stargazing. Beyond its impact on human visibility, light pollution endangers the nation's nocturnal creatures by impacting their orientation and navigation. Australia's official 'dark sky places' cover four bushwalk-friendly regions: Warrumbungle National Park (NSW), The Jump-Up (Queensland), River Murray Dark Sky Reserve and Arkaroola Wilderness Sanctuary (both in South Australia). Each reserve offers secluded, low-light camping options. When staying overnight, help preserve the celestial ambience by minimising artificial light, but keep a torch nearby for safety.

HOW MUCH FOR A NIGHT IN A...

Public Camp Site
Free-$15

Cabin
$100-220

B&B Double room
$180-280

## National Parks

Soak up the Aussie bushwalk aura by waking up alongside the trail, roused by a chirpy chorus of critters. Unpowered camp sites are a convenient, wallet-friendly accommodation option throughout Australia's national parks. Most will have toilets and running water. You can claim your patch of designated dirt (and the odd character cabin) via the state parks' online portals. Plan ahead, especially during peak holiday periods.

## Caravan Parks

Australia's countryside caravan parks have upped their game over the last decade. These grassy grounds include affordable powered and unpowered sites, self-contained cabins and, more recently, child-free glamping. You'll readily find well-kept camp kitchens, coin laundries and shower blocks, with an increasing number featuring waterparks, tennis courts and elaborate play zones. At the pricier end, they're more like resorts and come with a luxuryprice tag.

## Motels

Consider drive-up motels for comfortable and cost-conscious stays in the countryside; though do your research, experiences can vary. Typically found on a town's periphery, they seldom offer discounted rates for solo hikers and better service group bookings, with midweek rates the most economical. Budget from $120 a night for a no-frills room equipped with a kettle, wi-fi, bar fridge, TV, air-con and a bathroom.

## B&Bs

Elevate your hiking experience with a cosy B&B overnighter, complemented by a hearty breakfast to bridge the gap to your first trail snack. Australia's rural regions brim with restored heritage houses, beachside retreats and outback estates, but these properties don't come cheaply. You can expect to pay several hundred dollars per night; weekday getaways and off-season steals soften the financial blow.

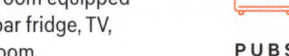

## PUBS

From modest setups in rural outposts to chic boutiques in trendy hotspots, Australia's pubs span the accommodation spectrum. Regardless of class, they are a welcome sight for post-hike eyes and stomachs. Pro tip: check kitchen hours before hitting the shower; you don't want to miss the dinner bell! Be aware that some simple taverns will only provide shared facilities; others, labelled 'hotels', may no longer offer overnight stays.

# Hiking

### Gear Rental

You'll likely already own much of the essential gear for an Australian day walk: a trusty hat, sunglasses, a long-sleeved shirt, pants and sturdy shoes. However, if your route takes you on remote, secluded trails or areas with dicey reception, consider renting a Personal Location Beacon (PLB) for added safety. In emergencies, activating a distress signal from this device helps rescuers pinpoint your location. Macpac offers PLB rentals at their stores nationwide, subject to availability.

For longer or more demanding hikes, or overnight camping, you can readily rent gear such as trekking poles, tents, backpacks, sleeping pads and cooking equipment. Each state and territory presents a selection of rental options, and Rooze ships hired gear to several metro cities across the country.

### Trail Etiquette

Even on short jaunts, your choices impact the environment, local wildlife and fellow bushwalkers; choose to tread lightly. Follow the Leave No Trace principles, emphasising the need to carry out what you bring in, from tissues to mandarin peels and sanitary products. Never bury rubbish (even biodegradable items), as it disturbs the soil and ground cover, leading to erosion. Animals will likely excavate buried leftovers, triggering territorial showdowns and even aggression towards humans. Likewise, avoid feeding wildlife, to prevent reliance on human-supplied snacks. If nature calls, you can dig a small 15cm (6in) cathole to do your business, at least 100m (320ft) from the nearest watercourse – remember a shovel! Once you're done, cover with soil and a rock. Clearly marked toilets are common in Australian parks, so it's much easier to pop in before you pop off.

On well-trodden trails, keep noise to a minimum, silencing phones and ambience-destroying beats. Walk single file with friends (allowing fellow hikers to overtake on your right), and be a considerate paparazzo, letting others snap their masterpieces sans photobomb.

---

#### AllTrails
*alltrails.com.au*
Freemium website/app featuring trails, photo previews and hiker ratings.

#### Trail Hiking Australia
*trailhiking.com.au*
A comprehensive archive of Australian trails, tips, blogs and GPX maps.

#### We Are Explorers
*weareexplorers.co*
Australia-centric hiking, conservation and all-round-adventure stories.

THP CREATIVE/SHUTTERSTOCK ©

# Health & Safe Travel

### Snakes
Many new hikers are concerned about encountering Australia's venomous snakes. Very few species are aggressive, so the likelihood of being bitten is low unless you provoke or accidentally step on one. Stay vigilant, walk heavily (snakes feel vibrations), and if you spy a snake on the trail, slowly back away and let it slither into the bush.

### UV Rays
When the sun is out, wear clothing that covers much of your body, especially during summer's high-UV months. Wear a broad-brim hat, sunglasses and a light, collared long-sleeved shirt made from merino wool or moisture-wicking synthetics. Apply sunscreen to any remaining exposed skin. At night, cover your arms, legs and feet to prevent bites from mosquitoes and other pesky insects.

### Heat Exhaustion
Bushwalking in Australia poses a genuine risk of heat exhaustion. Symptoms include dizziness, fainting, fatigue, nausea and pale, cool, clammy skin. If these signs appear, find a cool, shady spot and replenish your fluids with sips of water or electrolyte drinks. Avoid walking during the peak of very hot days, and ask locals or rangers for advice on how much water to carry before setting off.

### Bushfires
Nearly every Australian summer brings forest fires, with bushfire seasons extending due to the warming climate. On Total Fire Ban days, avoid lighting camp stoves, BBQs or campfires and stay updated on local conditions. If you smell smoke, act quickly. Your local ABC radio station provides real-time reports of unsafe areas – visit abc.net.au/radio for frequencies.

> **IN CASE OF EMERGENCY**
>
> **Police**
> 000
>
> **Ambulance**
> 000
>
> **Fire Service**
> 000
>
> **Text Emergency Relay Service**
> For those with hearing or speech impairments, the text emergency service number 106 reaches police, fire or ambulance via textphone

#### INSURANCE
Most comprehensive travel insurance will cover leisure walks, but it may exclude more extreme overland add-ons such as mountaineering or outdoor rock climbing. Check your policy wording and consult your insurer to clarify hiking-related claim questions. If necessary, upgrade to a more inclusive coverage.

# Responsible Travel

## Climate Change & Travel

It's impossible to ignore the impact we have when travelling, and the importance of making changes where we can. Lonely Planet urges all travellers to engage with their travel carbon footprint. There are many carbon calculators online that allow travellers to estimate the carbon emissions generated by their journey; try resurgence.org/resources/carbon-calculator.html. Many airlines and booking sites offer travellers the option of offsetting the impact of greenhouse gas emissions by contributing to climate-friendly initiatives around the world. We continue to offset the carbon footprint of all Lonely Planet staff travel, while recognising this is a mitigation more than a solution.

### Welcome to Country
*welcometocountry.com*
Digital platform highlighting authentic Aboriginal and Torres Strait Islander experiences.

### Leave No Trace Australia
*vslnt.com*
Australia's national minimal-impact program educates about responsible travel and recreation.

### Bureau of Meteorology (BOM)
*www.bom.gov.au*
Stay ahead of the weather with real-time updates, forecasts and warnings.

### FIRST NATIONS PERSPECTIVES
Deepen your understanding of the land's cultural heritage on Aboriginal-led walks such as the 90-minute Kuku-Yalanji Dreamtime Gorge Walk in Mossman Gorge or the two-hour Sacred Canyon Tour through Wilpena Pound.

### BUY LOCAL
Satisfy your post-hike hunger pangs at local eateries championing regional, seasonal produce and Australian beer and wine. Similarly, scout out unique handcrafted souvenirs from local artisans over mass-produced fridge magnets.

### KEEP WILDLIFE WILD
Preserve nature's balance by keeping snacks to yourself. Feeding wildlife can lead to poor animal nutrition, disease and loss of foraging instincts. This includes carrying out your biodegradable food scraps.

LEFT: VISION WILDLIFE/SHUTTERSTOCK ©, RIGHT: TOTAJLA/SHUTTERSTOCK ©

# Nuts & Bolts

**CURRENCY: AUSTRALIAN DOLLAR ($)**

**GOOD TO KNOW**

**Time zones**
Three mainland zones (GMT+8, GMT+9½, GMT+10)

**Country code**
+61

**Emergency number**
000

**Population**
27 million

### Cards & Cash

You can find ATMs across Australia, but be wary of hefty fees when withdrawing cash from credit cards. Consider searching out a better deal with a local currency exchange before jumping on your plane Down Under. Pre-paid cards from online banks, like Revolut and Wise, present a convenient alternative.

### Contactless Payments

Cashless payments have gained widespread acceptance in Australia, with a vast majority of businesses equipped for digital transactions. Predictions hint at a complete shift to digital payments within the next decade. Hence, carrying a chip and pin bank card for global use is highly recommended.

**ELECTRICITY 230V/50HZ**

Type I
230V/50Hz

### Tipping

While tipping isn't mandatory in Australia, it's commonly practised in high-end restaurants and bars. If you've enjoyed an exceptional dining experience, consider adding 5% to 10% as a gratuity. Throwing a few dollars in the cafe tip jar or rounding up your taxi fare is always appreciated but not expected.

### Tap Water

Water is typically safe to drink in Australia, but stay alert for warnings indicating otherwise, especially on remote trail tanks. As a fallback, pack a lightweight filter like the Sawyer Mini Water Filtration System.

### Toilets

Australia's toilets are sit-down Western style, with most public restrooms free and well maintained, although cleanliness may vary in isolated parks. Visit toiletmap.gov.au for facilities near popular trails, including those with disabled access.

### Network Coverage

For network reliability across Australia's rural regions, Telstra is the standout. However, don't rely on blazing transfer speeds beyond the outer suburbs and remember to download maps before hitting remote trails.

**HOW MUCH FOR...**

Coffee
$5

Taxi
$3/km

Energy bar
$4

Sunscreen 200ml
$20

# By Difficulty

## EASY

Prince Henry Cliff Walk ................... 24
Bondi to Coogee
   Clifftop Walk ..................................... 32
Florence Falls........................................ 96
Bungles Gorges ................................. 112
Mt Cope ................................................ 176
Squeaky Beach ................................. 188
Wreck Beach ....................................... 194
Dove Lake Circuit ............................. 202

## MODERATE

Wattamolla to Otford ..................... 26
Bouddi Coastal Walk ....................... 28
Tibrogargan &
   Trachyte Circuits ............................ 42
Mt Mitchell ............................................ 44
Mapleton Falls to
   Gheerulla Falls ................................. 46
Cape Byron ...........................................50
Minyon Falls Loop............................. 52
Mossman Gorge .................................60
Pine Grove & Broken River ........... 62

Best of Great Keppel Island ........ 64
Carnarvon Gorge .............................. 68
Valley of the Winds ......................... 78
Kings Canyon Rim............................80
Ormiston Pound .............................. 86
Above Standley Chasm................. 88
Edith Falls & Sweetwater Pool...90
Motor Car Falls .................................. 94
Emma Gorge....................................... 104
Punamii-Unpuu/
   Mitchell Falls ................................. 106
Bell Gorge ............................................110
Weano & Hancock Gorges .......... 116
Dales Gorge Circuit ........................118
Bluff Knoll............................................126
Nancy Peak & Devils Slide ..........128
Bald Head .......................................... 130
Nuyts Wilderness ...........................132
Hamelin Bay to
   Elephant Rock...............................134
Mt Remarkable Summit ................144
The Riesling Trail..............................146
Morialta Gorge Three Falls......... 148
Mylor to Mt Lofty ............................ 150
Belair National Park Waterfall ...154

Marion Coastal Trail .......................156
Blowhole Beach
   to Cape Jervis ................................158
Wonderland Loop ..........................166
Mt Stapylton .....................................168
Mt Buffalo Plateau..........................170
Lilly Pilly Gully & Mt Bishop........ 184
Oberon Bay .......................................186
Lorne Forests & Waterfalls ........ 190
leeawuleena/Lake St Clair ....... 204
Cataract Gorge Adventure ....... 206
Wineglass Bay &
   Hazards Beach ........................... 208
Organ Pipes Circuit........................ 210
Cape Hauy...........................................214
Crescent Bay......................................216
South Cape Bay................................218

## HARD

Jerusalem Bay Track ....................... 30
Mt Sorrow Ridge................................ 66
Mt Sonder............................................. 84
Mt Bruce...............................................114
The Razorback &
   Mt Feathertop ................................172

# Index

## A

Above Standley Chasm 88-9, **88**
accommodation 226, *see also individual locations*
activities, *see individual locations*
Adelaide 142
airports 224
Albany 124
Alice Springs 76
Apollo Bay 182

## B

B&Bs 226
Bald Head 130-1, **130**
bathrooms 230
beer 10
Belair National Park Waterfall 154-5, **154**
Bell Gorge 110-11, **110**
Best of Great Keppel Island 64-5, **64**
Bicheno 200
Blowhole Beach to Cape Jervis 158-9, **158**
Bluff Knoll 126-7, **126**
Bondi to Coogee Clifftop Walk 32-5, **33**
books 17
Bouddi Coastal Walk 28-9, **28**
Bright 164
Brisbane 40
Broome 102
Bungles Gorges 112-13, **112**
bus travel 225

Trails 000
**Map Pages 000 000**

bush trails
  Jerusalem Bay Track 30-1, **30**
bushfires 228
Byron Bay 39-55
  climate 40
  festivals & events 41
  resources 41
  transport 41

## C

Cairns 58
camping 226
canyon trails
  Kings Canyon Rim 80-3, **81**
  Wonderland Loop 166-7, **166**
Cape Byron 50-1, **50**
Cape Hauy 214-15, **214**
caravan parks 226
car rental 225
Carnarvon Gorge 68-71, **69**
cash 230
Cataract Gorge Adventure 206-7, **206**
city trails
  Bondi to Coogee Clifftop Walk 32-5, **33**
Clare 142
climate 14-15, 22, 40, 58, 77, 102, 125, 142-3, 164, 183, 200, 229
climate change 229
coastal trails
  Bald Head 130-1, **130**
  Best of Great Keppel Island 64-5, **64**
  Blowhole Beach to Cape Jervis 158-9, **158**
  Bondi to Coogee Clifftop Walk 32-5, **33**
  Bouddi Coastal Walk 28-9, **28**
  Cape Byron 50-1, **50**

  Cape Hauy 214-15, **214**
  Crescent Bay 216-17, **216**
  Hamelin Bay to Elephant Rock 134-7, **135**
  Marion Coastal Trail 156-7, **156**
  Oberon Bay 186-7, **186**
  South Cape Bay 218-19, **218**
  Squeaky Beach 188-9, **188**
  Wattamolla to Otford 26-7, **26**
  Wineglass Bay & Hazards Beach 208-9, **208**
  Wreck Beach 194-5, **194**
Coastrek 15
costs 225, 230
credit cards 230
Crescent Bay 216-17, **216**
customs 224

## D

Daintree 57-73
  climate 58
  festivals & events 59
  resources 59
  transport 59
Dales Gorge Circuit 118-19, **118**
dark sky reserves 226
Darwin 76
Dove Lake Circuit 202-3, **202**
driving 225

## E

Edith Falls & Sweetwater Pool 90-3, **91**
electricity 230
emergencies 228
Emma Gorge 104-5, **104**
events, *see* festivals & events

# F

festivals & events 15
    Adelaide 15
    Alice Springs 18
    Byron Bay 41
    Coastrek 15
    Daintree 59
    Fleurieu 143
    Flinders 143
    Grampians 165
    Great Ocean Road 183
    High Country 165
    Kimberley 103
    North Queensland 59
    Outback 77
    Pilbara 103
    Southwest Western Australia 125
    Sunshine Coast 41
    Sydney 15, 23
    Tasmania 201
    Wilsons Promontory National Park 183
films 16
Fleurieu Peninsula 141-61
    climate 142-3
    festivals & events 143
    resources 143
    transport 143
Flinders Ranges 141-61
    climate 142-3
    festivals & events 143
    resources 143
    transport 143
Florence Falls 96-7, **96**
forest trails
    Lilly Pilly Gully & Mt Bishop 184-5, **184**
    Lorne Forests & Waterfalls 190-3, **191**
    Nuyts Wilderness 132-3, **132**
Foster 182

# G

gear rental 227
gorge trails
    Above Standley Chasm 88-9, **88**
    Bell Gorge 110-11, **110**
    Bungles Gorges 112-13, **112**
    Carnarvon Gorge 68-71, **69**
    Cataract Gorge Adventure 206-7, **206**
    Dales Gorge Circuit 118-19, **118**
    Emma Gorge 104-5, **104**
    Morialta Gorge Three Falls 148-9, **148**
    Mossman Gorge 60-1, **60**
    Mt Buffalo Plateau 170-1, **170**
    Weano & Hancock Gorges 116-17, **116**
Grampians National Park 163-79
    climate 164
    festivals & events 165
    resources 165
    transport 165
Great Ocean Road 181-97
    climate 183
    festivals & events 183
    resources 183
    transport 183

# H

Halls Gap 164
Hamelin Bay to Elephant Rock 134-7, **135**
health 228
High Country 163-79
    climate 164
    festivals & events 165
    resources 165
    transport 165
highlights 6-13
hiking 227
Hobart 200

# I

insurance 228
internet access 230

# J

Jerusalem Bay Track 30-1, **30**

# K

Katherine 76
Katoomba 22
Kimberley 101-21
    climate 102
    festivals & events 103
    resources 103
    transport 103
Kings Canyon Rim 80-3, **81**
Kununurra 102

# L

lake trails
    Dove Lake Circuit 202-3, **202**
    leeawuleena/Lake St Clair 204-5, **205**
language 17
Launceston 200
leeawuleena/Lake St Clair 204-5, **205**
Lilly Pilly Gully & Mt Bishop 184-5, **184**
Lorne 182
Lorne Forests & Waterfalls 190-3, **191**

# M

Mackay 58
Mapleton Falls to Gheerulla Falls 46-9, **47**
Margaret River 124
Marion Coastal Trail 156-7, **156**
McLaren Vale 142
Minyon Falls Loop 52-3, **52**
Morialta Gorge Three Falls 148-9, **148**
Mossman Gorge 60-1, **60**
Motor Car Falls 94-5, **94**
mountain trails
    Bluff Knoll 126-7, **126**
    Lilly Pilly Gully & Mt Bishop 184-5, **184**
    Mt Bruce 114-15, **114**

Mt Cope 176-7, **176**
Mt Mitchell 44-5, **44**
Mt Remarkable Summit 144-5, **144**
Mt Sonder 84-5, **84**
Mt Sorrow Ridge 66-7, **66**
Mt Stapylton 168-9, **168**
Mylor to Mt Lofty 150-3, **151**
Nancy Peak & Devils Slide 128-9, **128**
Organ Pipes Circuit 210-13, **211**
Prince Henry Cliff Walk 24-5, **24**
Razorback & Mt Feathertop, The 172-5, **173**
Tibrogargan & Trachyte Circuits 42-3, **42**
Mt Bruce 114-15, **114**
Mt Buffalo Plateau 170-1, **170**
Mt Cope 176-7, **176**
Mt Mitchell 44-5, **44**
Mt Remarkable Summit 144-5, **144**
Mt Sonder 84-5, **84**
Mt Sorrow Ridge 66-7, **66**
Mt Stapylton 168-9, **168**
music 17
Mylor to Mt Lofty 150-3, **151**

# N

Nancy Peak & Devils Slide 128-9, **128**
national parks
  Belair National Park 154-5, **154**
  Border Ranges National Park 55
  Bouddi National Park 28-9, **28**
  Cape Hillsborough National Park 72
  Cape Le Grande National Park 139
  Carnarvon National Park 68-71, **69**
  Cradle Mountain-Lake St Clair National Park 202-3, **202**
  Daintree National Park 60
  Dinden National Park 73
  Douglas-Apsley National Park 221
  Freycinet National Park 208-9
  Grampians National Park 166-7

Trails 000
**Map Pages 000 000**

  Great Otway National Park 190-3
  Hartz Mountains National Park 221
  Ikara-Flinders Ranges National Park 160
  Kalbarri National Park 120
  Kondalilla National Park 47
  Ku-ring-gai National Park 30-1
  Lamington National Park 55
  Lane Cove National Park 37
  Leeuwin-Naturaliste National Park 135-7
  Litchfield National Park 96-7
  Main Range National Park 44-5
  Mapleton National Park 48
  Mitchell River National Park 106-9
  Mt Buffalo National Park 170-1
  Mt Remarkable National Park 161
  Mt William National Park 220
  Nightcap National Park 52, 54
  Nitmiluk National Park 90-3, 99
  Porongurup National Park 128
  Purnululu National Park 112-13
  Royal National Park 26
  Southwest National Park 218-19
  Sydney Harbour National Park 36
  Tamborine National Park 55
  Tasman National Park 214-15, 216-17
  Torndirrup National Park 130
  Tully Falls National Park 73
  Watarrka National Park 80-3
  Wilsons Promontory National Park 184-5, 186-7, 188-9, 196
Noosa 40
North Queensland 57-73
  climate 58
  festivals & events 59
  resources 59
  transport 59
Nuyts Wilderness 132-3, **132**

# O

Oberon Bay 186-7, **186**
Organ Pipes Circuit 210-13, **211**
Ormiston Pound 86-7, **86**

Outback 75-99
  climate 77
  festivals & events 77
  resources 77
  transport 77

# P

Parrtjima – A Festival in Light 15
Pilbara 101-21
  climate 102
  festivals & events 103
  resources 103
  transport 103
Pine Grove & Broken River 62-3, **62**
planning
  clothes 16
podcasts 17
Port Campbell 182
Prince Henry Cliff Walk 24-5, **24**
Punamii-Unpuu/Mitchell Falls 106-9, **107**

# R

Razorback & Mt Feathertop, The 172-3, **173**
responsible travel 229
Riesling Trail, The 146-7, **146**
Rockhampton 58

# S

safe travel 228
Sculpture by the Sea 15
snakes 228
South Cape Bay 218-19, **218**
Southwest Western Australia 123-39
  climate 125
  festivals & events 125
  resources 125
  transport 125
Squeaky Beach 188-9, **188**

Sunshine Coast 39-55
climate 40
festivals & events 41
resources 41
transport 41
sustainability 229
swimming 11
Sydney 21-37
climate 22
festivals & events 23
resources 23
transport 23

## T

Tasmania 199-221
climate 200
festivals & events 201
resources 201
transport 201
Tibrogargan & Trachyte Circuits 42-3, **42**
Tidal River 182
tipping 230
toilets 230
Tom Price 102
trail etiquette 227
train travel 225

travel seasons 14-15, 22, 40, 58, 77, 102, 125, 142-3, 164, 183, 200
travel to/from Australia 224
travel within Australia 225

## V

Valley of the Winds 78-9, **78**
valley trails
Ormiston Pound 86-7, **86**
Valley of the Winds 78-9, **78**
visas 224

## W

Walpole 124
water 230
waterfall trails
Belair National Park Waterfall 154-5, **154**
Edith Falls & Sweetwater Pool 90-3, **91**
Florence Falls 96-7, **96**
Lorne Forests & Waterfalls 190-3, **191**
Mapleton Falls to Gheerulla Falls 46-9, **47**
Minyon Falls Loop 52-3, **52**
Morialta Gorge Three Falls 148-9, **148**
Motor Car Falls 94-5, **94**

Punamii-Unpuu/Mitchell Falls 106-9, **107**
Wonderland Loop 166-7, **166**
Wattamolla to Otford 26-7, **26**
Weano & Hancock Gorges 116-17, **116**
weather 14-15
wildlife 6
wildlife trails
Pine Grove & Broken River 62-3, **62**
Wilsons Promontory National Park 181-97
climate 183
festivals & events 183
resources 183
transport 183
wine 10
Wineglass Bay & Hazards Beach 208-9, **208**
wine trails
Mylor to Mt Lofty 150-3, **151**
Riesling Trail, The 146-7, **146**
WOMADelaide 15
Wonderland Loop 166-7, **166**
Wreck Beach 194-5, **194**

## Y

Yulara 76

# Notes

NOTES

NOTES

NOTES

## THE WRITERS

This is the 2nd edition of this guidebook, updated with new material by Josh West. Writers on previous editions whose work also appears in this book are included below.

**Josh West**

Josh is an avid hiker, paddler and cyclist who can be found traipsing long distances searching for nature's enlightenment or a well-camouflaged cache. Find Josh on Instagram @trekkingwest.

**Contributing writers**

Anna Kaminski, Monique Perrin, Charles Rawlings-Way, Glenn van der Knijff, Steve Waters

## SEND US YOUR FEEDBACK

We love to hear from travellers – your comments keep us on our toes and help make our books better. Our well-travelled team reads every word on what you loved or loathed about this book. Although we cannot reply individually to your submissions, we always guarantee that your feedback goes straight to the appropriate writers, in time for the next edition. Each person who sends us information is thanked in the next edition.

Visit **lonelyplanet.com/contact** to submit your updates and suggestions or to ask for help. Our award-winning website also features inspirational travel stories and news.

Note: We may edit, reproduce and incorporate your comments in Lonely Planet products such as guidebooks, websites and digital products, so let us know if you are happy to have your name acknowledged. For a copy of our privacy policy visit **lonelyplanet.com/legal**.

## BEHIND THE SCENES

This book was produced by the following:

**Commissioning Editor**
Darren O'Connell

**Production Editor**
Amy Lysen

**Book Designer**
Clara Monitto

**Cartographers**
David Connolly, Julie Sheridan

**Assisting Cartographer**
Katerina Pavkova

**Assisting Editors**
Imogen Bannister, Nigel Chin

**Cover Researcher**
Lauren Egan

**Thanks to**
Ronan Abayawickrema, Melanie Dankel

**Product Development**
Amy Lynch, Marc Backwell, Katerina Pavkova, Fergal Condon, Ania Bartoszek

## ACKNOWLEDGMENTS

**Cover photograph**
Grampians National Park; David_Chrastek/Shutterstock ©